urban DESIGN

For planning to be successful, *design* must mean more than blindly following the dictates of legislation and regulation—yet losing sight of the importance of the design process is all too often exactly what has happened.

Ron Kasprisin has written a book for students of planning and urban design that reconnects the process of designing with outcomes on the ground, and puts thinking about design back at the heart of what planners do.

The book identifies the elements and principles of composition and explores compositional order and structure as they relate to the meaning and functionality of cities. It discusses new directions and methods, and outlines the importance of both buildings and the open spaces between them.

Mixing accessible theory, practical examples, and carefully designed exercises in composition from simple to complex settings, *Urban Design* is an essential textbook for classrooms and design studios across the full spectrum of planning and urban studies fields. Not only filled with illustrations and graphics of excellent projects, it gives students tools to enable them to sketch, draw, design, and, above all, to think.

Ron Kasprisin is an architect, urban planner, and artist with over 40 years of experience as a practitioner in urban design as Kasprisin Pettinari Design; and over 20 years of academic experience as Associate Professor in Urban Design and Planning, College of Built Environments, University of Washington, Seattle, Washington. Ron is also an accomplished watercolor painter with national recognition, awards, and exhibitions. Ron lives on Whidbey Island northwest of Seattle, Washington in Puget Sound, where he offers watercolor painting workshops at Kasprisin Ridge Studios, Langley, Washington.

urban DESIGN
THE COMPOSITION OF COMPLEXITY

Ron Kasprisin

LONDON AND NEW YORK

First published 2011
by Routledge
2 Park Square, Milton Park, Abingdon, Oxon, OX14 4RN

Simultaneously published in the USA and Canada
by Routledge
711 Third Avenue, New York, NY 10017

Routledge is an imprint of the Taylor & Francis Group, an informa business

© 2011 Ron Kasprisin

The right of Ron Kasprisin to be identified as author of this work has been asserted by him in accordance with sections 77 and 78 of the Copyright, Designs and Patents Act 1988.

Typeset in Adobe Garamond by
Florence Production Ltd, Stoodleigh, Devon

Printed and bound in Great Britain by
Ashford Colour Press Ltd, Gosport, Hampshire

British Library Cataloguing in Publication Data
A catalogue record for this book is available from the British Library

Library of Congress Cataloging-in-Publication Data
Kasprisin, Ronald J.
  Urban design : the composition of complexity / Ron Kasprisin.
    p. cm.
  Includes bibliographical references and index.
  1. City planning. 2. Design. I. Title.
  HT166.K359 2011
  307.1'216—dc22   2010027920

ISBN13: 978-0-415-59146-1 (hbk)
ISBN13: 978-0-415-59147-8 (pbk)
ISBN13: 978-0-203-83376-6 (ebk)

Graduate urban planning and design students contributed examples for Chapter 8, a portion of which are included, specifically Figures 8.5 through 8.11 and 8.13 through 8.18. They include: Christy Alexander, Eric Alskog, Ion Arai, Diana Benson, Nick Bond, Erica Huang, Hiroko Matsuno, Hannah Jane McIntosh, Eddie Hill, Rueben McKnight, Craig Montgomery, Davila Parker-Garcia, Jessica Stein, Zhi Wen Tan, Kenn Teng, Clay Harris Veka, Adam Webber, and Jason Woycke. If any names have been omitted, please accept our apologies and contact the publisher for inclusion in future reprints.

All other images are copyright of the author.

CONTENTS

Foreword and acknowledgements   vii

1   **Introduction**   1
    A dual mission   1
    The audience   2
    Connecting design to reality: urban meaning and urban functionality   6
    The foundation for design: the interactions of culture, space, and time   8
    Composition of complexity for planners and designers   8
    Design as compositional order and compositional structure   8

2   **Definitions and fundamentals of urban design in culture**   10
    (The many) definitions of urban design   10
    Manifestations of urban design in civilization and culture   12
    Expanding urban meaning: space, culture, and time/history   13
    The emergence of design in culture   15
    Modernist corporatism   18

3   **Urban design language and parameters**   20
    The language of design   20
    Essential graphic language techniques   20
    Parameters of design   27

4   **Elements and principles of design composition**   30
    Form as community relationship   30
    Design elements: "the nouns"   30
    Design principles: "the verbs"   38

5   **Relationships in composition: organization and structure**   45
    Definitions related to composition   46
    Organizational relationships in composition   47
    Structural relationships in composition   48
    Compositional structures   51
    Spatial reference frameworks   68
    Additional spatial characteristics of composition   79

CONTENTS

6   **Transformations of form: elements and composition**   81

Dimensional transformations   81
Subtractive transformations   83
Additive transformations   83
Merging transformations   87
Bridging transformations   92
Other spatial transformational techniques   97
Design opportunity in the limits of form   98

7   **Context, program, and typologies**   107

Context: the spatial container of reality   107
Program (need and opportunity)   110
Form typology related to urban design   110
Selected examples   138
Final thoughts on typology   147

8   **Experiments in composition: the basis for place-making**   151

Understanding and working with primary shapes   152
Compositional structures   159
Experiments in the transformations of form   160
Spatial reference systems   168
Typology exercises   171
Increasing complexity: urban design projects   176

9   **Theoretical considerations**   184

The composition of complexity   184
An overview approach   191
Conflict (or the positive use of polarities)   193

Appendix I: Drawing types for urban design   199
Appendix II: Working with people: the politics of urban design   213
Appendix III: Remnants, bridging, hybridity, and edges   232

Index   238

FOREWORD AND ACKNOWLEDGEMENTS

I have two aspirations in writing this book: first, to increase the knowledge, skills and ability of students in urban studies to enable them to engage in the design process—making spatial compositions in urban design; second, to explore the essential connection between urban design and the complexity of cities—interactions among people and people with their environments. Many professionals will say that urban designers already engage this connection. I argue that too many, albeit well intentioned, do not; they understand the connection and are remiss in engaging that connection—the built form suffers accordingly. The second exploration provides the basis for the spatial composition process.

Human settlements, from hamlet to metropolis, are messy. Working in the *trenches* for 40 years has exposed me to the complicated and complex nature of human settlements—human behavior, politics, economic forces, capitalism, and more. In many instances, the urban design contribution is superficial band-aid applications, small alterations and tinkering to dynamic complex patterns and large-scale drastic interventions—large-scale architecture that is misconstrued as urban design.

The urban meaning and functionality of towns and cities are the basis for design and they demand attention and awareness of reality: the sensual nature of cities that lies between the planning quantification data units. Cities are real and filled with stories of achievement and dysfunction. Urban design is a translation of those stories.

I have long appreciated the credo of Pablo Neruda in his "Some Thoughts on Impure Poetry" excerpted from *Pablo Neruda: Residence on Earth* (2004, New Directions Books (NY) with an Introduction by Jim Harrison, pp. xii–xiii):

> It is worth one's while, at certain hours of the day or night, to scrutinize useful objects in repose: wheels that have rolled across long, dusty distances with their enormous loads of crops or ore, charcoal sacks, barrels, baskets, the hafts and handles of carpenter's tools. The contact these objects have had with man and earth may serve as a valuable lesson to a tortured lyric poet. Worn surfaces, the wear inflicted by human hands, the sometimes tragic, always pathetic, emanations from these objects give reality a magnetism that should not be scorned.
>
> Man's nebulous impurity can be perceived in them: the affinity for groups, the use and obsolescence of materials, the mark of a hand or a foot, the constancy of the human presence that permeates every surface.
>
> This is the poetry we are seeking, corroded, as if by acid, by the labors of man's hand, pervaded by sweat and smoke, reeking of urine and of lilies soiled by diverse professions in and outside the law.
>
> A poetry as impure as a suit or a body, a poetry stained by food and shame, a poetry of wrinkles, observations, dreams, waking, prophecies, declarations of love and hatred, beasts, blows, idylls, manifestos, denials, doubts, affirmations, taxes.
>
> (Neruda, 2004, pp. xii–xiii)

FOREWORD AND ACKNOWLEDGEMENTS

As designers, we seek to improve the built form of human settlements: to make them work effectively and to make them desirable places to inhabit among this reality described by Neruda. Designers make spatial metaphors of cultural meanings for contemporary society with historic connections. Those metaphors are spatial constructions or compositions dancing with the stories and needs of humans and their settlements. We must understand both partners in the dance.

I have architecture and landscape architecture colleagues who refer to themselves as urban designers. With all due respect, I ask them to look beyond the "scale" component of "urban" and the conventional models of design they over-utilize. I urge them to engage the complexities of cultural, historic, time, and spatial aspects of concepts of *urban* or *community*. I urge them to let the design emerge from this complexity as a process of design discovery not certainty. So this book is also for them in the hopes that the work can inspire an awareness of the meaning and functionality underlying urban design–of the rich underlying forces affecting spatial compositions. As I discuss in Chapter 7 on typologies, there are established building and development configuration patterns that are used on a daily basis because they work and provide convention and effectiveness to the design and construction of the built environment. And some are obsolete (as in standard residential subdivisions), some are devoid of meaning as in theme-towns, and others are relied upon in excess, becoming expedient and corporately franchised applications. Our role is to challenge that expediency, forging hybrids that reflect the contextual reality of communities to the best of our abilities.

When we as designers engage the reality of community, what I refer to as the culture/space/time matrix (CST), derived from the work of Edward Soja, Henri Lefebvre, Manuel Castells, Charles Johnston, Fritjof Capra and others, we begin a search to be creative, moving beyond what is known in design. As designers, our role is to fashion urban design spatial compositions that are responsive to the meaning and functionality of community. This takes us beyond form for form's sake and conventional typologies that are easily packaged and financed. I hope I can contribute to the bridging of design composition and urban meaning and functionality while assisting urban planning and urban studies students (from public affairs to real estate) in understanding the elements and principles of design composition.

I am appreciative of the many discussions with my graduate students regarding the approach of this book: from the practical to the theoretical. They are my audience. And I thank my business partner, teaching colleague, and friend, Professor James Pettinari (University of Oregon, retired), for support and critical dialogue. Technical support has been graciously accepted regarding computer issues from Ande Flower and Mary Bellone, both of whom came to my rescue. And of course, I owe treats to Whidbey, my yellow Labrador retriever, who diligently slept under my feet during this entire process, keeping me company.

Chapter 1

INTRODUCTION

I wrote this book for my planning and emerging design students who want to participate in the design aspect of urban design. And for all those people interested in urban design who desire access to design— to make urban design compositions, to test planning policy, to educate and inform citizens of development implications, and to explore the making of place. Surprisingly, many planning-based urban design programs teach students about urban design, not *how to design*. Reasons given for this lack of design education range from "not enough time in a two-year curriculum" to "insufficient resources". Because design is a process of exploration and discovery, design as a compositional "making" process must be inherent in *urban design—for all students*. I hope this book can provide a resource base for students and beginning designers in understanding and engaging urban design in all aspects.

A dual mission

There are two critical missions in this book: the first deals with the instruction of the elements and principles of design and composition—a necessary starting point and often not taught in planning programs; the second deals with the challenge of applying design composition principles and methods to the complex nature of cities—often a messy and complicated array of forces, influences, politics, and social pressures facing the design process. Bringing these two missions together for students is a key aspiration of this book.

The discussions on theory and the complexity of urban reality can assist established designers— architects and landscape architects—to better apply their design skills to the rich characteristics of cities, going beyond form for form's sake and attaining a new level of design composition that understands and responds to urban complexity.

Urban design defines the intentional forming of the spatial dimensions of human settlements, both from direct design actions and as influenced by public policy. These actions and policies are based on the stories, meanings, and functional needs observed in and assessed from the integral forces within human settlements: culture, space and time (CST) (Soja, 1996). They are inseparable and provide the foundation for exploring the focus of this book—design composition. Design composition is a part of urban planning that has been minimized in the planning process, and treated as a separate "artsy" fringe application to planning.

Why focus on design composition? Because in my experience and study as an architect and urban planner for over 40 years, not enough people who affect urban form are knowledgeable about design; they cannot engage in its exploratory and evolutionary nature; they can only talk about it in generalities, leading to mediocre built form at best. And by increasing the number of people who can engage design composition within this complex CST trialectic, hopefully the quality of the built environment can be significantly improved through the multiplicity of daily decisions affecting the built form. Consequently, this book is targeted at urban planners, beginning designers, elected officials, developers, and citizens. This book addresses design composition in an instructive process beginning with basic semi-abstract elements and principles and advancing to more complex compositional challenges with the multiple dimensions in human settlements.

Design, the making of spatial constructs, is an integral part of this trialectic, deriving from it the basis for its metaphors, stories, and meaning. Too often, urban design is left to chance, accident, guided by vague policies, minimized in the larger planning analytical process, and often perceived by too many planners and academics as "drawing" or graphic representation of predetermined planning concepts. Architects in turn can focus solely on design with insufficient attention to the socio-cultural-historic aspects of human interactions, in the same way that planners diminish the spatial aspects. We see this represented in design based on nostalgia and themes in many countries. We are bewildered when sound planning processes result in compromised and mediocre built form, in large part because "design," the act of making built form, is privy to too few.

Urban Design: The Composition of Complexity addresses the importance of design as a vital link to quality built form that must survive the complexities of this multi-dimensional CST trialectic, from competition for basic needs, to the search for community identity, to the complications of urban politics, and must, in my opinion, involve a lot more people beyond the design professions. As we expand the underlying n-dimensional matrix of community (CST), we require more informed design-sensitive decision makers.

We are not superhuman. This composition of complexity requires interdisciplinary engagement; more time and involvement in the analysis of human settlement issues and the spatial patterns associated therein; more design testing of policy and development impacts. I teach urban design as a trialectic: intentionally making urban form; testing urban policy; informing, involving, and engaging the people who inhabit that form.

The audience

I began writing this book for my urban planning students: intelligent, motivated, curious and, I realized after too many "talking circles" in urban design studios, lacking an understanding of design process, methodology, and skills. This lack prevented them from truly engaging the design exploration process, relegating them to "data analysis," meeting facilitators and wallflowers. Talking about urban form and design is not enough. It requires engagement, even "play" as I discuss later. Here's to you gang, to your desire to be a part of the design process, and to your increased understanding of design composition through hands-on experimentation with the elements, principles, relationships, and methods of design composition in complex urban situations.

As I ventured further into the work, and discussed the projected audience with planning colleagues, elected officials, and developers, the book's usefulness for these other urbanists became apparent. Applications of the book's content to site design, design review, design guidelines, and form-based zoning strategies were all mentioned in these discussions. Hopefully the ideas and exercises can increase the non-designer's engagement in the design process through a working knowledge of design composition, further increasing the quality of urban design dialogue across the built form spectrum.

"Composition" and "complexity" are the key words and are the subjects of this book—creating form for diverse and complex urban meaning and functionality, referenced throughout the book. Composition and its organizational and structural relationships are the foundation for cityscapes. From planning policy to design review, design composition organizes and structures this meaning and functionality into rich, creative, and coherent wholes. Planning and design decision makers can be more of a proactive part of the urban design process.

Access to design

There was . . . an international force for change of dramatic potency that never appears in discussions about the roots of modern art and is only rarely mentioned as an influence on the movement's pioneers. The Victorian childhood of the seminal modernists and their audience at large coincided with the development and widespread embrace of a radical educational system that was a catalyst in exploding the cultural past and restructuring the resulting intellectual panoply with a new world view . . . It has been largely ignored because its participants—three- to seven-year olds—were in the primary band of the scholastic spectrum. It was the seed pearl of the modern era and it was called *kindergarten*.

(Brosterman, 1997, p. 7) (my emphasis)

The beginnings of design in some cultures began very early, as a part of life, not as a profession and career. In North American educational programs, we have lost some of that engagement with design in our everyday lives. Children play digital games, not with blocks and paper, glue and scissors—more sensory play. And for many adults it is not too late to start playing again. Design and play, a magical combination worthy of pursuit for us all, and a requirement for engaging with this work.

Is urban design the purview of architects, urban designers, and landscape architects only? Traditionally, yes. And I argue that if many more people can understand the basis for composing forms as spatial relationships representing meaning and functionality, at least a working knowledge of design can place them at the decision-making table—as emerging designers.

This book takes the reader on an incremental and progressive process in design, from abstract compositions to applications and experiments with more challenging urban design compositions in complex spatial contexts. Engaging these experiments and exercises can bring reticence, doubt, and fear. Let's begin with fear.

The fear of making/creativity

Mrs. Anna Lloyd Wright . . . was one of the many visitors (at the Centennial Exposition in Philadelphia in 1876) . . . and . . . was fascinated by the systematic clarity of the toys and games and intrigued by the theoretical notions of "unity" expressed by . . . the young teacher in charge . . . and observe(d) the children engaged in active play . . . in focused concentration, seated at long, low tables with orthogonally gridded surfaces, creating geometric designs from small pieces of wood, colored paper, thread, or wire.

(Brosterman, 1997, p. 10)

These young children were immersed into the play aspect of design early in their education, building excitement and confidence long before the fears of later years took root. For many, creative play became a part of their cognitive thought process that carried through life and flowered in many various creative ways (Brosterman, 1997).

My intent in this book for young planners, emerging designers, and interested lay people is twofold: to guide them through a playful learning process for design, and to connect that design process to the complexities of human settlements. In order to explore design as a play-full process, everyone needs to confront the many aspects of fear: reticence, fear of failure, fear of success, fear of comparison, fear of engagement, and so on-—all natural feelings and all manageable. A student in my painting class asked me what "fear of success" meant. Based on years of observation, some students who are shy or more inward do not want to have attention called to themselves, thus avoiding the limelight with less notable work. There are many forms of fear.

Most people encounter some form of fear when they participate in what is referred to as the creative design process: making something that is new, innovative, exploratory, and uncertain; especially when it requires a hands-on crafted process. Welcome to the real world, you are not alone.

- Talent
- Fear
- Working through fear
- Failing
- Play-work
- Creative actions
- Uncertainity.

Let's redefine *talent. Webster's Dictionary* defines it as "a natural ability or power; a special, superior ability in an art, science, craft, etc." I don't agree on the "superior ability" or the "natural ability" parts. Based on my experience with students in design and painting, I argue that talent is a developed ability based on an openness that enables a person to "let go," to engage the act of making something with fewer barriers, fueled by an immersive joy rather than reticence or fear of engagement. Here is another definition from my perspective and experience: talent is *a state of creative and playful energy that emanates from the reduction or overcoming of fear; where fear is replaced by confident motivation that emanates from a fear-reduced crafting/artful process (writing, drawing, dancing, singing, playing music, etc.).*

With less fear, people are more able to engage and develop skills that increase confidence, which increases motivation that increases the quality of those skills and their application in art. This does not say that "talented" people have no fear; quite the contrary—and many find an oasis of passion, a "freedom," and joy in a particular craft/art that replaces fear and allows open and motivated access to that craft/art— once they learn how to play.

In my watercolor classes, an important underlying effort is to reduce that fear in various forms (a lot of bad jokes for a start!); specific and constructive critiques not criticisms; building confidence in essential techniques through supportive guidance; thereby increasing the motivation and engagement in those skills that can lead to creative (talented) endeavors. Many of these students reach a certain plateau of technical ability with positive guidance. That is when there can be a significant increase in confidence and motivation and subsequent quality results. Are they talented?

Years ago I was guiding two friends of my daughter, early teenage students, in basic drawing. One eagerly sat down and drew an exact representation of a horse from a photograph; the second did some avoidance exercises (retrieved some snacks from the kitchen, moved tools around on the table, etc.) then began drawing while fretting about someone looking at the work, already comparing that work to the first student's efforts. The observation and interaction with the subject, the horse, was broken and disrupted; fear had intervened in the focus and engagement. Needless to say, the drawing was cartoonish, distorted (from memory), and hesitant. Was one more talented than the other? No. Watching them both, I concluded that the first had little or no fear of drawing (and little previous experience), and was able to see and translate what was observed clearly and directly to the paper. The other was being too mental and self-critical, demonstrating a fear of comparison and fear of failure, preventing that student from engaging the drawing.

Frank Webb (1990), an American impressionist watercolor painter, states that fear is a necessary ingredient inherent in art and its making; an ingredient to recognize and engage. That is why I tell students that "failing" is really a part of exploration and innovation (assuming the work energy is real). In watercolor painting, for example, I ask students to push a color past its darkest value and make it fail or break or go opaque. Why? So they know its limits! Being conservative, hesitant, and timid keeps their efforts in the mid-range, the mediocre center with little or no growth.

Which brings us to *play-work*! Play-work is a phrase I use with students that encompasses both the openness, freedom, absorption, and exploration of play (as in our childhood) and the work energy required in that play to apply ideas and concepts through the crafting process into *something made*. I cringe when I hear educators state that it is either *process or product*. It is both! In every process, from social interactions to arts and crafts, there is an emerging physical/spatial outcome, a design inherent in all aspects of process and manifested at given time intervals, made apparent to the senses, revealed in real spatial terms. Play enables us to openly experiment and explore, moving wooden blocks and sticks around in uncertain and curious fashion, just as Anna Wright's son learned to do, discovering new directions through that play, directions not apparent from a solely mental or intellectual process. Hopefully the exercises in this book can restore or initiate that play-work sensation in many readers.

To create is to bring into being (something that did not exist before); *creative* is to be imaginative and inventive. This requires an understanding of basic principles, experienced conventions, and the limits of a design problem in order to push those limits outward into a new state of being, a state where old boundaries have dissolved and new boundaries are emerging only to be challenged again. Fear, failing, play-work are all a part of that process/product. Jump in the water. And creativity requires a capacity for creative energy, something that needs nurturing—reduce the fear and increase the capacity for creativity.

Uncertainty is in my experience an important positive principle in design. Being uncertain of the outcome enables the designer to focus on the creative energies within the process, where that process leads to discovery and *creates* the outcome. Working toward a predetermined outcome is simply filling in the spaces or shapes—painting by numbers. The principle of uncertainty is well stated by Charles Johnston (1984/1986, 1991)—there is no goal (as outcome) and the aspiration (of the process) is to maintain the integrity of the dynamics (creative energy) of the process. Years ago while attending a writing workshop in La Conner, Washington, led by author Tom Robbins, I listened as Tom explained his approach to writing; he crafted each sentence and paragraph with as much creative energy and imagination as possible, with those crafted passages aiding in and leading to the formation of the next paragraph and concept, building toward an uncertain future. Tom explained that he had a contract for a 650-page book and at page 600 still had little idea of how it would end. And the book came to successful fruition.

In grounded theory (Strauss and Corbin, 1998), the analysis and insight from the data leads to the outcome, more than proving or disproving an existing hypothesis. This fosters more creative discovery in the process. There are recognized behaviors associated with creative thinking and include:

- being open to multiple possibilities
- generating lists of options
- exploring various possibilities before choosing one
- making use of multiple avenues of expression (art, music, and metaphors) to stimulate thinking

- using nonlinear forms of thinking such as going back and forth, and circumventing around a subject to get a fresh start
- trusting process and not holding back
- putting energy and effort into the process
- having fun while doing the effort.

(Strauss and Corbin, 1998, p. 13)

This is similar to the design process—discovery not certainty. The same applies in the public involvement processes: going into a public workshop with a predetermined goal to be tested by the public leaves little room for creativity, interaction, and innovation or public authorship. Moreover, going into a workshop with a range of aspirations and avenues for dialogue, having an area of study, without a predetermined outcome, most likely will result in creative "thirdspace" solutions (see Appendix II).

As a final setup for the main contents of the book, design composition needs to be connected to the real world, to the foundation for design rationale: urban meaning and urban functionality.

Connecting design to reality: urban meaning and urban functionality

As discussed below, design is a part of a larger dialogue about the main components of human settlements: *culture*, which entails the patterns of human behavior from basic habitation patterns, to social relations, to economics, to politics, and so on; *space*, which encompasses the physical reality of our settlements from built form to natural environments; and *time*, extending from history to the emergent present and to future probabilities. This book is about the act of form-making, composing the results of this dialogue into multi-dimensional spatial realities, so often referred to as *place*.

For the beginning designer, it is important to understand the role of design composition as an inherent part of this dialogue and not simply a representational or pictorial rendition of planning dialogue. The design process diagram summarizes the role of design composition in this larger dialogue. Design's role is not linear but inherently entwined in the trialectic of culture, space, and time (CST).

- *The n-dimensional matrix.* Reality is observed as a complex matrix of human–environment interactions, the CST matrix that is a tool of understanding by the design communities using a multitude of planning, sociological, and urban form methodologies.
- *Urban meaning.* This produces an emergent story or *urban meaning* that in turn expresses issues in time and requires needs, desires, and resources relative to those issues. This meaning leads to the CST program.
- *Urban functionality.* This represents the needs and operational aspects of human settlements, from waste recycling to transportation and circulation.
- *The CST program.* The CST program specifies the needs and resources required by human settlements and their associated urban meaning in terms of *what, how much, and where*. In architecture, the program is often referred to as the space program, used for institutional design, public projects, and as market analyses in housing development. This program is essentially the ingredients list for a larger recipe.
- *Organizational relationships.* The CST program is only an ingredients list and requires action to place the ingredients in relationships—a complex and critical planning function. The organizational relationships establish the underlying principles for function and meaning separate from the spatial context. The extent and dimension of these principles are specified as a result of

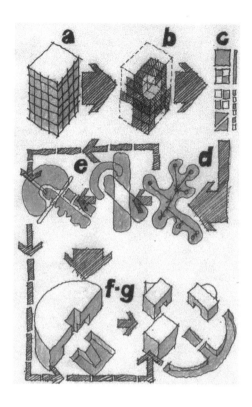

Figure 1.1. Design process diagram.
The design composition process begins in the understanding of reality—the cultural, spatial and temporal/historic (CST) interactions of real life— the n-dimensional matrix (a). Within this matrix emerge a multiplicity of stories describing the meanings and functions occurring in and over time, referred to here as urban meaning and functionality (b). From this matrix the community and designer(s) identify and specify needs and resources required for this meaning/functionality, the CST program (c): what, how much and where? Once established, they are arranged in coherent organizational relationships, (d), exhibiting compatibility. These organizational and functional relationships are then interacted with the spatial context of site, neighborhood, district etc. to extend the organizational relationship into a functional "fit" with that context (e). The task of making form-decisions in meaningful compositional patterns and structures begins (f) as need, organization, context, and form are playfully integrated and structurally assembled—constantly eliciting emergent patterns until a healthy composition takes shape, (g).

the CST program. Essentially, the "organization of the chair" and the basic sizes or requirements of the basic components required for "seating" are now known to the designer. The meaning and function within these organizational relationships are often defined as clusters within clusters, or places within places (Kasprisin and Pettinari, 1995)—a network of coherent and meaningful arrangements of activities expressed as organizational relationships.

- *"Fit" of organizational relationship to context.* The form begins to take shape as the organizational principles, compatible within themselves, are now interacted with reality, the physical–spatial components of context; the organizational relationship changes and adjusts to new compatibility requirements with the larger context.

- *The structural relationship.* The role of form-maker becomes critical in this phase as the organizational relationships are brought more intimately into interactions with the physical dimensions of reality or context, from bio-physical conditions, to jurisdictional, to administrative, to user conditions, all relative to context. The compositional process has begun in earnest. The principles of the "chair's organizational relationships" take form by assembly or structuring, expressed in materials, form, and structural relationships.

- *Play-work and design testing.* Design composition is not complete once a structural assembly occurs. The exploration of more appropriate and context-responsive design options requires a crafting and testing process with a strong dose of uncertainty in order for the design composition to evolve and hold up to the complexity of the requirements of the n-dimensional matrix or urban meaning(s).

And this description barely scratches the surface . . .

The foundation for design: the interactions of culture, space, and time

There are three significant dimensions that *interactively* craft human settlements, *culture, space, and time (history)* (Soja, 1996). A fourth factor, one that is assumed but not mentioned, is the *socio-biological,* the actions of human biology on socio-cultural factors. These interactions produce "urban meaning" and "urban functionality" (Castells, 1983), the containers for the complex stories, metaphors, traditions, emergent patterns, and needs in human settlements. Often, planning decisions are made with only one or two of these dimensions actively considered. Thus we have built-form by-products emanating from culture and history, and monuments and crafted artifacts from spatial emphases. None may really enable a quality built form. One of the longer-term goals as a "planner" or "designer" is to understand all three influences on the making of human settlements in order to integrate them into good city form—the emergent product or spatial pattern at a given time interval.

The explorations of this book focus on the spatial aspect of human settlements without losing sight of the other co-ingredients in the above trialectic, which together constitute urban meaning and urban functionality. Adequately engaged, this trialectic can lead to better design decisions, decisions required in the making of cities, instead of leaving their form-building energies to accident and expediency (more on this in Chapter 9).

Composition of complexity for planners and designers

When the spatial potentials of design are expanded by the culture/space/time trialectic, or interaction, the design framework of context, program, and composition expands as a multi-dimensional matrix of possible outcomes—daunting and exhilarating. As designers, we can only take in so much information. Hopefully this book's guidance can enable new designers to move beyond the semi-abstraction of planning; to deal with these complex CST patterns; to enter into the magical world of composing spatial relationships that address and interpret this complex urban meaning and its functionality. The more information we encounter the more complex the process becomes: and the more in need the process is of new methodologies.

Design as compositional order and compositional structure

This work explores many definitions of urban design, summarized in Chapter 2, striving to bring them into a large related coherence, beginning from the basic building blocks of *compositional order* as the main focus and evolving to the integration of form, use, motive (Lynch, 1989), culture, space, and time (Soja, 1996), through the use of *compositional structure*—where these building blocks and elements are put into spatial relationships.

(Urban or community) design is both intentional and unintentional, performed directly by trained designers and indirectly by politicians, the marketplace, engineers, and people in their everyday activities. As practicing planners, your everyday decisions *do* affect and influence the built form, making you urban builders—and maybe designers.

Most planners, community leaders, and developers know little about design. They rely extensively on consultants or mimic other communities' work; examples of what others have identified as "preferred" and "not preferred"; or examples of designs from other urban contexts. *All* have the capability of engaging design as process and product. But we must go beyond the discussion of design to its essence—the crafting of meaning into form. This is called the "eidetic form" (Friedman, 2000) where form and idea become one, resulting from an exploratory process beyond the mental; where the original *idea as mental notion* evolves into the eidetic form.

Some readers hopefully will pursue additional design instruction and experiences; others may use an increased awareness of design to augment their own non-design career paths. For all, the basic question is: can each of you, with your present inexperience in "design", begin to participate in the geometry (earth measure) and compositional ordering of physical space as so-called non-designers with preparation and guidance in design composition? My answer is yes, with work and motivation.

This book sets out to advance your capability, without previous design education, as participatory designers. The book seeks to go beyond the rhetoric of design examples ("good and bad," "preferred and not preferred"), introducing you to design elements, principles, and composition through a combination of discussions, information sharing, and hands-on crafting processes. Design needs to be experienced; it is both an application of theory and principle as well as trial and error, all evolving together. It involves fear and failing as well as euphoria and success. "Failing" is okay, when it is a concerted effort to put geometry to a stated need or program in a given physical situation that doesn't quite work. Of course, it really is *not failing but exploring*. As we shall discuss in the beginning, it is a playful experience, abstract and real, conceptual and measured. You are asked to assist your own learning process by actively and intently engaging the readings, discussions, and exercises.

You will teach yourself how to design by engaging the crafting process, and I am your guide.

A final word: in urban design, we seek to integrate the orders of composition with the meaning of culture and community over periods of time. The "order" does not mean regimentation or rigidity; it brings a coherence and effectiveness to the making of the built form—from strategy to assembly. The "meaning" is the underlying story that drives the "what, how much, and where." Dealing with time and context challenges the order of composition, adding a richness to design and its meaning, and requiring the designer to juggle, adjust, and adapt.

Bibliography

Brosterman, Norman, 1997: *Inventing Kindergarten*: Harry N. Abrams, Inc., New York.

Castells, Manuel, 1983: "The Process of Urban Social Change." In *Designing Cities: Critical Readings in Urban Design*: Cuthbert, Alexander R. (ed.), 2003, Blackwell Publishers, Cambridge, MA.

Friedman, Jonathan Block, 2000: *Creation in Space: A Course in the Fundamentals of Architecture, Vol. 1: Architectonics*, Kendall Hunt Publishing, Dubuque, IA.

Johnston, Charles MD, 1984/1986: *The Creative Imperative*: Celestial Arts, Berkeley, CA.

Johnston, Charles MD, 1991: *Necessary Wisdom*: Celestial Arts, Berkeley, CA.

Kasprisin, Ron and Pettinari, James, 1995: *Visual Thinking for Architects and Designers*: John Wiley & Sons, Inc., New York.

Lynch, Kevin, 1989: *Good City Form*: MIT Press, Cambridge, MA/London, UK.

Soja, Edward W., 1996: *Thirdspace*: Blackwell Publishers, Cambridge, MA.

Strauss, Anselm and Corbin, Juliet, 1998: *Basics of Qualitative Research*: Sage Publications, Inc., Thousand Oaks, CA.

Webb, Frank, 1990: *Webb on Watercolor*: North Light Books, Cincinnati, OH.

Webster's New World Dictionary, Second Concise Edition, 1975: William Collins & World Publishing Co., Inc.

Chapter 2

DEFINITIONS AND FUNDAMENTALS OF URBAN DESIGN IN CULTURE

I am amused at the many times I have been with urban design colleagues and the definition of urban design enters the dialogue—no consensus and lots of viewpoints. And that is a good place to start because the term *urban design* represents a wide array of agendas, points of view, approaches, theory etc., and in short there is no one definition. So I begin this section with the basic premise that urban design, like architecture, landscape architecture, industrial design etc., is about making or comprising something physical—a composition with *urban* dimensions ranging from the residential community or hamlet scale to large metropolitan scales. And I discuss why urban design is more than a dimensional focus—in fact, it is a design process that translates the complex dimensions and relationships of *urban meaning and functionality* into physical compositions. There is our challenge.

(The many) definitions of urban design

Urban design has as many definitions as there are faculty members in a design curriculum, and more. They all have relevance and they all contribute to a larger design perspective. Understanding the range of definitions assists students in identifying the varying agendas and perspectives (yes, politics!) that are positioned within and influence the urban studies disciplines.

Urban design is a broad term with many interpretations: design is generally understood to deal with physical quality and aspects of the environment, such as the spaces between buildings, the relationship of buildings to open space, and the larger structure of cities as defined by the infrastructure of utilities, streets, and block layout. To a lesser extent, urban design encompasses urban beautification, pedestrian and bicycle circulation, and building styles.

Definitions of urban design vary dramatically depending upon the background(s) of the designer or physical planner, from geography to landscape architecture, to architect, to sociology.

Urban design schools have produced practitioners whose major focus is the making of form— form-making on a large scale; others with less design background focus on the relationships between and among culture, where urban design is a function of those cultures. These perspectives are all valid and comprise the larger definition of urban design. As I discuss in the book, the foundation of urban design is both design (spatial) and culture (human behavior) in time over time.

> Community design (is) concerned with the organization of human communities . . . (focusing) on "organization" and only later on "form" to stress the systematic basis of community design . . . based on good technical knowledge, imagination, analytical understanding of the systematic nature of cities, and political commitment to social justice and democracy.
>
> (Lazano, 1990, p. 2)

Under (the) concept of urbanism, the physical design of urban areas is an extrapolation of the activity of individual building design, based more often than not on the same compositional rules … the application of compositional rules—originating on the scale of buildings—to urban-scale complexes is the basic characteristic of urbanism, regardless of stylistic differences … (and) the relative inexperience of professionals in dealing with community-wide design problems, as well as their lack of analytical insight, lead to mechanistic justifications to support a compositional image … Urbanism, in merely transposing architectural compositional rules to urban complexes, restricts urban design to the choice of a single powerful compositional idea.

(Lazano, 1990, p. 23)

Design as a function of culture and the larger civilization is an art as well as a quantitative and technical construction process. The art requires play and creativity to deal with the complexity of the urban scale. Playing in creative ways leads to exploration and discovery beyond the quantitative process; and encompasses both the qualitative and quantitative, the intuitive and rational aspects of thought. As we shall see in this book, the cognitive perception component of thinking (thinking with the senses) along with the intellectual counterpart (thinking with the mind) is essential to form-making and the design of spatial constructs. Design requires a use of the medium of space, i.e. drawing, constructing models, playing with clay, paper and cardboard. These are not the tools of dinosaurs. I refer to the entire process as whole mind–body thinking.

Form is measured through geometry, the earth measure. Design is the forming of compositional order (Goldstein, 1989) integral with the *creative reality* of human cultures and their settlements.

The term *urban design* is in reality an umbrella term under which all of the above are represented. For this discussion, I consider urban design's foundation to be in the dimensions of community, and as such, I argue that urban design can be expressed as:

The spatial composition of a multi-dimensional complexity of community as translated (by the community with the assistance of designers) from the observed (urban) meaning of community.

I provide multiple examples of definitions for urban design at the beginning of this chapter. Let's begin our understanding of this spatial composition with a real basic understanding of the terms without the politics and embellishments.

Urban is a word defining scale, meaning a physical "characteristic of the city as distinguished from the country"; "constituting a city or town". In this vein, terms such as "regional" and "rural" have the same importance to design simply at a different scale connotation. I often use the term "community design" because it defines a group of people in association or in social units within a space that is not scale-specific. Whatever scale term is used, remember to add "meaning" and "function" after it to reference and connect the culture/space/time trialectic to the scale, a factor in complexity.

Design is a process of making something (physical in our case) that inherently has emergent products or spatial patterns in given time-frames that manifest the ever-changing realities in a community (Johnston, 1991) occurring within the process. They are connected and not separate realities. This is not a debate about form following function or vice versa; or process versus product. If I ignore the product component of design, the process never gets tested and advanced.

Key issues on design from various authors are:

1   The design of space is a function of culture (need, identity, function, form, manufacture, decoration, and symbols) (Lazano, 1990); in reality one does not follow another but are intertwined.

2   Design is a process of making or shaping physical forms through cognitive perception (senses) (Arnheim, 1969)—it is not simply an intellectual process nor can it be; this is critical for the beginning designer to understand: the act of "crafting"—playing with the elements and principles of composition—is an act of thinking, leading to exploration and discovery beyond the mental thought process. Design is not linear and constitutes a sensual engagement with reality (not virtual reality).

3   "The explicit, programmatic goal of the early kindergartens was to awaken the senses to what Fredrich Froebel considered to be the . . . structure underlying all growth—from animal, vegetable, mineral—in nature" (Brosterman, 1997, pp. 12–13), *where Froebel makes an early connection to ecological principles.*

4   Design consists of *elements* (building blocks or spatial nouns), *principles* (rules of assembly or spatial verbs), *relationships* or interactions and connections among elements and their resultant configurations in composition (the connective outcome of two or more assembled elements exhibiting a set of principles or rules of conduct, telling a story or representing a metaphor).

5   Design becomes the "third space"; the whole that is different from the sum of its parts; the uncertain outcome of creative action; the eidetic vision where form and function meld into one formation, not as a compromise or blending but as a spatial dance of form and idea.

6   Design is founded in real life and the physics of that reality. Thus I suggest additional readings in creative systems (Capra, 1982; Johnston, 1984/1986) and ecology (Maturana and Verala, 1980; Bateson, 1972).

Manifestations of urban design in civilization and culture

The reality or meaning of human settlements

The reality or meaning of human settlements is an intricate dance, comprising the basic rationale for design. Understanding this reality requires both *quantitative and qualitative processes working in synchronicity,* exploring the spatial pattern probabilities. The dance is at times coherent and synchronized and at times in conflict as a part of changing dimensions and new interactions. By themselves these processes are merely forms and numbers of incomplete measurement. In design, they comprise *a continuing interactive pursuit that seeks to bring order to these complex interactions and is neither predictable nor governable by long-range goals (a journey without goals), viewed more as emergent probabilities.*

For the pursuit of a basis for composition in the book, I reference the work of Manuel Castells, Edward Soja, and others as they clarify the dance.

- *Urban meaning* is "the structural performance assigned as a goal [directional aspiration] to cities in general . . . by the conflicting process between historical [and contemporary] actors in a given society."
- *Urban function* is "the articulated system of organizational means aimed at performing the goals assigned to each city by its historically defined urban meaning."
- "Urban meaning and urban functions jointly determine urban form" (Castells, 1983, p. 24).

Castells and his colleagues do not argue that economy determines urban form; they are underscoring the relationship and hierarchy between historic meaning, urban functions, and spatial forms. They describe *urban form* as "the symbolic expression of urban meaning and of the historical superimposition of urban meanings (and their forms) always determined by a *conflictive process* (my emphasis) between historical actors." The conflicts by these actors occur over the definition of urban meaning, over the adequate performance of urban functions from the varying perspectives of different interests, values, and approaches, and over the adequate symbolic expression of urban meaning and (or) functions.

Consequently, they define *urban planning* as the negotiated adaptation of urban functions to a shared urban meaning; for our purposes here, they define *urban design* as *the symbolic attempt to express an accepted urban meaning in certain urban forms.* The metric tensor (Kaku, 1994) or complexity matrix begins. Alexander Cuthbert (2003) goes to great lengths to emphasize that urban design is a wholly contextual process, not just a process of "skills" as perceived by some planning academics; that we place our emphasis not on core skills, but on core "knowledge"—stressing the reflexive relationships between actors, processes, concepts, and traditions.

In order for this to be translated into the "making of something," I argue that we do need the core skills in concert and they need to adapt in their type and application in accordance with the complexity affecting that composition. Those skills are affected by the integration of culture and time to space. Based on this complexity in defining meaning and functionality, we need a new language to convey this complexity.

Expanding urban meaning: space, culture, and time/history

Edward Soja's work in *Thirdspace* (1996) and *Postmetropolis* (2000), sets the stage for understanding the community-reality base for design: the trialectic of space, culture, and time/history.

Space

Here are some definitions of space used in urban design for discussion purposes. The bottom line is that space is inherent in all aspects of life and living; and the design of space needs to reflect and manifest that life and living in its meaning, form, and materials—intellectually obvious and yet challenging to achieve with integrity.

1   Space as enclosed behavior, a concept that moved to the forefront of urban design in the 1960s with the ecological movement and the embracing of environmental psychology by the design community.

2   Space as enclosed need and function: the basis for what and how much in urban functionality.

3   Space as living system—an ecological design process where design product and pattern emanates through and from an ecological process, and does not stand alone as "green product" or eco-design hardware or "sustainable design": if the process is not ecological in nature neither is the outcome.

4   Space as ordered form through geometry: shapes in relationship (shape components, values, color, composition).

5   The existential purpose of building is to make a site become a place to uncover the meanings potentially present in the given environment *because we exist in it and are a responsible part of that environment.*

6   Spatial structure orients through assembly the concrete objects of identification as organizational relationships (this is the "how" of making something).

7   Space possesses enclosure and extension and connection to other space.

8   Space is a real form manifestation of meaning and function, and once made "concrete," begins to change again in meaning and function: the emergent reality.

The above descriptions of space represent work from Edward Hall (1966), Christopher Alexander (1964), Robert Bechtel (1977), Paul Spreiregen (1965), Eduardo Lazano (1990), Hamid Shirvani (1985), Edward Soja (1996), Geoffrey Broadbent (1990), and others.

Culture

Culture is multi-faceted and complex. Let's begin with *Webster's Dictionary*:

> . . . the ideas, customs, skills, arts, etc. of a given people in a given time period . . .

Within these ideas, customs, skills, etc. Soja and others include economics, politics, social issues, and interactions all as functions of culture. Culture also leads us into a discussion of who designs cities! This involves the aesthetic ideology in urban design (Rubin, 1979, p. 23), representing a polarization in Western civilization between urban function and urban "culture," where many students of culture have been unable to come to terms with the city—the modern city—as a symbolic manifestation of values mediated by form (Rubin, 1979).

The umbrella term "culture" requires an interdisciplinary approach to community observation and analysis. And, as I discuss further, the design process must be open to the community in ways that are interactive and provide community members with genuine authorship within the design process. This does not lessen the role of the urban designer—it greatly expands that role (see Appendix II).

Here is a clear role in design for the many components of urban studies—assessing the interactions of space, culture, and time.

The metric tensor builds again—more complex.

Time/history

Think of time as periodicities, lengths of time within which actions occur and new forms emerge from those actions; to change once again as a new periodicity occurs, most likely with a new context and new limits. These periodicities are containers of time, framing and marking with cultural symbology the emergent realities or forms resulting from the *salmagundi*. The containers are measurements of time in direct relation to the cultural customs and ideas manifested in emergent forms, in the architecture, manufacturing, and arts of the period.

The time component includes and goes beyond the aspect of historic preservation and protection. Protecting aspects of community for historic significance provides a connection to the past cultures and styles but does not necessarily bridge that past to the emergent present. So time provides designers with three components: history and knowledge; present and emerging patterns; and probable and uncertain aspirations and outcomes.

Later in the book I refer to the importance of "remnants" as opposed to artifacts as ways to bridge the past, present, and future. Simply put, artifacts are objects remaining from a past time; remnants are relational patterns. These patterns are often composed of physical/spatial elements and configurations left over from a larger historic pattern and reflect an imprint of the historic time period's culture (sociology, politics, crafts, materials, meaning, etc.). These remnants may have enough energy and creative capability to bridge the time gap, historic to contemporary, contemporary to future, being reconstituted or reinvented into a meaningful part of contemporary composition. I enlarge on this in Appendix III.

The emergence of design in culture

Let's return to design and review its fundamental basis in history and the human dimension. Many students now enamored with the digital world often forget or overlook the basic origins of design—as a function of culture.

The human experience and measurement

Design constitutes innovations involving urban meaning and urban function from camp to village to city, based on real experiences of food production, defensibility, family unit needs, and services, expressed in the basic cultural needs of survival:

- land division for plowing: the amount of land a person can till (non-mechanically) in a work day, i.e. the acre (about 209 sq. feet or 66 sq. metres)
- plotting of settlements (families, clans, trades, subsistence)
- lots into squares, yards, and gardens: for common shared lands (pastures, food production), security, and a social hierarchy (in Pompeii, for example, a family may own a villa with a street-front shop backed by a common courtyard for the shop and apartments in the front followed by a smaller private court in the rear for the master family)
- defense: the camp, the moat, and the wall (the habitat and the edge)
- made to human measure, that is within human "parameters" or to human scale, constructed by humans within their "reach" and limits of their tools; and remember the historic origins of dimensions as the average Roman legionnaire was four feet six inches in height and his thumb was an "inch"; the classic Roman tile pattern was the extent that a craftsman could reach, etc.
- the city designed with an optimum size in design (Greeks).

The Greeks viewed the design of their towns from a sense of the finite, the human dimension, essentially understandable and workable to city dwellers (Spreiregen, 1965).

Beyond human need and measurement—abstraction, the power of grandeur, and the defensible space

Enter the later Romans: the cultures of the god-Caesar, the module or system of proportions:

- the major and minor street: arterial and collector
- the expanded use of the grid: dispersed and efficient circulation
- the monument: the rise and expression of political power and influence on design

- the enclosed urban space: privacy and security
- inspiration for the Renaissance
- the importance of infrastructure as space organizer
- the sewers of Rome: grand and failed engineering.

The medievalists, the emerging cultures recovering from the collapse:

- the remnant bishoprates dominated by church and monastery
- the castle towns and cities (defense, city states, turf wars)
- fortifications, churches, guild halls, and burgers' houses
- wall surrounding wall surrounding wall; edges and containments.

Medieval architects designed within the existing context—irregular and evolving according to cultural and economic pressures of the time, including security and a growing merchant class (Spreiregen, 1965). The complexity of context! The metric tensor builds again.

The Renaissance brought ideal city designs, connections between monuments, and found design ideas in the classical orders and ornaments, expanding their use and introducing the "colossal" or "gigantic" order, where buildings are seen from afar as well as close up. And the merchant class and patron matured, the forms of emerging capitalism.

The industrial era and the cultures of technology

The emerging mechanical era and the culmination of the Cartesian approach to design:

- ideal towns
- worker towns
- "hygeia" for health and fresh air; Jefferson's grid park scheme
- English planned industrial towns
- Pullman, Illinois (1879), Port Sunlight (1887), Gary, Indiana (1906), Kohler, Wisconsin and Lowell, Massachusetts (1822).

The technology of the industrial era: railroads, highways, transit, airports, the emergent infrastructure or assembly framework of contemporary cities. This was the age of the public works directors; the urban function was dominant as catalyst in building cities.

Spreiregen (1965) cautions designers on the superficial embracing of technology, urging an evaluation of its usefulness to society and the quality of urban life, and avoiding its use through expedience or novelty.

The reaction to the industrial era: Garden City movement and the nature conservationists, the emerging cultures of reform and ecology awareness, placing man back in a position of cooperation with nature.

Friedrich Froebel easily assimilated the concepts of biological interconnectedness (ecology) into his work: "I could perceive unity in diversity, the correlation of forces, the interconnection of all living things, life in matter, and the principles of physics and biology" (see Brosterman, 1997, p. 18).

The American experiment

The pragmatic American era: Pragmatikos from the Greek—doing business, seeking out what works from various systems, not necessarily aligned, practical, the emerging cultures of the eclectic.

The City Beautiful movement: A reform movement, led by Daniel Burnham, in North American architecture and planning in the 1890s and early 1900s, which focused on European grandeur in design. Advocates believed the beautification brought about by this urban grandeur promoted moral and civic virtue (Broadbent, 1990).

The rise of the public works directors, engineering feats and large urban infrastructure, urban renewal.

The (early) New Communities movement, Radburn, New Jersey.

The changing and expanding urban region, post-Second World War and the dispersal of American cities: the suburb (flight from the grid) and rush to paradise.

Post-modern, nostalgia, New Urbanism and searches for new boundaries (Frank Gehry) and Postmetropolis (Edward Soja)

Post-modernism in architectural theory is a style; in literary theory it is referred to as a method. While there is no consensus on the debate, many in the fields of music, film-making, architecture, and art consider post-modernism as inherently a visual apprehension of the world. It emerged in conjunction with a new and vibrant, varied and pluralistic culture in the 1970s. The "style" has produced superstar projects and superstar architects all linked to capitalism, and "there is both similarity and continuity with the modernism that represents (and opposes) the 'high' capitalism of an advancing industrial age" (Zukin, 2003, p. 52). Maybe we can call this the culture of social differentiation?

New Urbanism (neo-traditional in Britain) has been described as "basically driven by a fundamentally economic and political agenda" embraced by capitalism, reactionary, localized, and historicist in nature (Cuthbert, 2003, p. 5). On one side of the debate, New Urbanism is seen as a rejection of suburbia and a return to a more formal urban framework; another perspective, mine included, views it as a conservative, formalized addition to suburbia. There are many aspects of New Urbanism that have been collected from other approaches and theories that have merit, so this criticizes more the rigid typologies, their packaging and selling. Contributions are in the area of packaging specificity in urban design implementation regulations, such as form-based zoning and more urban mixed-density concepts that have application in the small town and semi-rural landscapes (more on this later).

Frank Gehry and the new technologies of architecture: Frank Gehry has infused new design software technologies from the military and the space program into the process of architecture. The boundaries of form have taken new directions. Gehry's style is labeled as deconstructivist or DeCon Architecture based on the sculptured structural independence of the forms disconnected from local context and functional necessity.[1]

A search for meaning and connection and a return to the human dimension in urban design

Postmetropolis—after the mother city: Edward Soja discusses the break of suburban and outlying towns and cities from the historic mother city. Connections are stronger between and among these suburban and exurban communities than are their ties to the major cities of their regions. Freeways, loop highways, mega-malls, "big-box" intercept centers, and outlying employment campuses have all contributed to this cutting of the umbilical cord. Major new cities like Los Angeles and Las Vegas are emerging with entirely new patterns of urban form, new hybrids from the more traditional east coast and Midwestern cities.

A new regionalism: David Miller (2005) describes the emergence of a new regionalism in the Pacific northwest that breaks away from the international style that promoted a universal approach to design. Miller portrays this new regionalism as an architecture that is conceived out of local conditions; it resists being totally absorbed by the global imperatives of production and consumption. This critical regionalism adds to the growing metric tensor by adding contextual complexity to replace formalized models such as New Urbanism. Miller quotes architect Harwell Hamilton Harris on this regionalism, and I will use it as an argument for a responsiveness to contextual complexity: "to be expressed, an idea must be built. To be built, it must be particularized, localized, set within a region." Miller also refers to Kenneth Frampton's 1982 essay on critical regionalism that argues for an architecture that is conceived out of local conditions, and resists being totally absorbed by the global imperatives of production and consumption, where fashion is the enemy of integrity in design (Frampton, 1982).

Modernist corporatism

An ending point is the emergence and dominance, since the Second World War, of national and international corporations, entities disconnected from local community interests. These corporations contribute to a rise of corporate architecture and urban design as represented in shopping malls and plazas, office developments, and packaged retail outlets. Their focus on investor financial return leads to a packaging and marketing of products in space for consumer consumption, with less interest in the meaning of functionality of individual communities. American cities can have the same shopping center model repeated along major arterials every mile or so with the same retail and entertainment establishments—retail corporations—repeated in each center.

The packaging and marketing aspects of corporate urban development encourage predictable and repeatable forms from the big-box warehouse retail giants, to the *leisure centers* still occupied by franchise corporate retail outlets, to thematic or nostalgic residential development models. The gathering places of communities are now on private land, in *consumer capture spaces*, controlled and secured and policed by private entities. This is a powerful force in community development, architecture, and urban design, often replacing civic roles and responsibilities with corporate intermediaries.

The conflicting natures of modernist corporatism, the new regionalism, and creative urbanism are a part of the urban development pattern, part of the urban complexity. The urban designer has choices: accept and promote national and international models for expediency and packaging, or step beyond the models and re-enter the complexity of the ever-changing community organism for rich and innovative criteria or design.

Note

1   Frank Owen Gehry, born Frank Owen Goldberg in Toronto, Canada in 1929, recipient of the Pritzker Prize, Order of Canada, AIA Gold Medal and others, is a Los Angeles architect known for works such as the Guggenheim Museum in Bilbao, Spain; the Walt Disney Concert Hall in Los Angeles; Experience Music Center in Seattle and many others.

Bibliography

Alexander, Christopher, 1964: *Notes on the Synthesis of Form*: MIT Press, Cambridge, MA.

Arnheim, Rudolph, 1969: *Visual Thinking*: University of California Press, Berkeley, CA.

Bateson, Gregory, 1972: *Steps to an Ecology of the Mind*: Ballantine, New York.

Bechtel, Robert B., 1977: *Enclosing Behavior*: Dowden, Hutchinson & Ross, Inc., Stroudsburg, PA.

Broadbent, Geoffrey, 1990: *Emerging Concepts in Urban Space Design*: Spon Press, London.

Brosterman, Norman, 1997: *Inventing Kindergarten*: Harry N. Abrams, Inc., New York.

Capra, Fritjof, 1982: *The Turning Point*: Simon & Schuster, New York.

Castells, Manuel, 1983: "The Process of Urban Social Change". In *Designing Cities: Critical Readings in Urban Design*: Cuthbert, Alexander R. (ed.), 2003, Blackwell Publishers, Cambridge, MA.

Cuthbert, Alexander R. (ed.), 2003: *Designing Cities: Critical Readings in Urban Design*: Blackwell Publishers, Cambridge, MA.

Frampton, Kenneth, 1982: *Modern Architecture and the Critical Present*: Institute for Architecture and Urban Studies, New York.

Friedman, Jonathan Block, 2000: *Creation in Space: A Course in the Fundamentals of Architecture, Vol. 1: Architectonics*: Kendall Hunt Publishing Company, Dubuque, IA.

Goldstein, Nathan, 1989: *Design and Composition*: Prentice Hall, Inc., Englewood Cliffs, NJ.

Hall, Edward T., 1966: *The Hidden Dimension*: Doubleday, Garden City, NY.

Johnston, Charles MD, 1984/1986: *The Creative Imperative*: Celestial Arts, Berkeley, CA.

Johnston, Charles MD, 1991: *Necessary Wisdom*: Celestial Arts, Berkeley, CA.

Kaku, Michio, 1994: *Hyperspace: A Scientific Odyssey through Parallel Universes, Time Warps, and the Tenth Dimension*: Oxford University Press, Oxford, UK.

Lazano, Eduardo E., 1990: *Community Design and the Culture of Cities*: Cambridge University Press, Cambridge, UK.

Lynch, Kevin, 1989: *Good City Form*: MIT Press, Cambridge, MA/London, UK.

Maturana, Humberto and Verala, Frank, 1980: *Autopoiesis and Cognition*: D. Reidel, Dordrecht, Holland.

Miller, David E., 2005: *Toward a New Regionalism*: University of Washington Press, Seattle, WA.

Rubin, Barbara, 1979: "Aesthetic Ideology and Urban Design". In *Designing Cities: Critical Readings in Urban Design*: Cuthbert, Alexander R. (ed.), 2003, Blackwell Publishers, Cambridge, MA.

Shirvani, Hamid, 1985: *The Urban Design Process*: Van Nostrand Reinhold, New York.

Soja, Edward W., 1996: *Thirdspace*: Blackwell Publishers, Cambridge, MA.

Soja, Edward W., 2000: *Postmetropolis*: Blackwell Publishers, Cambridge, MA.

Spreiregen, Paul D., 1965: *Urban Design: The Architecture of Towns and Cities*: McGraw-Hill, New York.

Webster's New World Dictionary, Second Concise Edition, 1975: William Collins & World Publishing Co., Inc.

Zukin, Sharon, 1988: "The Postmodern Debate over Urban Form" In *Designing Cities: Critical Readings in Urban Design*: Cuthbert, Alexander R. (ed.), 2003, Blackwell Publishers, Cambridge, MA.

Chapter 3

URBAN DESIGN LANGUAGE AND PARAMETERS

The language of design

Language is the ability to communicate, in most cases by a set and composition of symbols ranging from words representing objects and ideas constructed as graphic symbols representing sounds, to shapes and lines representing forms and spatial elements. The specifics of language vary based on the culture or group of people defining and attaching meaning to the symbols and their emphasis.

Design as a process has a language—a language of exploration and discovery, not simply of representation. This language communicates spatial relationships and consequently consists of symbols and shapes representing form rather than letters, and words that represent sounds. The methods include drawing and model making. Most importantly, the language of design has two major tasks: internally, communicate emerging form explorations and discoveries to the designer during the process, and, externally, communicate emerging design patterns to others (clients, community, team members, etc.).

To my students, I emphasize that urban design cannot be simply talked through, approached intellectually without the dimensions of cognitive perception—thinking with the senses. There are constant discoveries only perceived through the play process, the crafting process.

Design's alphabet is composed of spatial elements (shapes, lines, dots, color, values, and their constructs such as planes, volumes, etc.); most importantly, the relationships between and among those elements. The "word," "sentence" and "paragraph" of a graphic language are *relational assemblies* composed from spatial principles that guide the organization and structure of the composition. For example, a composition may have "directional movement," implying elements forming a path or pattern that may be diagonal, vertical, curvilinear, etc. The grid and radial burst are types of geometric structures that assemble compositions. And each of these relational assemblies has an underlying spatial storytelling or spatial metaphor process.

The symbols and images related to design were formed over eons of interpreting the ways and means of building human settlements. These symbols were and still remain connected to the human experience and scale: they are about us and from us ... something to be reminded of as the culture moves into a digital machine age, where there can be a significant separation or disconnect between spatial thinking and the human dimension.

Essential graphic language techniques

The following section briefly summarizes the key language types and techniques used in design composition. They are critical to the visual thinking process. I am including this summary because I have discovered that many planning students and even professionals are unversed in these basic drawing types and are becoming overly dependent upon digital graphic programs, disconnecting them from the sensory experience of visual thinking. Experienced designers can move on to the next section.

I include graphic examples in Appendix I. I encourage all those not familiar with the types of drawing applicable to urban design to review both the example graphics and the discussion of their techniques.

This is not a drawing book and the drawing types cannot be ignored as they are necessary ingredients in the design composition process. For planners, the axonometric drawing, the section, and plan diagram are essential to three-dimensional thinking and communication, and I recommend that is where they place their focus.

Orthographic and paraline drawings

Orthographic drawings are straight-on views, right angles, correct, or standard views. Orthographic drawings have little or no distortion (some in aerial photography) and therefore are used for the standard and measureable graphic study and representations in design and construction. Because they can be measured they are quantitative as well as qualitative. The plan, section, and elevation drawing types are all orthographic.

Paraline drawings are drawings where lines parallel to one another always remain parallel and do not distort as in a perspective. The axonometric drawing is a paraline drawing that is of particular value to the designer and planner, in that it illustrates at least three planes of a volume and is measurable, as there is no perspective distortion. Essentially all lines that are parallel in plan, elevation, section, etc. remain parallel in the axonometric drawing.

Plan drawing

Basic to the architect, engineer and landscape architect, the plan drawing is a straight-down right-angle view of a horizontal plane, illustrating relationships on that plane (house plan, office layout, block parcels, etc.). The plan is an orthographic and quantitative graphic vital for standard reference and measurement. A *conventional* scale[1] is assigned to the drawing for measurement purposes and is always represented in graphic mode as well as numbers, so that the scale can be determined regardless of the plan's enlargement or reduction in size and therefore in scale. A plan is also a horizontal section where the section line cuts the vertical "view" at standard altitudes. In a house plan, the horizontal section is "cut" four feet above the floor, meaning that all walls are four feet high maximum from floor to the cut. Why? So that windows and door openings can be observed in the cut (vertical) walls. A city scale plan can have a designated horizontal cut line depending upon the information to be expressed. For example, an altitude of 50 feet can be established to cut through all vertical objects 51 feet or more in height from the base horizontal plane.

Section drawing

A section is a view from a horizontal plane (0–180 degrees) looking straight (orthographically—90 degrees) at *vertical planes* and objects within them (below grade, at grade, above grade). A site section begins with a cut through the site perpendicular to you the observer, *and* you observe in elevation any vertical (including slanted) plane within your line of sight beyond the cut. You choose the relevant view and establish the cut line for reference and orientation.

Figure 3.1. Pelican plan drawing. *The plan drawing is referred to as a "base map" when the plan contains basic graphic reference and orientation information. Additional information can be added to advance the level of analysis. The base map is always retained as an original reference source. This simple example of the small southeast Alaskan fishing village of Pelican displays key features of the village form. Remember: in urban design, analysis spills out over the project area boundaries, requiring an analysis of multiple scales of information and input. The base map is in reality a series of maps from the project area outward until an adequate context is identified and assessed for design clues.*

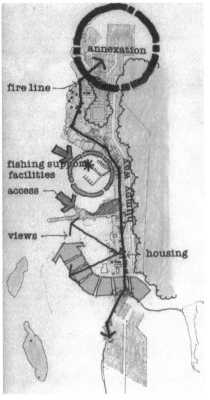

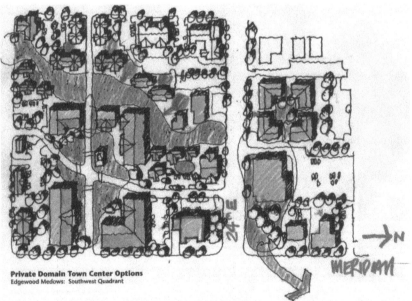

Figure 3.2. Edgewood concept plan drawing. *The plan drawing is also used as a straight-down or orthographic view from above (at 90 degrees). "Edgewood" is a part of a public information series of plan drawings used in public workshops to explore ideas and options with the community.*

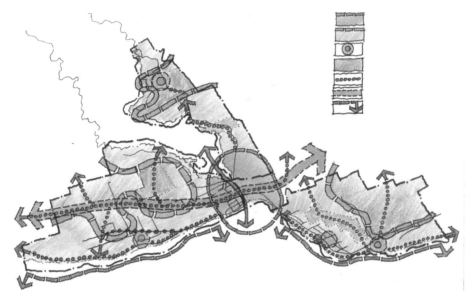

Figure 3.3. Sechelt BC plan diagram. *The plan diagram is drawn as an overlay on the base map. For example, a base map at conventional scale with standard reference material (streets, curbs, topography and buildings, graphic scale and north arrow, etc.) becomes a plan diagram when land use, demographic, land values, building conditions, etc. or other information in graphic form is added as an overlay onto the base map. The base map is now a part of an analytical process, establishes a record, provides a base for manual and/or digital comparison, etc. In this example for Sechelt, British Columbia, the plan diagram summarizes major design components on a neighborhood level.*

- The cut line is like a sheet of vertical glass that you have your nose against; you are looking straight at it similar to an elevation.
- Except . . . everything along the cut line, all horizontal and vertical planes that are cut through, as with a skill saw, are emphasized as cuts, usually with darker value lines than elevation lines.
- The foreground, everything between the observer and the cut, is gone, leaving only the mid- and backgrounds.
- If a building in the distance, beyond the cut line, is partially blocked by another structure in front of it, between you the observer and the distant building, you will only see that portion of the distant building not obstructed (by a straight-on view) by the closer structure.
- A section is both a cut and an elevation, graphically revealing the materials, horizontal and vertical (and sloped) planes actually cut through and all other vertical planes behind the cut but not actually cut; this includes planes above the ground, below the ground (basements and garages), and the ground plane itself.

In urban design, the site section is useful in portraying vertical and horizontal relationships. Building sections are more detailed and the cut areas may contain detailed construction information. A building can be cut in a number of locations to view the interior vertical relationships not perceived on an elevation view (interior courtyard or lobby relationship with surrounding interior spaces). A site can be cut in a number of locations to view outdoor and topographical features in relationship to surrounding buildings), again indicated on a horizontal plan view for reference.

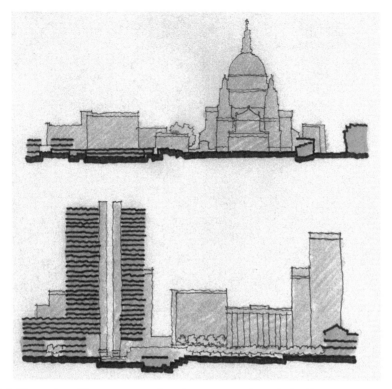

Figure 3.4. Site section. *The site section utilizes the same principles as the building section. Based on the decision where to cut through the site and the direction of the view, the section illustrates the cut horizontal and vertical planes including sub-grade features (underground parking, utilities, water depth, etc.) and above-grade natural and building features. Physical features behind the cut line are indicated in lighter value lines. The lighter value lines are maintained for all features in elevation and the darker and bolder lines are used for vertical and horizontal planes that are cut through (ground, walls, floors, parking lots, streets, water features, etc.) only along the cut line. Retraced from Okamoto and Williams (1969).*

A section is always accompanied by a plan view with the sectional cut location and direction specified at a conventional scale.

Diagrams

Diagrams are semi-real graphic representations that can utilize various types of drawings: plan, section, axonometric, and perspective. They dramatize or summarize ideas, information, and analysis, filtering out information not relevant for that analysis or scale. Diagrams are best communicated with reference and orientation information such as direction, scale, and sufficient notes.

I use diagrams in summarizing the big patterns in design analysis, or key factors in contextual analysis. They provide an excellent format for presenting and discussing ideas and information in workshops, meetings, and design charrettes. They also provide the designer with an assessment tool: as data are analyzed and synthesized, the diagram is used as a means of prioritizing and focusing information on a contextual drawing such as a base plan (see Figure 3.3).

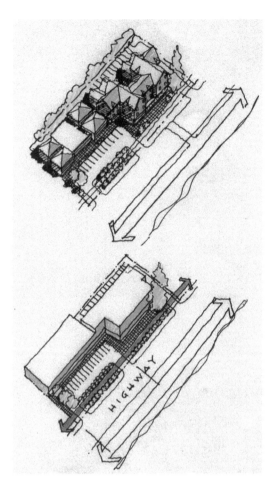

Figure 3.5. Sechelt BC axonometric diagram. *In "Visions for Sechelt" (2007), the axonometric drawing provided an aerial-like view of a proposed development site for the discussion of view corridor policies at public meetings and workshops. The drawing is semi-real in that it portrays building mass and open space, not architectural detail or style; an architectural example is provided along with the diagram for scale. The axonometric more closely resembles a form-based zoning envelope rather than a specific design.*

Axonometric drawing

The axonometric drawing is a paraline drawing, where lines that are parallel to one another in plan, elevation, and section remain parallel in the axonometric. Remember that the "plan" is always present in the axonometric. It does not distort. As described in Appendix I, I simply rotate the plan (final recommendation or conceptual scheme) at a 30/60 or 60/30 from the horizontal reference line (0–180 degrees) and raise the verticals to scale. Why rotate? Because I want to see at least two vertical planes of the volume, and in effect I will see three: the two side vertical planes and the top or roof plane. If I look at a cube straight on as an axonometric I only see the front vertical plane and the top horizontal plane. All lines that are parallel to one another in plan and elevation remain parallel. Again, this drawing type is one of the most widely used by designers where a "three-dimensional" view is desired without a perspective distortion, making the drawing both quantitative and qualitative.

As is evident in this book, I use the axonometric drawing extensively due to its equal views (not distorted by perspective views) and ease of construction. Perspectives always have a station or viewing point from which all parallel lines diminish toward a vanishing point, creating a hierarchy of shapes (larger in foreground and smaller in background).

25

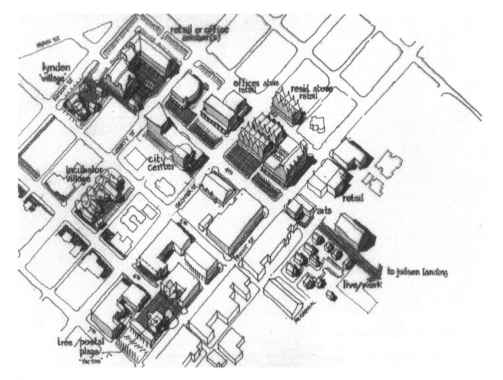

Figure 3.6. Axonometric drawing. *In the downtown design study for Linden, Washington, the axonometric drawing was used extensively to portray the overall design intent of various concepts. The axonometric drawings were reproduced and used as diagrams as well. Notice the orientation of the plan (30/60 or 60/30) and the basic requirement that all vertical lines are perpendicular to the 0–180 degree reference line—they are not slanted as can happen if the plan is not rotated. This slanting effect is confusing for most lay observers and can disrupt or distract the quality of public meetings.*

Perspective drawing

James Pettinari and I use aerial oblique (at an angle other than 90 degrees) perspectives extensively to portray the larger spatial context associated with specific projects. Perspectives are more qualitative in nature due to their distortion and limitations in quantification.

Contour drawing

I include contour drawing in this section for planners because it provides an easily learned tool for perspective drawing, particularly for field sketching. The basic concept is simple: you draw only what you see as the contours or edges of the subject's shape. You do not need to understand or be technically astute regarding perspective drawing. Thinking of perspective can actually be a barrier to quality contour drawing. Techniques in contour drawing are provided in Appendix I. They require focus and attention to train the eye to actually *look* at the nature and physical characteristics of the contour or edge conditions of a given subject. If you draw from memory or without close focus or observation of the subject, the mind and eye drift from attention to the object to a memory-fantasy and distortion results.

Figure 3.7. Aerial perspective drawing. *In this downtown study, the aerial perspective was used to portray the redevelopment of a major civic center nestled in surrounding high-rise office buildings. The aerial perspective provided a larger view of the downtown sector and surrounding context. These base perspectives can be reconstructed from various sources including aerial photographs. Design alterations or concepts can then be overlaid onto the base perspective view.*

I use contour drawing extensively in field observations and visual presentations. Why? I see and record more through my hand/eye/brain than through a camera lens because I am required, when I draw, to observe and focus on objects in the landscape. Photography is used as a backup resource.

Parameters of design

How did the dimensions and parameters of design originate?

As a prelude to design elements and principles, the reader is reminded that design is not an abstraction but rather an extension of us. Design as a function of culture is rooted in the human dimension and function. With increasing technology, manufacturing, shipping, and assembly changes based on that technology, the human dimension remains the fundamental principle for design. With increasing digital assistance in analysis and design, this human scale origination of design can be "lost in translation".

Humans did not start out with naming and then assigning dimensions and "things". They observed what worked in everyday life based on the senses and limits of the human body (at the time) and then named and quantified—empirically.

Design is the making of something (to fit the human physiology):

- a quart or liter is the amount of liquid that can be held out by an outstretched (historic and smaller) arm
- an acre is the amount of land a person can till in a day (manually)
- an inch, foot, yard are conventional ways to mark length using an element of the human body:
    - the thumb is (was) an inch (in ancient times for smaller folk)
    - a forearm is (was) a foot
    - a pace is (was) a yard.

The Greeks and gothic architects formalized the human dimension in architecture and community design. The Romans and Renaissance architects gave us abstraction and a larger order in addition to the human dimension: gods and power. Contemporary society and technology give us architecture based on handling, shipping, and assembly, which in reverse affects fabrication which affects manufacturing which affects design.

Design is also the making of things through indirect or unintentional actions. Design is the physical and geometric *manifestation* of underlying forces generated by human behavior and its interactions with the environment. The way you arrange your furniture in the living room to be "comfortable" is an act of design that has behind it significant underlying (cultural) forces and determinants (Hall, 1966).

Consequently, as we approach design in our culture, we have basic approaches and conventions for interpreting human behavior and needs into design form. These vary according to the circumstance of their application; they form the basis of established design and provide a departure point for innovation.

- People: need, want, aspiration, passion
- Program: what and how much of something satisfies the stated need
- Context: bio-physical, cultural, jurisdictional, historic/time, interrelationships
- Organization, structure, and process (physics)
- Design elements, principles, and relationships or compositions (art): space, enclosure, movement, and circulation
- Structure, manufacturing, and economy.

Understanding the importance of the human dimension in design is critical to understanding and applying the basic elements and principles of design composition. The language of design, the representation of the elements and principles of form in relationship, can influence your understanding of what people need and want and the design for that need. In contemporary design applications, a balance of digital and crafting methods can best serve the process of design. Simply because you can do something with the computer does not mean that the computer is the most appropriate tool. In the remaining portions of the book, I use hand-drawn or crafted language types to explore and demonstrate. These methods and types are not obsolete nor are they out of reach of the contemporary student. They are, in my professional and academic experience, the most effective means of visual thinking.

Note

1   In graphic information systems (GIS) usage, many planners assign plan maps with non-conventional scales, causing problems of measurement for others involved in the process. The non-conventional scale can be used to measure data as calculated through the GIS program but cannot be used for measurement when using standard hand scales and other measuring devices (that are not going to cease in utilization because of computer technology). For example, when doing a downtown design, a standard scale based on the engineering (standard) scale can range from ten increments in an inch to 60 increments in one inch per the engineering scale, similar in metric scale—based on the meter as a measurement of length. These conventional scales are useful in fieldwork, team design work, workshops, etc. for hard-copy plotted maps. Many GIS maps are plotted out in non-conventional scales; one inch equals 462 feet, for example, and is little use to the team, client, or process.

Bibliography

Broadbent, Geoffrey, 1990: *Emerging Concepts in Urban Space Design*: Spon Press, London.

Edgewood, City of, 1999: "Town Center Plan: Community Character and Land Use Study": Kasprisin Pettinari Design and Dennis Tate Associates, Langley, WA.

Hall, Edward T., 1966: *The Hidden Dimension*: Doubleday, Garden City, NY.

Kasprisin, Ron and Pettinari, James, 1995: *Visual Thinking for Architects and Designers*: John Wiley & Sons, Inc., New York.

Okamoto, Y. Rai and Williams, Frank E., 1969: *Urban Design Manhattan (Regional Plan Association)*: The Viking Press, Inc., New York.

Sechelt BC, District of, 2007: "Visions for Sechelt": John Talbot & Associates (Burnaby, BC) and Kasprisin Pettinari Design (Langley, WA).

Chapter 4

ELEMENTS AND PRINCIPLES OF DESIGN COMPOSITION

Form as community relationship

The urban design process is often referred to as "place making," an interpretation of "urban meaning and urban functionality" (Castells, 1983) into spatial metaphors and sensory and sensual built environments that are considered special in the eyes of the observer. The more aspects of *urban meaning and functionality* incorporated into the process, the more complex becomes the challenge of place making. Integrating the rich stories of community with the compositional principles of art is a critical challenge for contemporary designers. Fashioning spatial compositions that respond to and structure this *urban meaning*, maintaining a compositional integrity within that complexity, begins the *art of urban design*, the use of elements and principles to compose these rich spatial stories. Urban design then becomes *form as community relationship*.

Along with understanding these elements and principles is the necessary act of artful play, design experimentation, the process of discovery through a crafting process. I talk about this crafting often in the book, as this process is an inherent ingredient in the design exploration of these community relationships.

Design elements: "the nouns"

As I build up the elements and principles of composition to a more complex level of application, the examples will initially be more abstract in nature, increasing in complexity and realism.

Element: a basic or fundamental component, part, or quality (of space)

Elements constitute the basics for the graphic design alphabet and spatial construction. We use symbols and shapes to represent a spatial language; we use shapes as elements to form spatial compositions. As an assignment in architecture school, we were required to construct the Roman alphabet, each letter, with compass, triangle, and T-square. Needless to say, I gained an understanding not of "A" but of the lines, circles, and squares that made up that "A" (as constructed by the Romans). The beautiful formal geometry of the alphabet as comprised of circles, angles, and straight lines became apparent! What is important for the designer is the flexibility and ability to manipulate in design composition these basic elements into meaningful form. Let's begin.

Dot: a point, small circular shape, and represented at other scales as:

• point
• circle

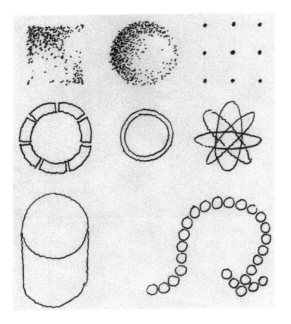

Figure 4.1. The dot. *Do not take the dot for granted—a speck, a slight circular mark. The dot is shape-defining and density-relevant. By itself, it is the speck or slight mark. In clusters of varying densities the dot makes shapes (squares and circles, for example) and portrays value in light and darks based on density. At larger scales, the dot becomes the circle, Stonehenge from the air; or the top of a cylinder, a sphere such as a basketball or part of a planetarium—and the form of a far-off galaxy seen in the night sky. Pretty impressive for a small circular speck.*

- cylinder
- sphere
- star (planet) in the night sky.

Line: a thin (relatively) linear shape characterized by a length that is substantially more than its width, also represented at other scales, beginning with the pen-made line and going to and beyond an interstate freeway:

- vertical (column, flagpole, high-rise building from afar, comet tail in the night sky)
- horizontal (axis, highway, shoreline)
- oblique (diagonal, not straight on, etc.)
- straight (curved, broken, edge, etc.)
- directional (arrow, graph, vector).

Shape (also a relationship of area to edge): any discernible bounded area defined by line, value, color, intensity, and/or texture and their contrasts or some combination; composed of a specified area, extent, or field and contained or marked by a boundary or edge (see edge). A shape can be direct as in the square or circle; semi-direct as in the "L"; and implied as in the separation or space formed by two elements, similar or different, in relative close association.

Varieties of shape

Shape has many physical characteristics as everything in nature is composed of shapes: "shape is content" (Arnheim, 1969):

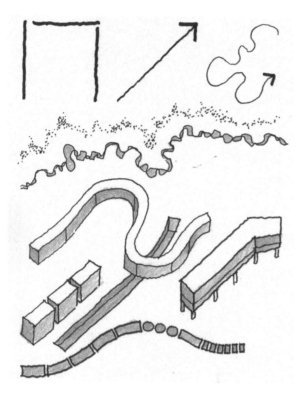

Figure 4.2. The line. *The line is a useful "shape" particularly as an axis, creating movement, direction, and force as in vector. As discussed later, the axis is a powerful compositional structure in design composition and can take many forms.*

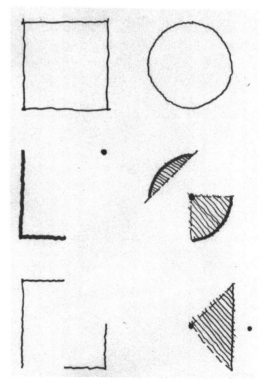

Figure 4.3. Shape. *Shape is enclosed, bounded, semi-bounded (even by implication) space or void (void is the absence of elements and is formed by some form of boundary). The hatched and dotted areas indicate implied bounded shapes.*

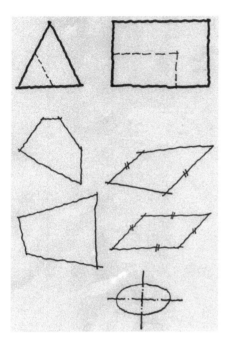

Figure 4.4. Derivative shapes. *Shapes that are derived from the primary shapes and/or departures from the primary shapes.*

- geometric: earth measure (implying a mathematical foundation), as in geometry
- organic: living system, growing, responsive to physical environment, whole system and fractal
- polarities: positive and negative/figure and ground/solid and void/lost and found
- ambiguous: uncertain, i.e. a pause in a changing pattern
- primary: first in order of development, from which others are derived:
    - circle
    - square
- derivatives: traceable to another (primary) source:
    - triangle
    - fractal/fractured
    - rectangle
    - polygons (enclosed shape especially with more than four sides/angles)
    - ellipse (the path of a point that moves so that the sum of its distances from two fixed points is constant)
    - trapezoid (four-sided shape with two parallel sides)
    - trapezium (four-sided shape with no parallel sides)
    - parallelogram (four-sided shape with opposing sides equal and parallel).

Planes and volumes: shape constructs from basic elements

The basic elements combine to shape both alphabet and spatial constructs from that alphabet. In design, these constructs shape the building blocks of (urban) design, including architecture and landscape architecture. They begin with two-dimensional constructs: planes, axis, fields, and three-dimensional constructs as volumes.

Planar shape (plane)

- overhead (ceiling, roof)
- vertical (wall, fence, window, hedge)
- horizontal (base, footprint, floor, path)
- oblique or angular (tilted plane, ramp, shed roof, slope)
- multiple vertical planes in relationship-contiguous, parallel, oblique:
  - L-shape
  - oblique
  - parallel
  - orthographic
  - U-shaped
  - enclosed
- curved vertical planes:
  - equal radii
  - undulating (changing radii) and/or changing centers
  - S-shapes (repeating but reversed equal radii)
  - enclosed cylinder with flat horizontal plane at top and bottom
  - enclosed sphere with all curved surfaces of equal radii.

Axis (line)

- overhead (contrail, light string, ceiling panel)
- vertical (elevator shaft, rocket exhaust, skyscraper)

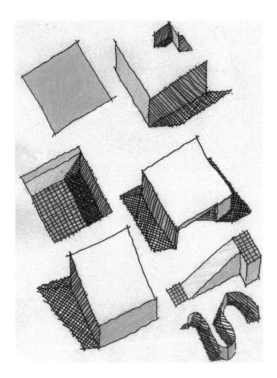

Figure 4.5. Planar shapes. *The combinations of planar shapes create volume, enclosed and semi-enclosed, or bounded space.*

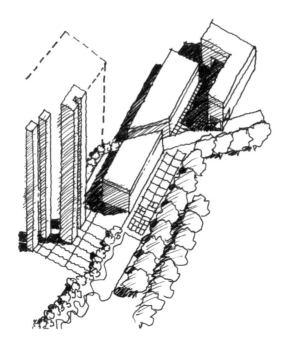

Figure 4.6. The axis. *Movement, direction, and force are key characteristics of the line or axis in design. As discussed in compositional structures, the axis assembles and structures compositions. The axis can consist of horizontal pathways, formed by building masses, landscaping, and can be vertical towers, elevator systems, etc.*

- horizontal (corridor, street, sidewalk)
- oblique (off ramp, switchback trail).

Field or pattern (dots)
- pebble field
- rock wall
- texture
- grain.

Volumes
Volumes constitute three-dimensional shapes constructed from combinations of two-dimensional shapes and/or elements where at least three elements define length, breadth, depth, or are defined by mass displacing space:

- space displaced or defined by mass (solid such as bowling ball)
- space contained or enclosed by planes or mass (enclosed stadium, dome, sunken plaza, channel, tunnel, building)
- sphere
- prism
- cone
- cylinder
- pyramid
- cube.

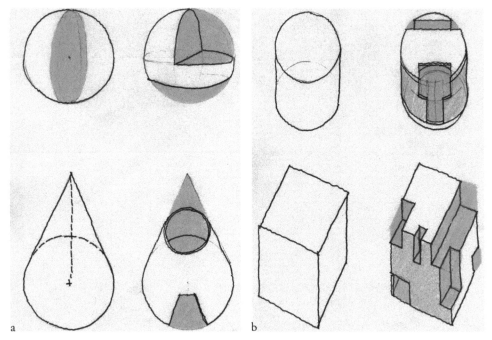

Figures 4.7 a and b. Volumes. *These are the volumes that constitute our built environment in primary and hybridized forms. Sphere: any round body with a surface equally distant from the center at all points; prism: a solid whose ends are equal and parallel polygons and whose sides are parallelograms; cone: a solid with a circle as its base and a curved surface tapering to a point; cylinder: a solid with parallel and equal circles as ends; pyramid: a solid with a square base and four sloping sides meeting at a point; cube: a solid with six equal square sides.*

Color

I include color as a design element, often overlooked and reduced to neutral grays in architecture and city design. Color is powerful in that it can generate mood, temperature, recession, procession, and intensity.

Color or hue: an element (wavelength) on the spectrum of light that is distinguishable by temperature (warm or cool), by brightness or intensity or lack thereof, by transparency (ability to absorb or reflect light), and by the purity or mixture of its elements (there are a number of primary or pure colors in various palettes generally defined by red, yellow, and blue); secondary colors defined by combinations of any two primaries: red plus yellow equals orange, red plus blue equals purple, blue plus yellow equals green; tertiary colors are essentially colored grays that have a mixture of all three primaries, i.e., olive green (yellow plus blue plus a bit of red).

The conventional families or palettes of color, i.e. watercolor, are as follows.

Delicate transparent palette
- rose madder
- cobalt blue

- Aurelian or azo yellow
- viridian green is a mixing green (cooler).

Intense staining palette
- pthalo red or alizarin red (cooler): also known by manufacturers' names (Winsor Red, etc., or grumbacher Red, etc., or Intense Red, etc.)
- pthalo blue
- pthalo yellow
- pthalo or Winsor Green is a mixing green (intense).

Opaque palette
- cadmium red
- cerulean blue
- yellow ochre
- and many more variations of the three primaries are available.

Value increment in color (value is also a relationship): one of three to five to nine (in the visual arts) increments between lightest and darkest or white and black; a basic value scale is composed of *light, middle, dark*, expanding to *light, mid-light, middle, mid-dark, dark*; nine value scales are not used as often.

Characteristics (descriptors) of elements

- *Size:* dimensional appearance in relation to other shapes
- *Texture:* a surface characteristic implying a touch response or visual appearance as a surface interacts with light or other variations to its surface features
- *Grain:* a density of surface characteristics (five dots per inch vs. 500 dots per inch)
- *Direction:* a movement to or from somewhere (N, S, E, W); horizontal, vertical, diagonal, circular ("circle the wagons")
- *Transparency:* light and image are apparent through a material
- *Translucency:* light is apparent, image is diffused through a material
- *Opacity:* light and image are prevented from passing through material, either absorbed or reflected
- *Position:* location in relation to other shapes; see center of interest
- *Orientation:* exposure, implies direction
- *Stability:* relationship to ground plane, gravity.

Focus or center of interest: the main descriptors of elements are self-evident. Focus and center of interest are often overlooked in design and emanate from the golden mean, a point or area of emphasis in a composition. The CI can be the climax, the point of most drama, and is supported by the other elements and principles in composition (see Figure 4.8).

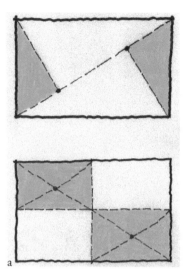

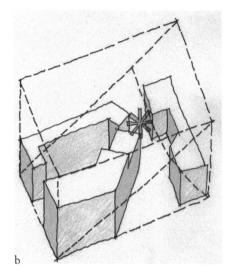

a   b

Figures 4.8 a and b. Focus or center of interest (CI). *Center of interest (CI) is the "aha," point of highest drama, or main aspect of a design story; in painting the CI is usually located at one of the quadrant centers or at a location along any diagonal where a perpendicular line intersects the diagonal from any corner.*

Design principles: "the verbs"

Principles are rules of conduct, fundamental laws (not universal) that explain an action. They are often perceived as outcomes when in reality they are the conduct that causes the outcome. In composition, principles instruct or guide elements into relational compositions. The following principles result from centuries of artistic exploration and apply directly to most aspects of design, including urban design. They can assist the beginning designer particularly in activating objects or elements into dramatic arrangements and compositions.

These require practice and exploration, not memorization.

- *Alternation:* the repeated use of two or more shapes, sizes, etc. usually in succession as in ABABABAB.
- *Angle of view:* the amount, range, dimension or extent of view framed by two straight lines that meet; the space between those lines defined by an extension of those lines to the horizon; also, the angle of view from the observer—all things are seen and observed through the observer's eyes.
- *Axial movement:* a line between two or more points by the very nature of orientation indicates direction and movement; a line that organizes other shapes around and along the extent of distance and width of the line; this movement can be straight, bent, curved, broken, channeled, etc. The axis exists both as an element (as line) and as a compositional structure exhibiting design principles of organization and assembly.
- *Balance/symmetry:* a state of equilibrium of a total work (does not have to be mirror images); balance and weight are similar expressions of the same principle.
- *Bridging (polarities):* the act of integrating polarities (contrasting or conflicting elements or relationships) with minimal compromise.
- *Compositional structures:* these are design principles aligned with structuring and assembling forms and form the backbone or framework of design—the guts of design—based on the basic shapes

and components of the square and circle. I include them here as an introduction and as complex sets of principles.

- *Datum:* things known or assumed; a common reference point that can represent or exist as a design principle—an organizing reference within a design composition.

- *Dominance:* an element or pattern having a recognizable strength or importance over others usually through size, value, weight, placement.

- *Edge transition:* an end and a beginning; a water edge, a change in color, a circumference, a cold front; I include "edge" as a principle of energy exchange, both in force and in form.

- *Gradation:* an incremental change (value, color, temperature, key or intensity, density) within a given shape or among a group or cluster of shapes.

- *Harmony:* an arrangement into an agreeable whole (easier to do in color if using one family or palette as a starting point); benchmarks are needed to establish what harmony is for design related to the context of the design; harmony can be culturally specific and not universal.

- *Merging:* bringing two or more elements, compositions, or relationships together at their edge transitions, creating a merged edge or perimeter with the retention of the essential characteristics of each original element or relationship; the transitional area can be quite significant as long as elements of the originals are still apparent.

- *Patterning:* repeated use of elements and compositions forming a larger whole; often composed of clusters of smaller design principles such as repetition with variety, gradation, etc.

- *Polarity identification:* establishing the limits of the design, dialogue, and shape potential, or design actions; often represented by minimal tension via *contrast* and maximum tension via *conflict*.

- *Procession:* to make something come closer, be seen (warmer colors), larger shapes, darker values, brighter and warmer colors, for example.

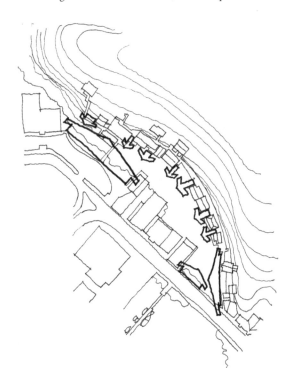

Figure 4.9. Angle of view. *In "Creek Street Historic District: Public Facilities Improvement Project" (1984), angles of view were assessed from key viewpoints along the boardwalk. The surface areas of historic buildings, contextual buildings, creek surface area, and other features were calculated and incorporated into an analysis of potential view-disrupting infrastructure elements.*

- *Recession:* to make something go further away (cooler colors), smaller shapes, and lighter values, for example.
- *Repetition:* a recurrence of an element or relationship at regular intervals.
- *Repetition with variety:* usually the same element repeated with variations in size, color, or other physical characteristic; AaAa or repeated circles each a diminishing size, etc.
- *Rhythm:* a repetition that is alternating in various and consistent intervals (AaaAaaAaa) or (AaaBBAaaBB repeat).
- *Symmetry:* similarity of form or arrangement on either side of a dividing line or shape.
- *Temperature:* warm to cool, hot to cold, warm to warmer, cool to cooler (all relative); can exhibit mood dominance.
- *Transformation:* changing shapes and compositions by a number of actions such as dimension, additive or subtractive actions, merging, bridging, and others.
- *Variety:* the difference between and among elements, compositions, and relationships.

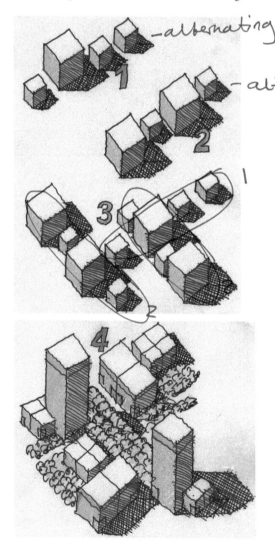

Figures 4.10 and 4.11. Alternation. *Two or more choices, repeating patterns composed of two or more elements alternating as every other or in sets or clusters of patterns. Alternation can be valuable when seeking coherence or consistency in complicated built form environments; they can break up monotonous forms in the manner of their alternation. In the illustrations, two different clusters of alternating forms (1) and (2) are combined in a 1, 2, 2 sequence (3). In (4), the same principle applies to larger-scale developments where repetitive programs permit.*

Figure 4.12. Dominance. *Dominance occurs when a shape, form, or pattern in a composition has more strength or importance in size, color, tone, etc. than other forms. Dominance may occur from a combination of elements rather than just one, see illustrations (a), (b), and (c): (a) has dominance by size; (b) by tone or value; (c) by difference.*

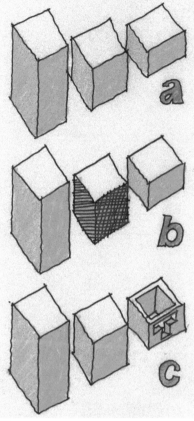

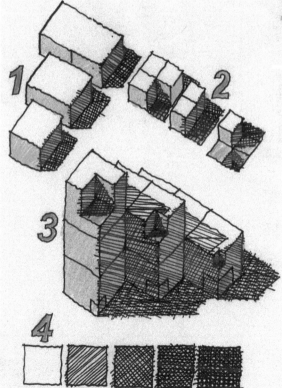

Figure 4.13. Gradation and repetition with variety and value. *The cube is repeated at different sizes (dimensional transformation) for a gradual increase in horizontal width (1); changed in increasing complexity using positive and negative quarter volumes (2); graded vertically in both overall volume and component details (subtractive transformation) (3). Gradation occurs in light patterns from light to dark. In art and design, a five-value scale is used ranging from light, mid-light, mid, mid-dark, and dark (4).*

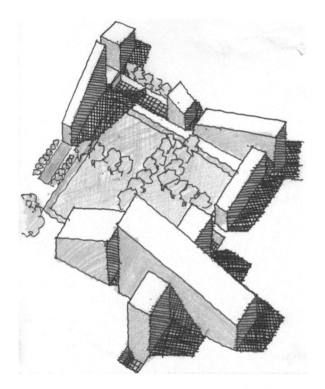

Figure 4.14. Harmony. *In painting, harmony can be achieved by using the same family or palette of colors dominating the composition. In design, a repetition of a family of volumes, like the sheds in the illustration, augmented by a directional movement and hierarchy of sizes can also instill a harmony to the composition.*

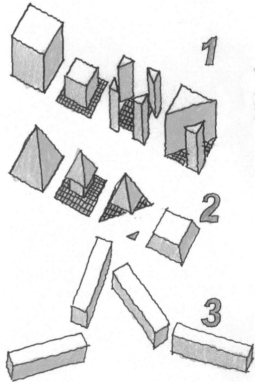

Figure 4.15. Repetition with variety and manipulation of primary shapes. *The cube (1) and pyramid (2) are repeated in principle; in various combinations with differing manipulations of key physical components (volume, corners, etc.). The rectangular volume (3) is repeated with differing placements and axial directions creating a sense of movement.*

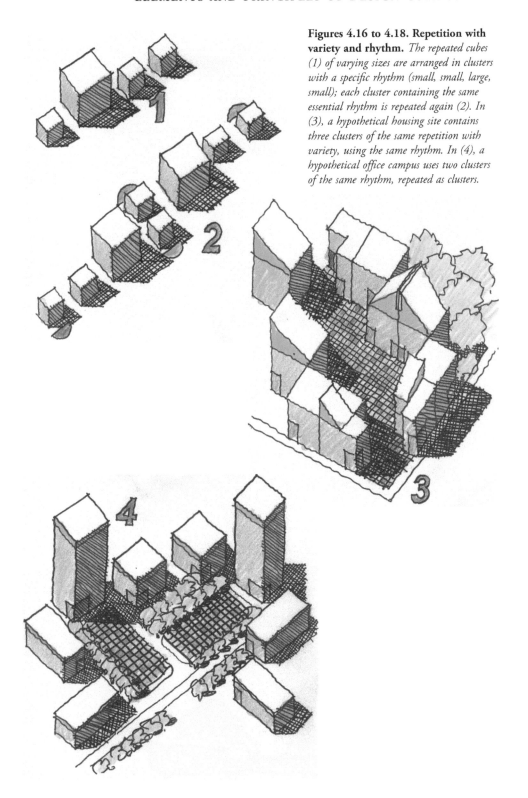

Figures 4.16 to 4.18. Repetition with variety and rhythm. *The repeated cubes (1) of varying sizes are arranged in clusters with a specific rhythm (small, small, large, small); each cluster containing the same essential rhythm is repeated again (2). In (3), a hypothetical housing site contains three clusters of the same repetition with variety, using the same rhythm. In (4), a hypothetical office campus uses two clusters of the same rhythm, repeated as clusters.*

Bibliography

Arnheim, Rudolph, 1969: *Visual Thinking*: University of California Press, Berkeley, CA.

Castells, Manuel, 1983: "The Process of Urban Social Change." In *Designing Cities: Critical Readings in Urban Design*: Cuthert, Alexander R. (ed.), 2003, Blackwell Publishers, Cambridge, MA.

Ching, Francis D.K., 1979: *Architecture: Form, Space and Order*: Van Nostrand Reinhold, New York.

Edwards, Betty, 1979: *Drawing on the Right Side of the Brain*: Houghton Mifflin Co., J.P. Tarcher, Los Angeles, CA (or any of her books that have a section on pure and modified contour drawing). Read the sections on contour drawing.

Freidman, Jonathan Block, 2000: *Creation in Space: A Course in the Fundamentals of Architecture*: Kendall/Hunt Publishing, Dubuque, IA.

Goldstein, Nathan, 1989: *Design and Composition*: Prentice Hall, Inc., Englewood Cliffs, NJ.

Kasprisin, Ron, 1999: *Design Media*: John Wiley & Sons, Inc., New York. Especially the chapter on fear and creativity.

Kasprisin, Ron and Pettinari, James, 1995: *Visual Thinking for Architects and Designers*: John Wiley & Sons, Inc., New York.

Ketchikan, City of, 1984: "Creek Street Historic District: Public Facilities Improvement Project": Kasprisin Hutnik Partnership with J.L. Pensiero and Associates/URS Engineers.

Spreiregen, Paul D., 1965: *Urban Design: The Architecture of Towns and Cities*: McGraw-Hill, New York.

Chapter 5

RELATIONSHIPS IN COMPOSITION
ORGANIZATION AND STRUCTURE

Composing is to put something in proper order and form, assembling a physical entity from small relational groupings or systems and their larger relationships; it is an aesthetically unified arrangement of small systems for a defined period of time (periodicity). Aesthetics of course are relative to culture and social agendas, and are major variables in composition—dependent upon the trialectic of culture, space, and time. In design, a composition is the arrangement (organization and structure) of elements in relationship representing a meaning or story, a spatial metaphor, with the process of its "making" evident in the composition, articulated in its physical dimensions or state.

The audience of this book comprises in large part emerging designers and lay people with an interest in design. Vital to this audience is an understanding of these key design principles. Most people in design review, making development policy in cities and writing form-based codes, are not designers—they are dedicated lay people (planners, lawyers, technicians). Their understanding and application in urban design can improve the quality of all these implementation mechanisms of urban design.

A good composition begins with a state of excitation about certain forms combined in a certain way, which, in our mind's eye at least, seems to promise satisfaction, both in the process of shaping the work into being, and in seeing our deeply felt creative interests in a resolved and permanent state that can be shared with others.

(Goldstein, 1989)

Let's discuss *design as a composed relationship* with definitions specific to the theory and experiments expressed in writing.

*   Design always has a meaning, a story, told through design as spatial metaphors whether in art, architecture, or urban design; shape *is* content (Arnheim, 1969).
*   Design comprises "parts" in relationship that can range from shapes in an order (classic columns: capital, shaft, pedestal) to social–cultural patterns and needs organized according to compatible interactions.
*   The "parts" in the relationship do not constitute the final design; more the functional needs of the design. An example is the chair: the chair has an organization of parts—vertical stand, seating area, and options such as a back support. These are critical needs organized to produce a functioning and generic "chair" (an organization of functional pieces into a relationship). They require "structure" to specify and complete their form.

- Consequently, design is also structure or assemblage, the manner in which the organized "parts" are brought together—four vertical stands versus three; a back support versus none; the many variations of these structural and material components. Structure and organization are dance partners, initiated by need and assembled as a set pattern in a specific context, i.e. designed.

Definitions related to composition

I use these terms throughout the book and introduce them as a fundamental language for urban design composition.

- *Content:* meaning, essence, idea, story.
- *Context:* underlying reality, that which influences an object lying within it and is changed by that object's actions and changes; complex reality, a constantly emerging physical setting or reality.
- *Organization:* arranging (design) components and their relationship into a program, function, or system. In design, a "program" is a plan or procedure specifying the "what and how much" of a problem-solving process; specifying a sequence of operations to be performed in solving a problem.
- *Order:* a hierarchal positioning, a style emanating from the organization of the parts, any of several classical styles of structure, and therefore important not to get "order" and "organization" confused.
- *Structure:* the assemblage of the organizational relationship—a relationship in and of itself, of organizational relationships to materials, elements, and principles of design, making one design of a similar organization distinguishable from the next similar organization (through its structure or assembly).
- *Process:* the art and science of creating an entity, system, etc. from organization and structure; approach or strategy.
- *Product/emergent reality:* the resultant form manifestation within the process, often referred to here as emergent reality (the product has a "life" over a given and limited time period); product and process are not separate entities or concepts: animal waste is an ongoing product of the living animal's process of existence, etc.; design as a building or plaza is a product of a larger process that expresses that process in real terms—as the process continues and further products emerge in different periodicities.
- *Periodicity:* a term I borrow from Johnston (1984/1986) that defines the specific period or extent of time that a relationship exists and is valid within before it breaks down and reforms.
- *Relationship:* to connect, show a connection between and among entities, elements, principles, and other relationships.
- *Meaning:* what is signified, intended, indicated, or important.
- *Functionality:* the normal, specific, or characteristic action of anything; a special performance in the course of work or activity.
- *Eidetic vision (emergent reality):* the eidetic vision occurs when the content and form become one, having a meaning manifested in physical form; I also include "emergent reality," as the meaning-form takes shape in the context of reality.
- *Parts:* "principles of creative organization" (Johnston, 1984/1986), expressions of relationship in design that cannot be further broken down without losing that relationship; a small system such as a creek shed in relationship to a larger watershed; and always viewed as a relationship in a connected cluster of other relationships.

- *Pieces or elements:* objects not in relationship, separate and not connected to a system.
- *Polarity:* two contrary qualities; being opposite; positive and negative, the differing limits of a given dialogue.

Organizational relationships in composition

Let's approach composition from the starting point of "relationship": where function and meaning are integrated and manifested in form. Compositional relationships are presented as a set of two relational clusters: *organizational* and *structural*. *Organizational* refers to the operations and functions of a composition; *structural* refers to the nature of the assemblage of those organizations into a physical whole.

As in the chair example, "parts" are arranged in relationships between and among other parts to fulfill a need or aspiration. These needs emanate from social–cultural–political interactions in human settlements. They represent the essence of urban meaning and function, or the drama created between or among people in dialogue. We can view these organizational relationships as functional directives for a design or art piece. They are critical in design when we bridge the gap between need and spatial accommodation of that need. Urban designers and planners often overlook this critical "space program" bridge between the statement of need and the implementation of a design in context.

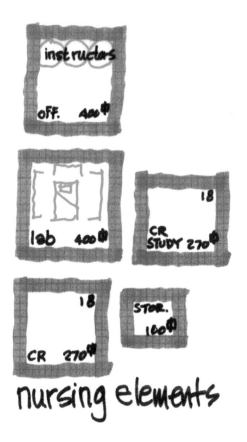

Figure 5.1. Departmental "pieces" and needed "elements". *Before relational assemblies occur, the basic needs and requirements are identified, made into lists of what and how much. These are important and are not relational.*

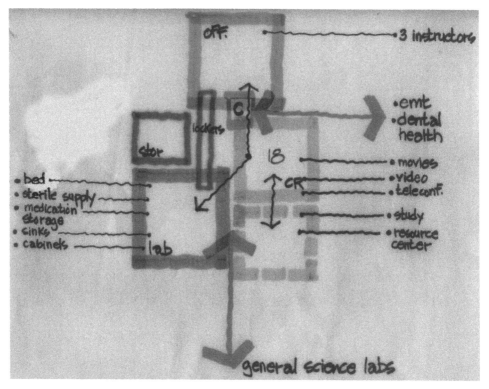

Figure 5.2. Departmental organizational relationship diagrams. *"Tanana Valley Community College Master Plan" organizational diagrams by academic department.*

In the design of a master plan for Tanana Valley Community College (Bettisworth and Kasprisin, 1982) in Fairbanks, Alaska, our design team interviewed each department head and catalogued projected needs for the successful functioning of each department. Within each department, "parts" were identified as functional requirements: classrooms for (x) number of students, offices, meeting rooms, laboratories, studios, storage, etc. all with quantitative requirements and sizes. These parts were then arranged through trial and error into functioning or larger workable organizations that met stated project needs. Each department arrived at this organization. Each was then organized into a larger functioning pattern where all departments formed a larger and workable whole.

Site context and structural assemblage are still not a part of this larger organization, and the design is incomplete.

Structural relationships in composition

The structural relationship aspect in a composition assembles the functional and operational relationships into a physical spatial composition, using forms to combine function and site context into a meaningful spatial metaphor. The structural relationships respect the organization and functional needs, respond to environment and seek the eidetic vision. In a design, there is usually one structural composition that is dominant out of numerous smaller assemblages, framing other smaller or supporting structures. Complex compositions have multiple structures in relationship, all performing a supportive action of a larger action.

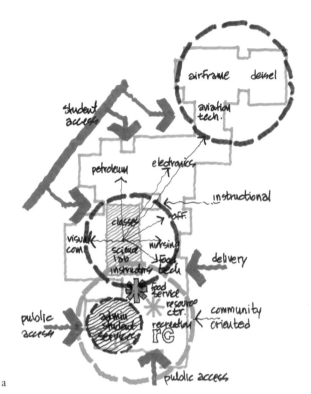

Figures 5.3 a and b. Facility-wide organizational relationship diagrams. *All academic departments are related in a series of facility-wide organizational options.*

a

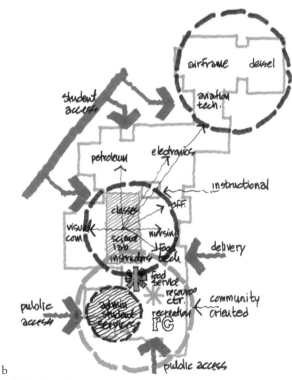

b

These structural relationships are the beginning stages of design composition and represent a phase in design where form takes on responsible and responsive meaning. In the following illustrations, the Tanana Valley Community College (Fairbanks) is represented in the evolutionary transition between organization, site fit, and physical assemblage.

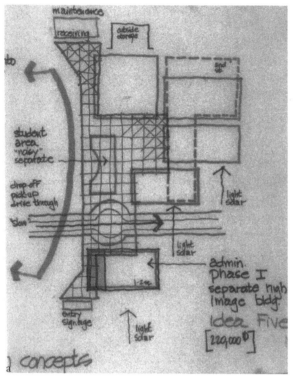

Figures 5.4 a and b. TVCC structural diagram options. *Each option diagram (a) explores various ways of structuring or assembling the organizational relationships into a form relative to site context. In (b), the larger composition emerges as a system of structures integrating buildings, uses, and open space.*

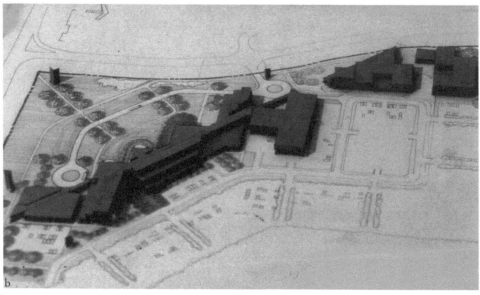

Compositional structures

Now the square, circle, and line become more than elements or shapes, they become structuring mechanisms for complex compositions.

Arnheim (1969) states that there are only two basic structural compositions: circle and square, from which all other compositions emanate. I add to this the line or axis, as it is inherent in both the circle and square and not always evident. Hybrids of each major structuring form include and are not limited to rectangles and grids for the square, radii, and radial bursts for the circle, and the axis for the line. These are explored here and in later chapters.

Why are these important? They provide *dynamic* structures or frameworks (assemblies of) for individualizing or giving *specification* to organizations. They always "beg" for a hybrid as they respond to context.

- *dynamic* (relating to change, physical forces in motion)
- *specifications* (peculiar to or characteristic of)
- *static* (stable, centered, not growing or changing as in *core values*)
- *periphery* (less stable, creative, changing, reactive).

Let's review the various characteristics of the three basic compositional structures as described in the primary shapes (see Figures 5.5–5.26).

Square characteristics

- four- to five-dot pattern (center plus four corner points)
- opposite right-angle corners pattern
- two parallel lines distant by their own measurement
- four identical quarter shapes
- two identical half shapes
- a cross of two equal lines implying four quarters.

Square derivatives

Grid:

- crisscross pattern
- orthographic pattern
- vertical and horizontal patterns
- types:
  - standard square grid
  - standard rectangular grid
  - broken grid
  - meandering grid
  - hybrid grid.

Rectangle:

- multiple squares
- portions of a square.

Triangle:

- two or three angles other than 90 degrees
- has a center along an apex or vertical axis
- directed and directional or centered as in an equilateral triangle
- the arrow is a triangle (directional)
- the vanishing point.

Diamond:

- intersection of vertical and horizontal lines
- or a composition of triangles
- four points forming four non-perpendicular angles
- in 3-D: two pyramids connected at their base.

Cross:

- with a center point
- with an off-set focal point
- angular with movement and non-perpendicular direction.

Diagonal:

- movement and direction
- 45-degree angle orientations
- the grid turned.

Horizontal/vertical:

- less tension and drama
- bars and pickets
- however, when mixed with diagonal (and 30/60) more drama and variety.

The "L" structure:

- turning a corner
- an end with options
- the illusion of diagonality
- deflection as well as end
- remember: the "l" can be standing or lying down, right or reversed.

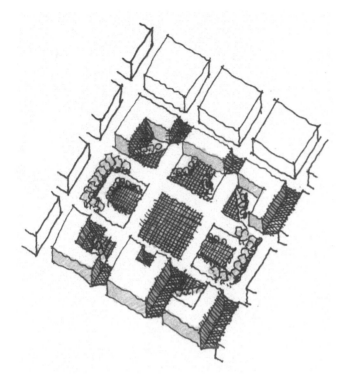

Figure 5.5. Compositional structure: the square. *The square is a powerful structuring form in urban settings, reflected in the conventional block grid and the assemblage of buildings and open spaces within that grid.*

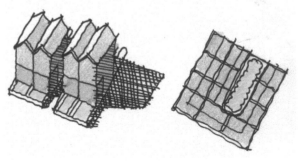

Figure 5.6. Applications of the square. *The square is the basic compositional structure for many human settlements. Examples include a downtown urban block with commercial buildings, a townhouse complex, a park design of curved walls, and a street grid pattern.*

53

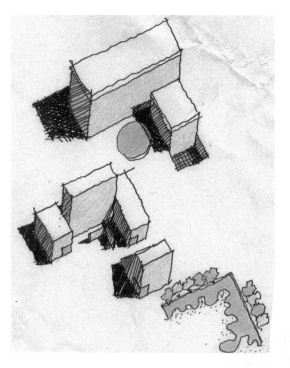

Figure 5.7. Compositional structure: the "L". *Another derivation of the square, the "L" is a common compositional structure used in urban design at all scales, from building and site development to urban block developments to landscape design. The "L" can be composed of many smaller shapes as long as the "L" structure is dominant.*

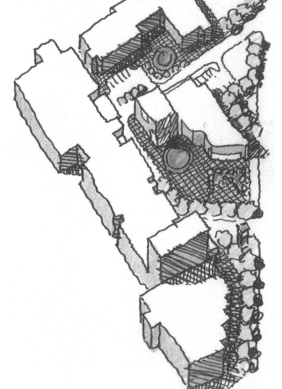

Figure 5.8. "L" as leisure center. *The "L" has many applications, especially on tight sites: composing a small leisure center retail complex on a triangular site, with one "L" nested in the larger "L".*

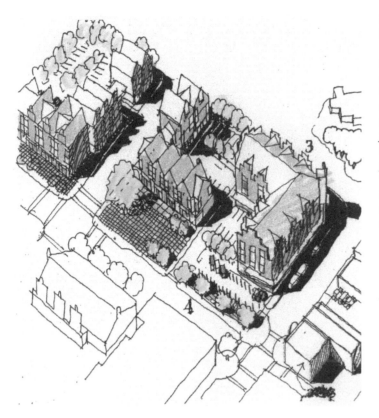

Figure 5.9. "L" as mixed-use block. *The "L" acts as an organizing structure in a mixed-density residential complex composed of townhouses above retail and stacked flats above retail, oriented toward a public commons. The "L" contains space in its corner configuration and has an open gesture to the outside.*

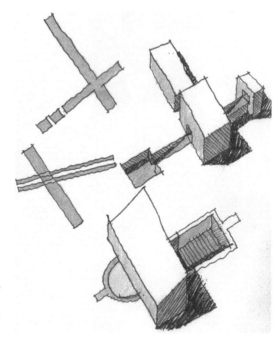

Figure 5.10. Compositional structure: the cross. *The cross structure consists of two (or more) intersecting shapes or patterns. The intersection can be perpendicular or at oblique angles. Each of the crossing shapes can be composed of different shapes, from buildings to open space components.*

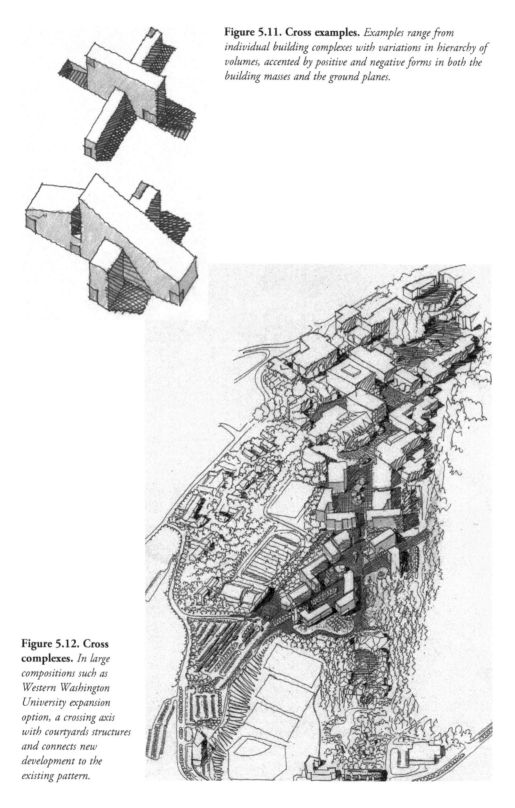

Figure 5.11. Cross examples. *Examples range from individual building complexes with variations in hierarchy of volumes, accented by positive and negative forms in both the building masses and the ground planes.*

Figure 5.12. Cross complexes. *In large compositions such as Western Washington University expansion option, a crossing axis with courtyards structures and connects new development to the existing pattern.*

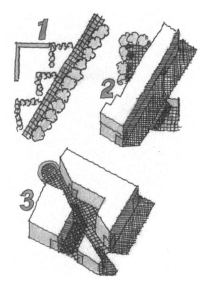

Figure 5.13 a. Compositional structure: the diagonal.
The diagonal is another derivation of the square and provides both a sense of direction and movement. As in the illustration, the diagonal can be an axis for movement in relation to a right-angle system, or it can appear as a positive building mass orientation and as a negative void within a building mass.

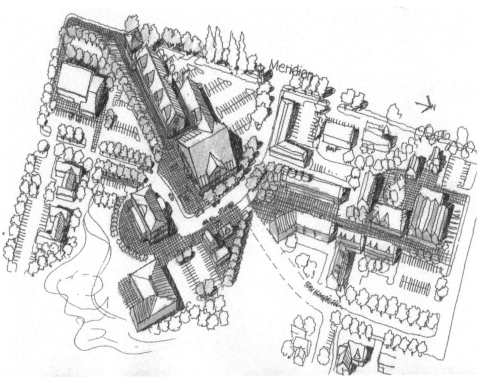

Figure 5.13 b. "Diagonal" application: Edgewood. *The Edgewood Town and Civic Center is connected to the main street intersection and related new town center developments with an axial diagonal pedestrian concourse. Civic buildings, new mixed-use commercial buildings, and a historic farm complex are visually and physically assembled parallel to and at the termination of the diagonal axis. As in all compositions, trees and landscape define space rather than simply occurring within space—as the trees strengthen and highlight the diagonal structure.*

Circle characteristics

- a center with equal distances to its edge
- center is a point of balance, not necessarily with equal radii
- of one object or a group of objects as a collective center
- curvilinear, circularity
- circle hybrids.

Circle derivatives

Two centered configurations:

- two configurations not touching or with minor contact, usually with one having dominance
- not united in some rhythm or movement
- confrontational
- creates tension and some degree of confrontation (can be positive if planned)
- three or odd number of centers may be easier to work with.

Radial burst structure:

- circular relationship in which the movement and direction of the radials overpower the center; do not have to be equal in length.

Curvilinear dominance:

- curves and spirals predominant
- "S," arcs, ovals, motion.

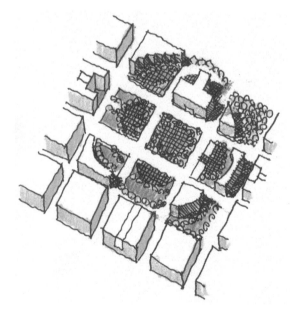

Figure 5.14. Compositional structure: the circle. *The circle is a powerful compositional structure, often used in formal ceremonial arrangements; superimposed over the grid (square) in urban settings it can be highlighted with buildings and open space components; and, when manipulated as a primary shape, presents flexibility for informal arrangements.*

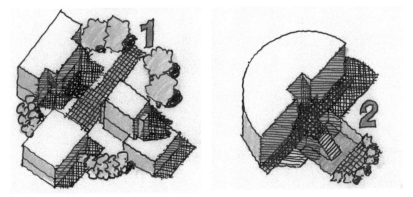

Figures 5.15 a and b. Circle examples. *The examples include: an office park with repeated rectangles varying in size (1) and (2) a circle and square combination with positive and negative levels. The circle provides the basis for many hybrids and derivations to structure compositions, from the radial burst to the serpentine.*

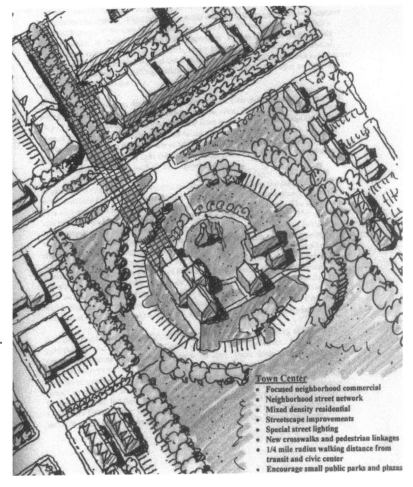

Figure 5.16. Civic center circle structure. *In Edgewood Civic Center, a circle structures the new civic center facilities connected to a commercial center with a pedestrian axis.*

Town Center
- Focused neighborhood commercial
- Neighborhood street network
- Mixed density residential
- Streetscape improvements
- Special street lighting
- New crosswalks and pedestrian linkages
- 1/4 mile radius walking distance from transit and civic center
- Encourage small public parks and plazas

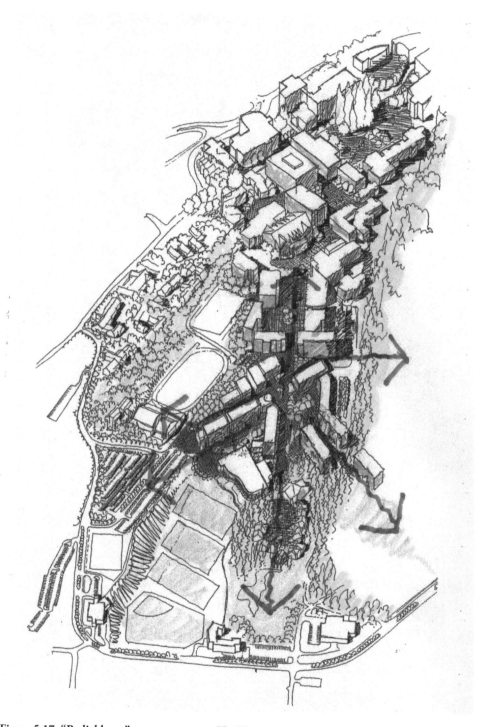

Figure 5.17. "Radial burst" campus concept. *The Western Washington University design charrette explored a radial burst structure to connect educational pods within the southern portion of the campus, connecting new and existing facilities with a radial burst pedestrian pattern.*

Line characteristics

The axis! As seen in previous examples, the axis is a powerful structuring device especially when combined with other compositional structures. For our purposes at this time, I suggest limiting the angles of axis to the following:

- 0–180
- 90
- 45–45
- 45–22.5
- 30–60 *or* 60–30.

Other angles are certainly valid. The conventional angles listed above provide workable mathematics in form without getting unnecessarily complicated. In order to challenge the rules, learn the basics first.

The axis as compositional structure is a strong linear force that acts as a positive organizing form (as buildings along a street) or as a void (the street as open space).

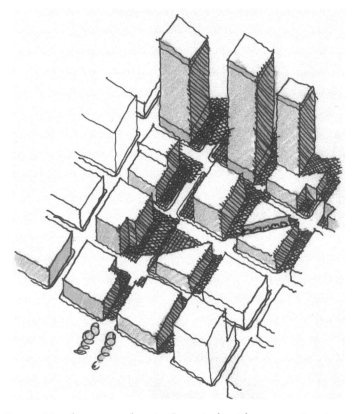

Figure 5.18. Compositional structure: the axis. *Streets in the grid are axes, as is a river and a freeway— a powerful linear force that assembles functional relationships within and along its movement and direction. In urban settings, they provide direction and penetration through dense building masses for orientation, reference, and movement, both with the grid and at angles to the grid. A progressive or graded axis structures the main avenue in the grid and a diagonal axis cuts across the grid.*

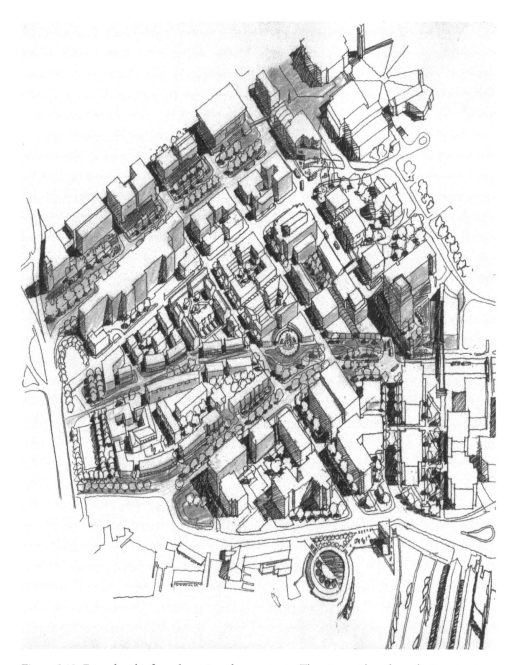

Figure 5.19. Formal and informal axes in urban contexts. *The axis provides order and orientation in dense urban areas. The axis can be a formal approach to important nodes (University of Washington campus), and can be a curving softer axis with landscaped oases along the way, intersecting with other axial structures.*

Figure 5.20. Axis as pedestrian concourse. *On a human scale, the axis provides clear movement channels through urban areas, connecting civic, commercial, and residential uses structured along the axis.*

Other compositional structures

Bridging structure:

- often two or more centers or foci joined by a connecting element or relationship
- bridging structures can be elevated, depressed, at grade level, and even vertical as in an elevator or funicular; examples include the elevated skywalk system or an underground shopping concourse in cold climate cities
- most bridging devices are physical but can also be implied via cultural histories related to a site, with remnants of past infrastructure, buildings, and other historic physical patterns
- bridging can be implied through a placement of opposites (solid/void, complementary colors, positive/negative).

Cantilever structure:

- a horizontal element supported at one end (diving board) or with one end projected beyond supporting elements
- usually used in support of other relationships and structures.

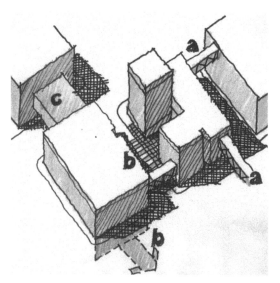

Figure 5.21. Compositional structure: bridging. *Bridging can occur with a conventional crossing (over, and in its polarity—tunneling under) of physical features (water bodies, freeways, etc.); urban blocks and building complexes as in the skyways of Minneapolis, Minnesota, and Spokane, Washington (both cold winter cities) (a); at-grade or below-grade "bridging" (b); by buildings as sometimes occurs within convention center expansions (c); and with cultural–spatial reclaimed remnant patterns (see Appendix III). Additionally, "bridging the gap" can be expressed simply as visually shared open space where both shared spaces are private and inaccessible except visually to the other space. This bridging is a form of visual connection and sharing while preserving territorial imperatives as occurs often in suburban communities.*

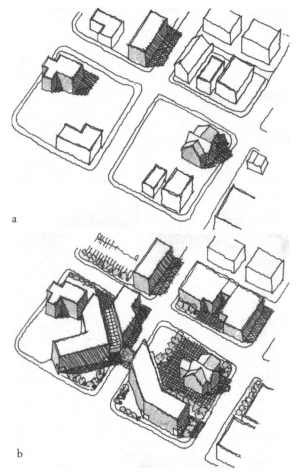

a

b

Figures 5.22 a and b. Bridging as connective device. *Bridging can be used to connect disparate uses and forms in an urban area, given land consolidation and other contextual issues. In the example, the existing urban form contains scattered office buildings and a historic library building. In the bridging example, the civic office forms are used to connect related uses and provide a focal area with the restored library building at the center.*

Figures 5.23 a and b. Compositional structure: the cantilever. *The cantilever is a suspension in space of one end of an element, extending out and over a space. In (urban) design, the cantilever can be a building extended out over an edge; a viewing platform over a waterfront (a); or a protrusion into another space, from hard streetscape to verdant stream-ravine, as in the Lake City Viewing Platform (b).*

a

b

Superimposition: To superimpose is to lay one element of pattern over another. The principle can also imply the dominance of one element or pattern over another.

- space within a space, e.g., a circle structure within a square structure, a sphere within a cube, etc.
- two spatial relationships brought together in an overlay pattern
- two conflicting relationships brought together in an overlay pattern, seeking a new outcome.

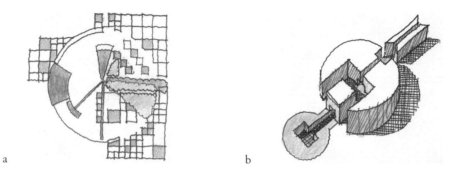

a   b

Figures 5.24 a and b. Compositional structure: superimposition. *Overlaying two or more different spatial structures can lead to new undiscovered and useful compositional resolutions as illustrated in these circle and square structural superimpositions, (a) representing urban patterns; and (b) representing a building complex. Here is an opportunity to play and explore.*

Clustering: Clusters are groups of spatial elements arranged around a common and shared element (park) or facility (parking), etc. They are connected to a larger spatial framework, such as additional housing clusters surrounded by open space and connected to a collector street network by private driveways and alleys. The clusters can be circular, square, etc. and can range from courtyard cottage housing to clusters with central parking areas or access roads. They can be composed of the same building type or mixed building (and density) types as in farmsteads.

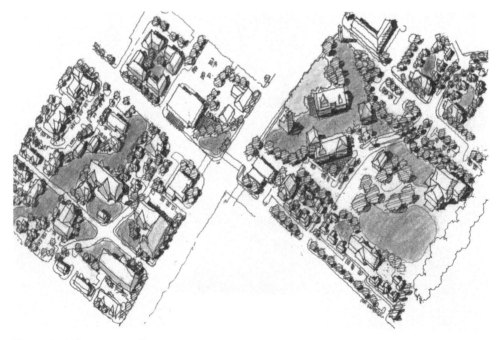

Figure 5.25. Compositional structure: clustering. *Clusters large and small in various patterns, ranging from residential groupings to office commercial campus-type clusters, are arranged around an open meadow connecting a new town and civic center to peripheral developments. More cluster examples are found in Chapter 7.*

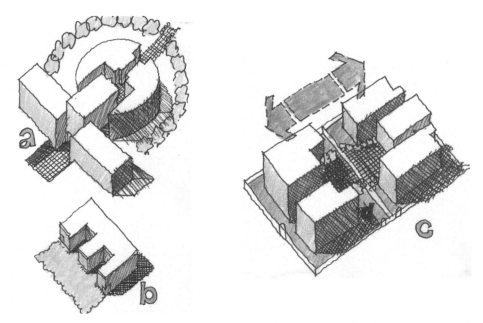

Figures 5.26 a, b and c. Compositional structure: interlocking structures. *Interlocking structures work well with positive and negative relationships as in these examples: for solid right-angle shapes into circular shapes (a), also using depressed planes penetrating above-grade masses; simple open space interlocks into building masses (b); and open space interlocking into adjacent building or neighborhoods forms (c). Interlocking in urban contexts can connect multiple building forms (1); act as a mirroring or positive/negative connecting device (2); transition one form to another with a vertical transparent courtyard; or, interlock the ground plane to a sub-grade plane.*

Interlocking structures: Interlocking is the integration of two or more shapes or patterns into one another, usually along their edges. Take the fingers of each hand and bring them together and "lock" together. The edges are hard and each shape or pattern penetrates the other, as in a saw-tooth pattern.

Playful exploration with compositional structures

I developed the following example for students to portray an exploratory search for a compositional structure for a complex of buildings. The structure, in this case a triangle, began to emerge as I played with the elements, the site, principles of repetition, and repetition with variety.

Some assumptions: this fictitious complex has an organizational relationship that translates into an initial radial repetition of buildings oriented toward the northwest along a lake edge, not unlike an institutional facility. Phase one is a given as in *initial design notion (a)*. The structural relationships are exhibited in the semi-radial *first design notion* and are deemed suitable for the functioning of the organizational need contained within the buildings.

Based on this first notion, the initial structural composition is interacted with the site context for an initial starting point. This is important for students: do not try to be "perfect" or final as you bring together the organizational and structural relationships with site context. *Second design notion (b) and (c)* are play efforts to protect the structural relationship (a) and expand the concept to the larger site, responding to northwest and southwest orientations along the water edge. Remember this is fictitious so use some imagination.

Notions (b) and (c) also provide emergent design opportunities as they interact with the site in different ways. I began searching for a larger compositional structure that had potential for providing a framework for future development, knowing that many designers will participate in the fulfillment of the master plan over an extended period of time.

The triangle as compositional structure: Based on the water edge form and the initial semi-radial structure of *notion (a)*, I tested a triangular compositional structure on the site, making efforts to have corners of buildings coordinate with the triangle edge. Based on some additional play, I decided to apply a more direct geometry to the initial semi-radial structure, maintaining the radial principle and strengthening the composition by using a common center point with radii emanating out to the centers of each building, adjusting them perpendicular to the radius. See *design notion (d)*. I then continued to play with the new radial structure, reversing it and doubling the complex with the same form, repeated with variety in orientation, *design notion (e)*. Both efforts fit into the triangular compositional structure and presented new opportunities for site development, as illustrated in *design notion (f)*, building shapes can vary as new phases adapt to changing programs and the compositional structure holds together.

Spatial reference frameworks

Using the compositional structures as underlying organizing frameworks

Spatial reference frameworks are structures that hold larger complex compositions together, provide a mathematical or quantifiable basis for design and implementation, and are not necessarily obvious or visual in the final composition, thus this separation from the previous discussion of compositional structures. The block grid in most cities is a visual–spatial structure that frames or provides a foundation for many different forms and is perceived visually in the built environment. A curvilinear form may have as its framing structure an underlying grid where the corners, half and quarter points and centers, etc. provide intersecting references or anchors for the curved forms, enabling a manageable implementation and assembly process—and is not (easily) visually perceived in the resulting form. Conversely, a radial structure such as Stonehenge is viewed as a circular form.

These frameworks are useful to the emerging designer in that they provide a quantifiable means of making complex form that is plausible, less complicated, and measurable. I refer to these as transparent or ghost structures—invisible. The difference between these and other structures is in their hidden role of assembly.

Compositional massing: form-based implementation

Massing diagrams

Compositional massing diagrams are the outer limit of preferred design envelopes in urban (and regional) contexts. They specify use (what), quantity (how much), location (where), and design amenities and/or features related to on-site conditions and off-site relationships. The compositional massing is use dependent in that land and building uses influence building typology. To assemble a form-based design massing diagram without knowledge of potential uses can lead to naïve or problematic implementation of reasonable development within the envelope.

Urban design often serves as a testing procedure for land use, zoning, and policy decisions by exploring and visualizing the potential outcomes of development. The testing begins with allowable zoning

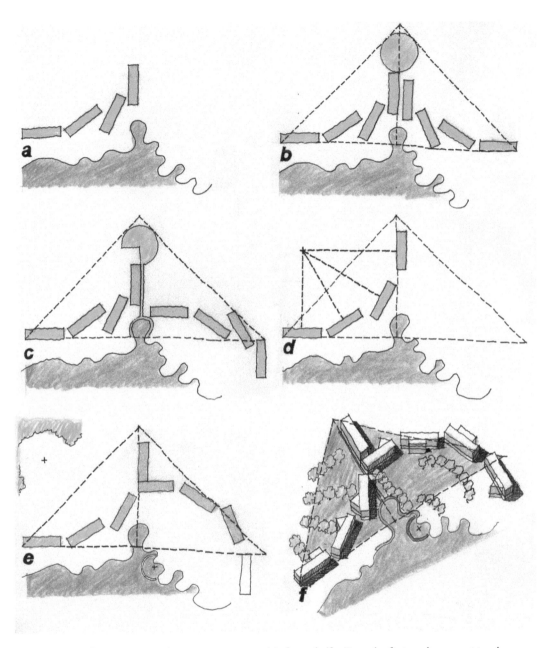

Figures 5.27 a–f. Compositional structure sequence (a) through (f). *Example of triangular compositional structure sequence for students.*

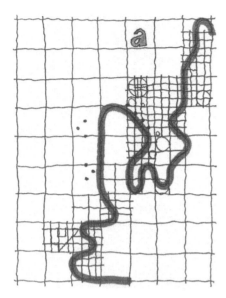

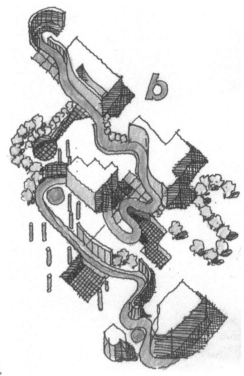

Figures 5.28 a and b. Transparent or ghost structures. *The playful illustration portrays a curvilinear organic configuration (b) with an underlying ghost structure (a)—a grid. In (a), the conceptual curvilinear form is superimposed upon a grid of varying size squares for more flexibility. In (b), a three-dimensional form is added to the base pattern.*

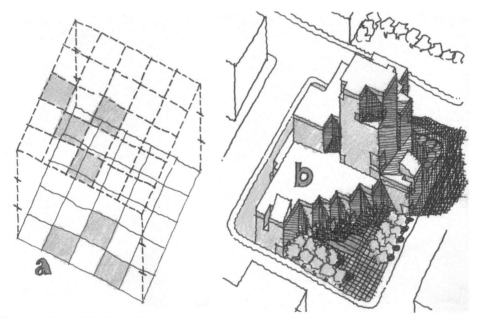

Figures 5.29 a and b. Three-dimensional grid frameworks. *A three-dimensional grid framework (a) is useful to carve out responsive forms in an urban context. The grid frame is more obvious in the outcome and provides a guide for adding and subtracting forms to accommodate site and program requirements (b).*

and proceeds through massing explorations relative to the site, resulting in form that is design-inclusive (as opposed to the conventional economic zoning envelope), and augmented by architectural examples for scale, style, and detail. Gordon Cullen used compositional massing in the 1950s and early 1960s as a tool in visualizing new built form within an existing and often historic context. His masterful perspective diagrams portray both existing specific built form and the larger massing envelopes, with historic buildings highlighted for reference and orientation (see Cullen, 1961, pp. 107, 214, and 231). They are not new and are valuable tools in form-based zoning.

Design implementation
Compositional massing plays a critical role in design implementation, particularly design standards and guidelines. Interpretation of design guidelines is an ongoing challenge to urban designers in that vagueness can lead to mediocrity, or worse to compromises; extremely specific details can thwart quality design. In design guideline projects, I used the following steps to provide clear intent, the ability for design flexibility in interpretation of the guidelines, and specific compositional massing. They include:

- *Design intent:* the directed and earnest aspirations of the guidelines regarding sensitivity to context and design approach to a specific location and/or place.
- *Design principles:* the guiding rules of conduct underlying the intent, specifically related to how the elements and compositions of the design proposal respond to and fit into the existing and/or emerging context.
- *Design actions:* the specifics regarding height, setbacks, access, orientation, connectivity, phasing, etc.
- *Design examples:* architectural and urban design visualizations of design interpretations that maintain the intent and principle underlying the guidelines. These can describe scale, style, and materials.

The compositional diagram provides the anchoring for these four levels of specificity. The following examples use compositional diagrams during the testing phase where proposals and policy are explored on specific sites and locations, and in the representation of final design guidelines. Examples include work from "Visions for Sechelt" (British Columbia), "Wharf Street Form-based Design Code" (Langley, Washington), and "Downtown Design Handbook" (Silverdale, Washington), respectively.

"Visions for Sechelt," British Columbia: Development along the Sechelt downtown waterfront has resulted in mixed-use buildings four stories high by one block in length, on long (parallel to waterfront) and narrow urban blocks, effectively forming a four-story dam blocking views of Georgia Strait and Vancouver Island from downtown. Views are not guaranteed in existing zoning envelopes for everyone near the Georgia Strait waterfront. However, neighbors and business people protested for a less massive and barrier-like built form. As a result, the vision process explored urban design options for a consensus position between the developers and community.

"Wharf Street Form-based Design Code": Langley, Washington is a village of 1,100 people along Saratoga Passage in Puget Sound, northwest of Seattle, Washington in the Pacific Northwest, a three-hour drive south of Vancouver, British Columbia. The Wharf Street area consists of a small marina, limited uplands between the water edge, and a steep bluff (200 feet or approximately 60 plus meters) for parking and tourist uses. Development pressure to build on the steep slope and along the toe of the slope was the catalyst for a detailed design testing process regarding development type and impacts, pedestrian access to waterfront, parking, and the use of the steep slope. Public workshops were held with

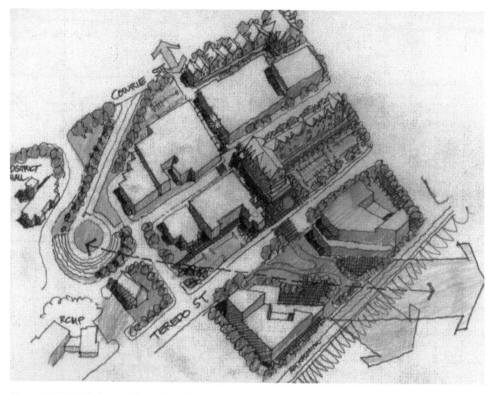

Figure 5.30. Sechelt waterfront development. *As part of a public information effort and as a testing mechanism for design implementation, compositional massing diagrams explored view corridors through development parcels, with special setbacks, varying heights throughout the parcels to compensate developer interests and other issues such as parking and pedestrian spaces. The example is one of a series of axonometric diagrams used to explore the various massing options. In the process of this exploration, the view corridor to Georgia Strait from the existing city hall and library gained prominence. In a later design phase, a new civic center park coordinated all civic buildings and parking demands and focused on the view corridor to the Strait.*

landowners, developers, citizens, and city staff to seek a consensus with limited compromise regarding a specific form-based design ordinance.

The following compositional massing diagrams are a few of over two dozen studies prepared for discussion in the workshops. Based on a near unanimous consensus of property owners, the City of Langley approved and adopted the results as a new form-based zoning ordinance for the Wharf Street uplands.

"Downtown Design Handbook": Silverdale, Washington is an unincorporated regional shopping center complex situated on the Kitsap Peninsula in Puget Sound north of Bremerton, Washington. The "downtown" consists of a regional shopping mall and many smaller shopping plazas and strip malls. They are served by a super-block arterial road network with minimal pedestrian amenities and few safe street crossings. Parking lots dominate the landscape and shoppers use their vehicles to travel from one plaza to another with little or no connectivity. The challenge was to develop an urban design aspiration or intent for the commercial center: transforming this suburban fragmented pattern into a functioning and meaningful downtown community.

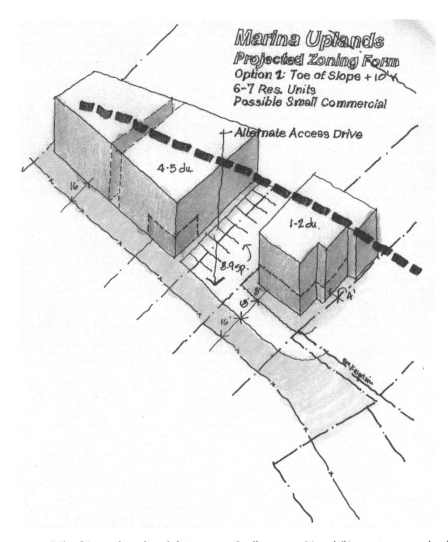

Figure 5.31. Wharf Street form-based design tests. *In illustrations (a) and (b), massing tests explored the fit and location of buildings, access roads and pedestrian corridors and gathering spaces within the Wharf Street uplands. Each test was accompanied by architectural interpretation examples to demonstrate scale and building features.*

The Silverdale illustrations represent the final compositional massing diagrams approved and adopted by the Board of Commissioners for Kitsap County, Washington. They encompass design intent and principles allocated for different design districts within the commercial center. These districts ranged from a salmon stream watershed and wetland area, to a historic downtown core on Dyes Inlet, to the surrounding suburban mall and plaza complex and office parks at the periphery. A local street network is incorporated into the guidelines as incremental redevelopment of older shopping plazas occurs due to competition and consumer demand. The compositional massing diagrams are accompanied by architectural examples.

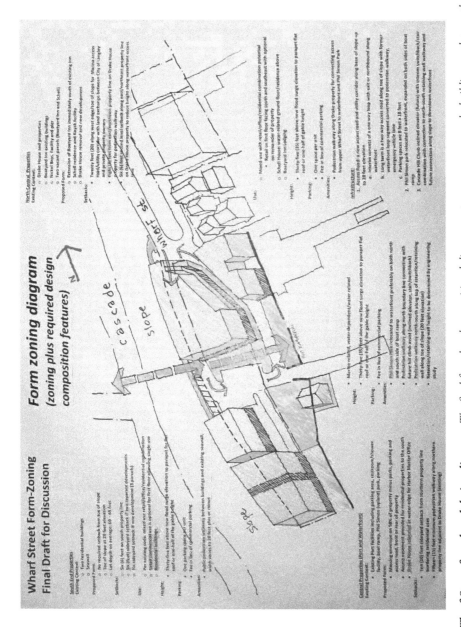

Figure 5.32. Wharf Street form-based design diagram. *The final form-based compositional diagram portrays new access roads, building envelopes, setbacks, pedestrian areas, slope hill-climb facilities, and other features. The diagram is the basis for the new zoning ordinance; the architectural visualization provides an example of build-out.*

SILVERDALE VILLAGE
COMPOSITION DIAGRAM

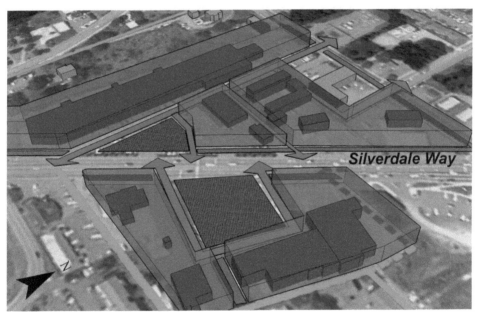

a

Source: KPD

Figures 5.33 a–d. Silverdale compositional diagrams. *The Silverdale compositional diagrams and accompanying architectural examples portray the redevelopment of aging shopping plazas into new town centers. In (a) and (b), the compositional diagrams highlight both internal form improvements and the relationship across the arterial of one shopping plaza to the other, both working in consort to create the downtown gateway. In (c) and (d), a gateway office park site, partially developed, is expanded to include new office space, the conservation of a wetland and stream, and orientation to new development to the south with pedestrian and open space connections.*

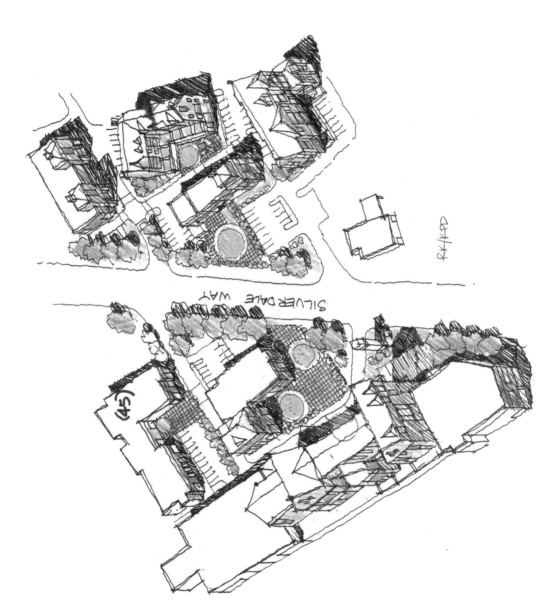

SILVER DALE WAY

(45)

RK/KD

b

SILVERDALE GATEWAY COMPOSITION DIAGRAM

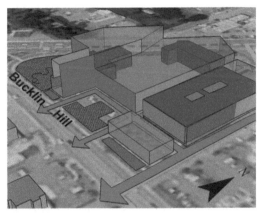

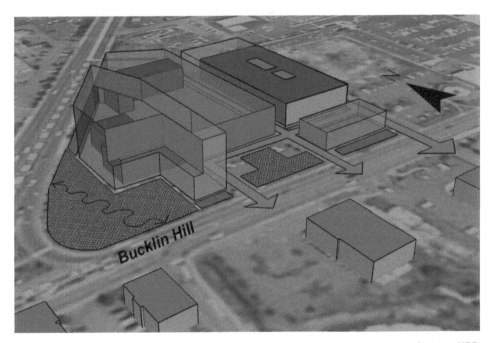

Source: KPD

c

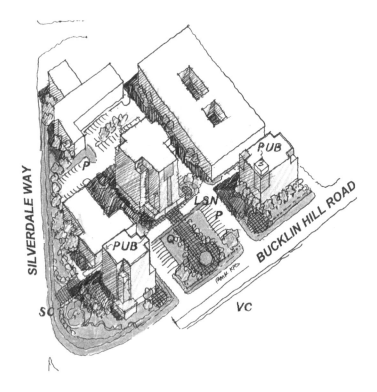

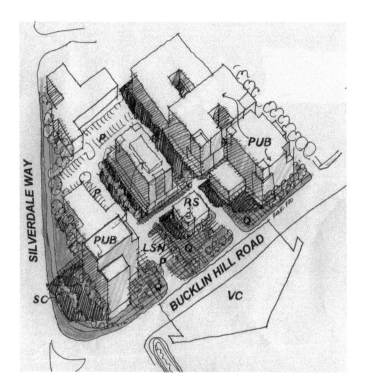

d

Additional spatial characteristics of composition

Proportions

Proportions create a sense of order through the equality of ratios (a fixed relationship between two similar things); a consistent set of visual relationships between the parts and the whole:

- natural material characteristics
- structural
- manufactured
- regulating lines.

Orders

Order is a fixed or definite arrangement of things. Often used in architecture to define classic and/or conventional arrangements of objects, not unlike a model.

- *Architectural:*
  - a classic column: pedestal four parts, shaft 12, capital three parts
  - a building with a base of two stories, a main mass of six stories, a cap of one story and a cornice.
- *Landscape architecture:*
  - a main pedestrian concourse 12 feet wide for four people to walk abreast in either direction; a smaller sidewalk of six feet for two people abreast.
- *Human:*
  - five feet six inches on average, etc.
  - three feet across allowable.

Scale

Scale is important to the human use of space in that the relationship between humans and their environment is either responsive or sensitive to human scale or overpowering and out of context. Buildings of monumental character can portray power and symbolism. They are generally intended to be separate from "human," to represent either a higher level of meaning or power or intimidation.

- *Generic scale* is generally the size of building relative to other forms in (existing) context
- *Human scale* is the built environment that is relative to the human body and includes all aspects of that environment:
  - windows
  - doors
  - height more than depth and width (churches)
  - shape, color, pattern of bounding surfaces
  - shape and location of openings
  - nature and scale of elements placed within space

- streets and pathways: the neighborhood street and sidewalks in comparison to the grand boulevard for visual scale
- parks and open space: the small passive park in comparison to the grand commons for shared community events.

- *Infrastructure or functional scale* is the scale required by the industrialization of our communities and is not necessarily human sensitive, for example:
  - spaces for motorized vehicles (parking lots, garages, freeways)
  - utility and rail corridors
  - airports, arenas, stadiums, etc.

Bibliography

Arnheim, Rudolph, 1969: *Visual Thinking*: University of California Press, Berkeley, CA.

Bettisworth, Charles and Kasprisin, Ron, 1982: "Tanana Valley Community College Master Plan": University of Alaska, Fairbanks, AK.

Ching, Francis D.K., 1979: *Architecture: Form, Space and Order*: Van Nostrand Reinhold, New York.

Cullen, Gordon, 1961: *Townscape*: Reinhold Publishing, New York.

Edgewood, City of, 1999: "Town Center Plan: Community Character and Land Use Study": Kasprisin Pettinari Design and Dennis Tate Associates, Langley, WA.

Goldstein, Nathan, 1989: *Design and Composition*: Prentice Hall Inc., Englewood Cliffs, NJ.

Johnston, Charles MD, 1984/1986: *The Creative Imperative*: Celestial Arts, Berkeley, CA.

Johnston, Charles MD, 1991: *Necessary Wisdom*: Celestial Arts, Berkeley, CA.

Kitsap County Department of Community Development/Kasprisin Pettinari Design (Langley, WA), 2006: "Downtown Design Handbook": Silverdale, WA.

Langley, City of, 2009: "Wharf Street Form-based Design Code": Langley, WA (design team: Ron Kasprisin AIA/APA; Dr Larry Cort, Planning Director; Fred Evander, Planner).

Sechelt BC, District of, 2007: "Visions for Sechelt": John Talbot & Associates (Burnaby, BC) and Kasprisin Pettinari Design (Langley, WA).

Chapter 6

TRANSFORMATIONS OF FORM
ELEMENTS AND COMPOSITION

Compositional structuring assembles elements and principles into meaningful form. Based on the complexities of the environment, manipulating form to respond to complex situations is also an integral part of design. Seldom can the primary shapes, volumes, and compositional structures be used in their pure state in urban design due to the complexity of the existing urban form, as well as the demands of the culture/space/time (CST) trialectic (Soja, 1996). There are conditions where the cube as house can be set in the landscape or the grid community can be set in a Greenfield due to a lack of significant constraints. In most urban or community situations, that physical simplicity or clarity is not possible. For urban designers, the compositional structures *et al.* require playful modification, imagination, hybridization, and manipulation to "fit" into and respond to existing and emerging context, maintaining the intended meaning and functionality of the "story" in a wholesome manner. Transformation principles are key design tools for this urban complexity and are discussed and envisioned in this chapter. They build upon conventional transformational actions used in the professional design fields.

With urban design applications in mind, review and experiment with these ways to change or manipulate form:

- dimensional
- subtractive
- additive
- integrative or merging
- bridging.

The first three (dimensional, subtractive, and additive) are existing conventions in design; see Ching (1979). Merging and bridging polarity transformations are experiments that emanate from my professional practice, the related applications of creative systems theory (Fritjof Capra, Edward Soja, Charles Johnston, etc.), and art. There are other hybrid variations including superimposition, edge transformation, reversing the positive and negatives, among others.

Dimensional transformations

Dimensional transformations consist of changing one or more measurements. The square may become a larger or smaller square, or become a rectangle. If the parent identity is to remain, all relative components are made larger or smaller.

Methods of transformation with dimensions:

- compressing or elongating an axis
- changing a base (as in triangle) dimension

- moving an apex of a triangle off-center
- changing height, width, depth on a cube and rectangular volumes
- extending or compressing a radius.

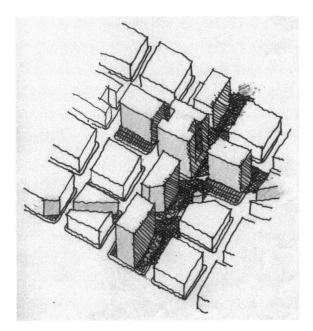

Figure 6.1. Dimensional transformation: cross and axis.
In these crossing compositional structures, each crossing volume is also a potential axis. Altering the dimensions of axial shapes provides a wide array of form possibilities that can respond to both site conditions and CST program requirements, and still maintains the crossing structure. The axis establishes or structures movement and direction in urban compositions. The cross can be used to celebrate and dramatize key intersecting spaces in urban areas. These can be highlighted by increasing axial dimensions and open space areas at the intersection, and by the positioning of key building forms.

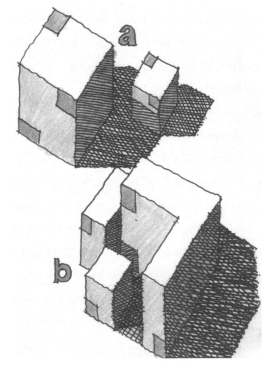

Figures 6.2 a and b. Dimensional transformation: cubes. *Using cubes, I transformed the larger cube to a smaller cube (a) by changing dimensions, a basic manipulation; and in (b) I superimposed the larger over the smaller, making the larger cube into a void surrounding the smaller cube, adding complexity to the transformation.*

Figure 6.3. Cubes in the urban pattern. *This illustration has a variety of urban cube transformations with dimensional changes including positive cube changes to larger positive/negative transformations using subtractive transformations as discussed below with the four towers comprising the cube. The parent identity is maintained even with the one lower tower.*

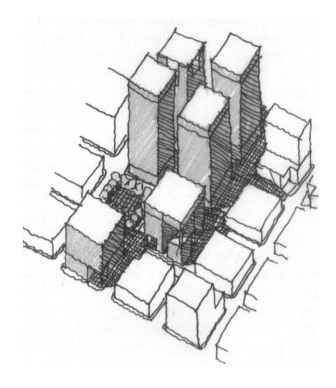

Subtractive transformations

Subtraction is the act of taking away a portion of an element or volume. At a certain point, the subtraction can stop in order to retain the original identity of the form; or continue and change the identity into something else. For example, a cube can be subtracted to a point where it becomes close to a pyramid.

Methods of transformation by subtracting:

- If you want to retain the original identity of the parent form, i.e. a cube, use caution on how you deteriorate the edges, corners, and overall profile.
- As a starting point and only a guide, in addition to removing other cubes from the larger original cube, experiment with subtracting other volumes such as the pyramid and sphere, still retaining the parent volume. Creating hybrids with them can be fun and creative and still retain plausibility of assembly. Uses include courtyards, entries, indoor/outdoor rooms, etc.

Additive transformations

Additive transformation consists of changing a form by adding to an existing form, keeping the original identity or major characteristic of the original (equal sides, for example). Maintaining the original identity of the primary form is the key principle.

Methods of transformation by adding:

- adding the same form to the original
- replicating the original form along adjacent surfaces in various sizes.

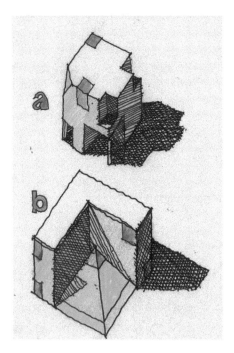

Figures 6.4 a and b. Subtractive transformations.
*My planning students enjoy this beginning exercise with
the cube because the subtractive actions enable them to
play with a "building" form (a) for the first time. The
cube becomes a two-story house with balconies and insets
and the variations are numerous. In (b), a pyramid
emerges from the cube and the cube is defined by the
boundaries of a void.*

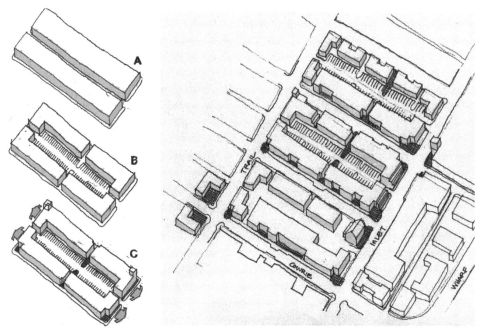

Figure 6.5. Subtractive zoning application sequence. *As a public educational exercise in "Visions for
Sechelt" (2007), the zoning mass for a downtown block (a) was transformed into a form-based zoning
concept by subtracting portions of the mass to make interior parking areas (b), pedestrian enclaves and eddies
(c), until the original mass becomes a context-specific urban block and blocks (d) with urban
design/community amenities.*

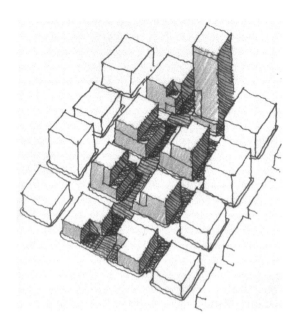

Figure 6.6. Subtractive urban block massing. *In larger urban centers, key streets, open space resources, significant buildings, etc. can be highlighted and supported by form-based design strategies. In this example, volumes are subtracted from larger office building masses to dramatize a key pedestrian axis.*

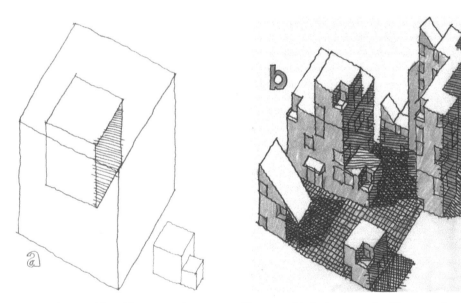

Figures 6.7 a and b. Additive transformations. *Illustration (a) displays a simple additive transformation of a small cube changing to a larger cube. Illustration (b) adds multiple cubes to the original cube and defines an even larger cube as a void, expressed in plan by the small grid pattern by adding cubes around the perimeter. Using repetition with variety, other cubes are playfully added to form a more complex composition with both dimensional change and the same forms adjacent to one another.*

These transformational actions apply to the larger and more complex compositional structures as well. In certain circumstances, the structural relationships of a larger complex can warrant additive transformations through expansion of previously used forms or same form additions to the underlying structural composition. As always, site conditions and the overall context require responsive forms.

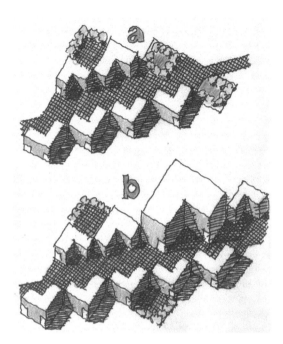

Figures 6.8 a and b. Additive transformations of structural compositions. *In this illustration, (a) represents a grid structural composition with a diagonal axis containing buildings and courtyards assembled by the grid and axis. In (b), the structural composition is transformed by adding both a dimensional change to the basic building form and added basic forms along the axis.*

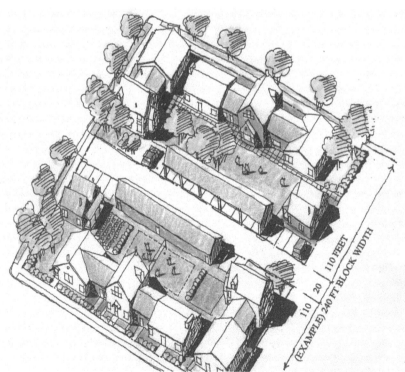

Figure 6.9. Additive residential cluster. *The additive residential cluster diagram portrays potential infill development with additive attached bungalow housing types. The one-acre parcel evolves from ten to 20 units per acre with the incremental addition of compatible building elements.*

Merging transformations

Merging consists of bringing two or more elements, volumes, or spatial relationships together (in contact at and within the edges or peripheries) where new characteristics are created within those edges and key aspects of each original (parent) are maintained. Merging can increase the complexity of a composition by introducing hybrids from the parents alongside them. Imagine taking a red and yellow and mixing them to form an orange; with the total mixture of the two, a uniform or monochromatic orange is formed. If the red and yellow are brought together and collided or interspersed within their peripheral areas, a mixture of red, yellow, and orange can result. The overall effect is "orange" and the actual mixture is a rich mingling of the orange and the parent primaries.

Let's try this with shapes and compositional structures. The following illustrations explore merging in an abstract way, then with more direct applications.

Methods for transformation with merging:

- colliding, integrating, interspersing two or more elements, volumes, or spatial relationships together with sufficient penetration, mixing, and superimposition to enable a co-mingling within the peripheral area (this area is relative in size as long as portions of the primary parent element are still present).

Figure 6.10. Merging transformational actions using watercolor. *Before we experiment with shapes and compositions, let's begin with merging as a watercolor technique: numerous colors are brought together in their peripheries to create a rich and complex color composite. In "Ravenous" (source: author), the ravens are "black" and yet have a richness within that hue that is made from multiple colors brought together not blended or homogenized—creating a new and fresh color effect.*

a

Figures 6.11 a and b. Merging transformational actions: abstract plans and volumes. *I began experimenting with this concept using simple black and white squares in a grid (a). What happens when the two are co-mingled or merged at their peripheral areas? In the second abstract illustration (b), I used a circle and grid patterns and experimented with merging the two, maintaining the original parent characteristics and constructing a transitional co-mingling composition. The circle varies from hard edge to void. The grid breaks down into smaller dimensions to articulate that void.*

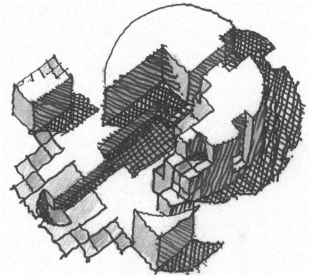

b

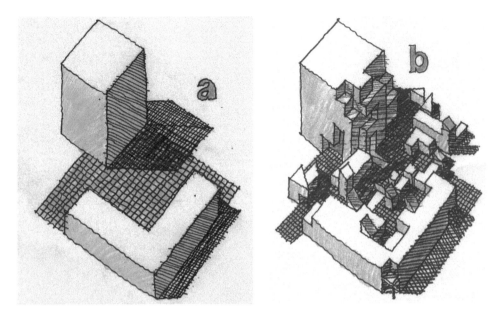

Figures 6.12 a and b. Merging transformational actions: abstract compositions. *Here a strong CST program can direct responsive forms for the area of integration. I gave this exercise to my students and asked them to envision a merging of two distinctly different housing types (a) (large high mass vs. low elongated mass) with supporting uses such as community center, health clinic, and supporting retail uses (b). The exercise can be further enriched by permitting a zero change in overall mass, where the merged area absorbs as additive transformation the subtractive transformation from the two larger masses.*

Merging as mixed-use transitions

Closer to reality, two urban design situations warrant the exploration of merging transformations: mixed-use and mixed-density development. Mixed use is commonly applied as residential and/or office vertically above commercial uses, or residential uses horizontally located behind street-oriented commercial uses.

Other applications can occur when two or more different use districts have a transition zone or seam, between residential and commercial and residential and industrial, for example. Live/work uses are often compatible transition mechanisms. In the United States and Canada, this seam is often a hard edge, a major arterial, with no transition.

Merging as mixed density

Mixed density can be found in examples ranging from European hamlet lots (three houses per lot typical), to the farmsteads of North America, to new applications of cluster housing in numerous Western countries. As a merging transformation (urban) design application, mixed density brings together a same-use cluster using a variety of building types. The application can provide a transition between established residential neighborhoods with different physical characteristics, and clusters of different building types in rural clusters, merging the conservation of open rural space with a tolerable development density and marketing diversity.

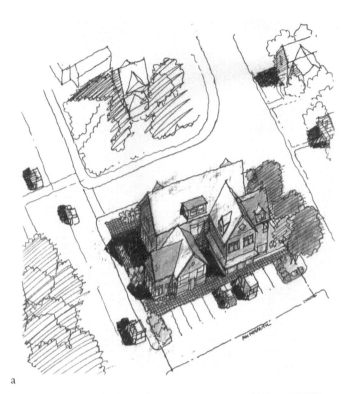

a

b

Figures 6.13 a and b. Merging transformational actions: neighborhood mixed-use applications.

Mixed-use illustration portrays a transition zone between a residential neighborhood and retail commercial street. The block is located along a small-town downtown entry arterial. The building forms in the neighborhood are historic Queen Anne/Victorian housing stock (two- to two-and-one-half stories, steep pitched gabled roofs with bay window extensions, landscaped front yard edge conditions). These massing characteristics are incorporated into a new neighborhood retail building complex. Residential units are located above retail uses facing the commercial arterial as well as at grade or ground level facing the established residential street. Uses and forms are merged into a distinctly different transitional composition within a compatible scale.

Figure 6.14. Merging transformational actions: mixed-use transitions. *This illustration portrays an integration of residential and light industrial live/work uses, via interlocking urban blocks of mixed uses (and mixed density, see below) including neighborhood or village retail/residential and single-use residential. Block (a) contains traditional single family detached residential with fenced front yards and rear alley parking. Block (b) contains single family detached residential buildings with "mother-in-law" rear yard cottages and single family attached residential with "mother-in-law" units attached to the main house. Multiplex single entry houses are on corner lots. Block (c) portrays large single family detached residential on a peripheral block. Block (d) portrays residential/light industrial/general commercial live/work buildings with common interior parking and street frontage orientation for shops. Block (e) portrays a more extensive live/work block with mixed building types ranging from attached larger buildings (residential on second level) plus smaller detached live/work houses. Finally, block (f) portrays a village center with retail commercial and residential uses both vertically and horizontally configured.*

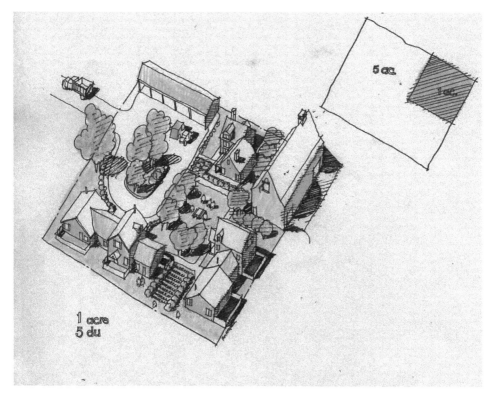

Figure 6.15. Merging transformational actions: mixed-density farmstead or urban cluster. *This example can be a higher residential density ranging from five residential units to 20 with shared accessory buildings. All units have private yards plus shared open space, garden areas, and other recreational space. Their application can be for urban-rural, or rurban, peripheral areas, or transition areas between different residential neighborhood typologies.*

In the previous mixed-use illustration, mixed density is also utilized to disperse the dominant or larger-scale housing and residential/light industrial/general commercial live/work buildings.

Bridging transformations

Bridging is the act of connecting two or more elements, volumes, or spatial relationships, usually contrasting or conflicting in nature while retaining the key principles of each relationship.

Methods for transformation with bridging:

- between two differing or conflicting compositions in present time, each separate in its function and meaning and in close proximity
- between current and anticipated patterns where adjacency and differences in meaning and functionality may occur
- between historic patterns (remnants) and new patterns, where activating or reinvigorating the remnant patterns can provide a bridge to the present.

Figure 6.16. Bridging transformational actions: making connections. *Bridging contrasting or conflicting compositions can employ numerous techniques such as merging and interlocking as described in this chapter. I used this illustration in "superimposition" and it applies to bridging as well. This illustration experiments with the circle and grid patterns as differing or contrasting elements. The challenge is to connect them without losing key aspects of their physical natures. In the illustration, the grid helps form the circle and the circle interlocks with the depressed rectangle (a portion of the grid); the axis provides movement, direction, and solidifies the overall assemblage.*

The act of bridging requires a concerted effort to minimize compromise. Compromise in design can lead to clichés, themes, and other borrowed meanings. Compromise can occur by blending 50/50 (each entity giving up 50 percent of principles), trying to solve the challenge with one form, or simply separating the composition into distinctly unintegrated parts. Unity within a composition is desired, and seeking unity with one form can be compromise. In 50/50, the design is compromised by eliminating 50 percent of the value of each entity in order to reach a design consensus. American planning is quite experienced at separating uses in the built form, compromising the built form with over-dominant functionalism.

Bridging: future connections

Bridging as a transformational action can integrate current development with uncertain future compositions by:

- anticipating connecting actions that can bridge differences, keeping them in relationship
- planting catalysts that can energize or stimulate an existing development pattern.

Anticipating connections can be as simple as providing a street connection for future development, or pedestrian trail hookups, or a visually and/or physically shared open space.

Planting catalysts can generate a ripple effect or attract energy for future development activity (Attoe and Logan, 1989). More than connections; catalysts have a market and design force to expand their quality meaning and functionality to other developments.

Making decisions for connective and catalyst devices in current time sets parameters for future and uncertain outcomes.

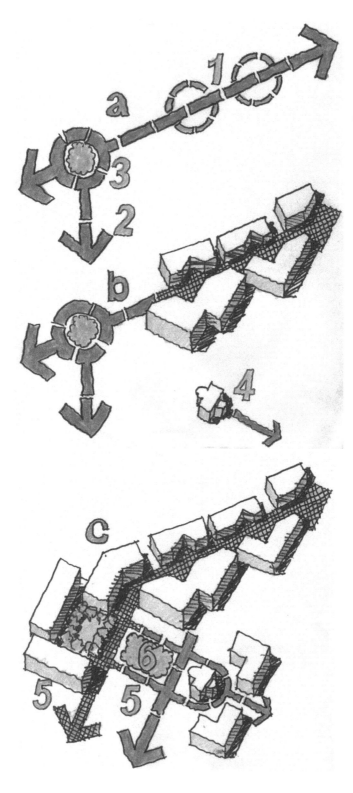

Figures 6.17 a, b and c. Bridging transformational actions: future connections. *Access corridors provide excellent examples of connections or bridges to the future. TVCC, a community college in Alaska that has a build-out span of 20 years, is structured around a semi-enclosed pedestrian service access corridor (1) flanked by the larger assemblage of building clusters. The corridor is the compositional structure and acts as a design policy statement, anticipating future expansion in probable directions (2) around an intersecting open space (3). A later decision earmarks an older building (4) for adaptive reuse as a part of the larger facility, not anticipated in the original program. The location and orientation of this building affects the planned orientation of the completed complex, with new building clusters changing in response to the additive program (5). The axis remains a bridging device in that the principles of direction, movement, and open space at the intercept are maintained, simply altered based on the new emerging context. The open space intercept is expanded (6) and the adaptively reused (historic) building gains prominence within the larger composition. The principles of the bridging connection held together and adapted to changing conditions. This example is abstracted and enhanced from a real situation in Fairbanks, Alaska only partially realized (Bettisworth and Kasprisin, 1982).*

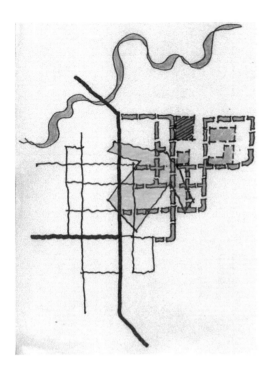

Figure 6.18. Bridging transformational actions: catalyst connections. *This is a hybrid concept diagram of Redmond, Washington's location of a new city hall and civic complex. Constructed over a decade, the new complex altered the direction of development in downtown and enabled the city to bridge the older center with a new civic and mixed-use district, with improved orientation to the Sammamish River. The initial city hall was constructed with limited infrastructure, awaiting peripheral development to cluster around city hall. Over time, as the complex and adjacent development matured, a new city hall was constructed, solidifying the new heart of Redmond.*

Bridging: remnant connections

The concept of remnants is discussed in Appendix II. Essentially, remnants are portions of historic physical compositions that remain in the contemporary built form. The parent pattern is obsolete and the remnants have fallen into dysfunction or been processed for other ancillary and unrelated uses. Remnants can be bridges from past to future.

The principles using remnants include:

- conserving the remaining physical artifacts
- identifying the original extent and characteristics of the parent pattern as a resource for design ideas
- reinvigorating the remnants from artifacts to functioning contemporary uses and patterns in conjunction with new development, i.e. bridging the past to the present with the remnants, forming a new and distinctly different built environment.

Options include:

- rehabilitation of existing portions of the remnant pattern
- reconstitution of the original parent pattern with contemporary uses
- reinvention of the original parent pattern as a spatial metaphor in new development. For example, a wood lot may be a remnant of a larger forested water recharge area, now surrounded and compromised by human development patterns. The remnant may be incorporated into new development patterns as a part of the open space design; the footprint of the larger parent pattern may be defined in a larger open space network as trails, landscaped patches, etc., where restoration is not possible.

Bridging: historic connections

Fort William H. Seward is an example of historic bridging with remnant patterns. The fort was constructed in Haines, Alaska around 1902–1910 by the United States Army to monitor the Yukon Gold Rush (and wield a "big-stick" toward Canada). Families, goods, and livestock traversed the trail over what is now the Haines Highway from Alaska to the Yukon Territories in British Columbia; hopeful miners scrambled over Chilkoot Pass from Skagway, 15 minutes from Haines as the crow flies and 371 miles by road. Fort Seward was purchased at auction after the Second World War by five families of retired military personnel, and became a composite of neighborhood, tourist facilities, and arts center, always teetering on the edge of extinction. The fort to this day contains a majority of original parent pattern characteristics: large duplex officer houses arranged around parade grounds, with barracks buildings and non-commissioned officers houses (Soap Suds Alley) cascading down to the waterfront where loading docks and warehouses front Portage Bay in Lynn Canal (deepest fjord in the North American continent).

The fort now operates as a tourist destination facility, with hotels, bed and breakfast facilities, restaurants, live theater (a reconstituted cannery—a remnant from the active fort), Alaska Native Arts center (masks and totem poles), residential uses, and ancillary commercial and tourist uses. The fort is

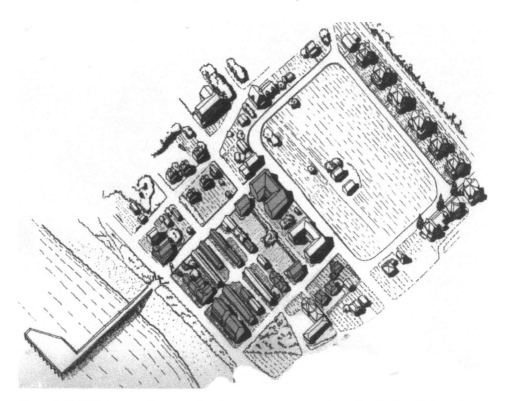

Figure 6.19. Bridging transformational actions: remnant connections. *Fort William H. Seward is a remnant pattern from a historic era (early 1900s for Alaska). Today, the fort complex is an active and evolving community within Haines with the larger compositional structure intact and serving as a basis for future additions. University of Washington (Seattle) graduate planning students prepared a historic district guideline and development strategy to assist the owners in improving the activities of the fort and maintaining the historic pattern.*

an adaptive reuse facility. More importantly, the fort stands as a bridge between the military history of the region and contemporary Alaska–Yukon Territory cultures and economies. The basic parent and remnant patterns provide a bridging device between past, contemporary, and future development patterns.

Many examples of remnants are hidden in contemporary built form waiting to be discovered. Years ago as I inspected salmon streams winding their way through the industrial waterfront of Ketchikan, Alaska, I observed a building on the creek with the creek coming out of the lower level of the building. Further investigation revealed a building constructed in the early 1920s over the salmon stream. Now used as a church, the building is surrounded by stacks of steel containers awaiting visiting freighters. The salmon stream and salmon are still present. What an opportunity to reclaim that area of the waterfront, conserve the salmon stream, and use the building and cascading stream as a bridging device for new development.

Other spatial transformational techniques

Other techniques to transform elements, volumes, and spatial relationships include how these forms are arranged in relation to one another. Here are some examples:

- *tension through separation*, with forms being relatively close to one another, usually sharing a common visual trait such as color, texture, shape, material
- *edge to edge*, sharing a common edge or point

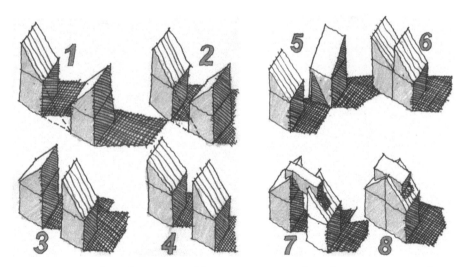

Figure 6.20. Tension through separation. *Tension is a strain or tightness between two or more elements, with a negative connotation. As the spacing between two or more elements closes, tension can increase. I have added diagonal forms to the cubes in the tension diagrams to give directional movement via the faces of the diagonals. This directional aspect influences the degree of tension present in the location of the cubes. The tension ranges from neutral or mild (1) spaced by a distance equal to the eight of the volume, to tighter (2) as that distance decreases, to less or more with the diagonals facing outward (3), to less with the diagonals facing in the same direction in (4) to less tension as the volumes are close together, even touching at the edges, and not facing one another (5). Face-to-face and touching volumes dissolves the tension, where the separate volumes are still evident and working together (6, 7, 8).*

- *face to face*, a variation of edge to edge also called adjacency and applies to forms with flat, planar surfaces that are parallel to one another
- *interlocking* through interpenetration where both forms need not share any other common traits; interlocking is described under both *compositional structures* and *transformational actions.*

Design opportunity in the limits of form

Design opportunity exists in the many ways form is perceived. The characteristics and limits of form are often overlooked by emerging designers and offer opportunity to dramatize, connect, and enhance compositions.

The limits of form and their opportunities and dynamics

Edges

Edges in art play an important role in defining shapes and integrating one shape into another. Edges contain shapes and the content they represent; they separate one shape from another, one content or meaning from another, and they integrate shapes through contrasts of size, value, intensity, and by merging various shapes into one another.

In urban design, edges define open space, courtyards, and plazas; they separate one district or use from another as in a commercial strip of buildings between a major arterial and a residential neighborhood; they can transition one land use intensity from another by different building and/or open space types.

Edges contain or separate one form from another, and are a part of each adjacent and nearby forms. Types of edges include:

- hard (wall, breakwater, dam, opaque)
- soft (fuzzy, textured transition, organic, hazy, transparent or translucent)
- lost and found or hard and soft combinations (a courtyard wall with gate or hedge, openings in a hedge, pathways through a building mass wall, a building wall with windows)
- interlocking (two different shapes come together and connect at the edges with penetration without merging—retaining their original characteristics as they lock together)
- merged (co-mingling within the periphery where a re-invention occurs with the original characteristics of each remaining beyond the periphery).

Keep in mind the *scale ladder* of edges in the region where you live. I live along a continental edge extending from northwest Alaska to British Columbia to California. My home is on Whidbey Island along and within the edges of Puget Sound, a part of a coastal sea extending from Prince Rupert to Vancouver, British Columbia to Everett, Seattle, and Tacoma to Olympia, Washington. Bays, fjords, straits, and sounds provide edges for a wide diversity of communities along the way, from fishing and lumber towns to tourist destinations and major metropolitan centers. This region has three of the most dynamic and wonderfully different cities along the coast: Vancouver, British Columbia, Seattle-Tacoma, Washington, and Portland, Oregon, a less than three-hour car trip between adjacent cities. They are all formed in strong part by their edge location and conditions, pinched between coastal mountain ranges and the Pacific Ocean. They are also all part of the Pacific Rim communities.

In our discussion of composition, this complexity of regional edge is critical regarding the contributions of land form, weather and climate, cultures, and edge-related industries all contributing to the (urban) meaning underlying that composition. From Southeast Alaska down through British Columbia, Washington, Oregon to northern California, the coastal edge weather is temperate, with small temperature differentials compared to the midwestern or eastern portions of Canada and the United States. This motivates design composition to take advantage of light and sun; to use the temperate outdoors during winter months; to celebrate the evergreen nature of the coastal forests—a critical regional force affecting design.

The urban waterfronts from small towns to the larger centers have a strong water-dependent industrial heritage: lumber mills, to canneries and fishing fleets, to mining and trans-shipment centers, to tourism and cruise ships. Jutting working wharves, cannery platforms, and contemporary cruise ship terminals interlock the land with the water. From metropolitan centers to small tidal river towns, public access once again competes for space among the warehouses and cargo container stockpiles. These edges are complex and dynamic in the relationships they bind together. Students are encouraged to investigate, observe, and explore the many versions and roles edges play in human settlements.

Linear edges can be composed of walkways, streets, and other at-grade axial elements; of water-land edge with the energies of the interaction of the two (waves, tides, erosion, etc.); of buildings and other solid masses forming a consistent edge as is common with building façades and even residential housing blocks (linear broken edge).

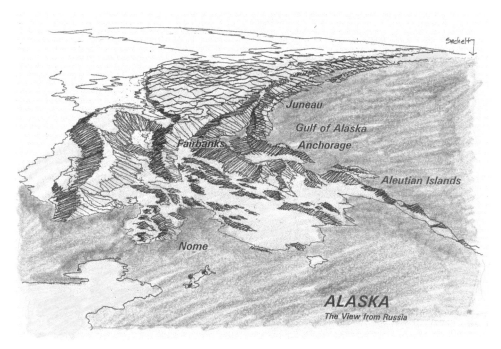

Figure 6.21. Edge opportunities: the view from Russia. *A major separating divide between America and Russia and yet a cultural transition zone for the indigenous peoples especially along the Arctic Circle. This is the beginning of a unique edge that nurtures a vast diversity of human settlement compositions.*

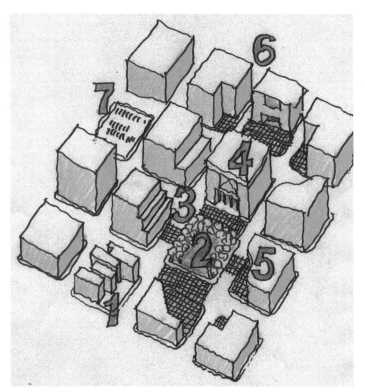

Figure 6.22. Urban edges. *Edges are powerful in dense urban settings and vital to bringing large forms together. They can be broken and haphazard (1); transparent and organic (2); textured and visually distinct as in the ground plane; stepped (3); porous as in building arcades (4); curved, providing movement and direction (5); concave (6); missing and/or open and undefined (7). Edges are a part of the overall mass, not separate and have their intensity affected by that mass (height, openings, opaqueness, etc.).*

Figure 6.23. Edge opportunities: block edges varieties. *Various block edges portray a few examples including a tall hard edge (1) with porous ground level; a deflecting edge (2), using movement to guide view and passage; a textured edge (3); a modulated edge (4); soft and organic edges (5); and soft deflecting edges (6).*

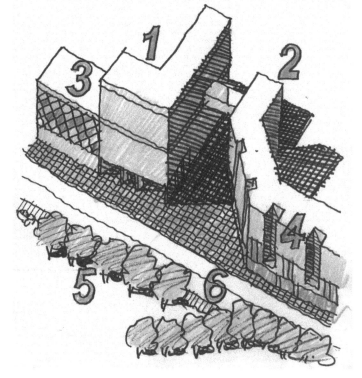

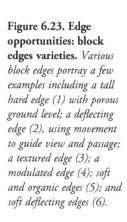

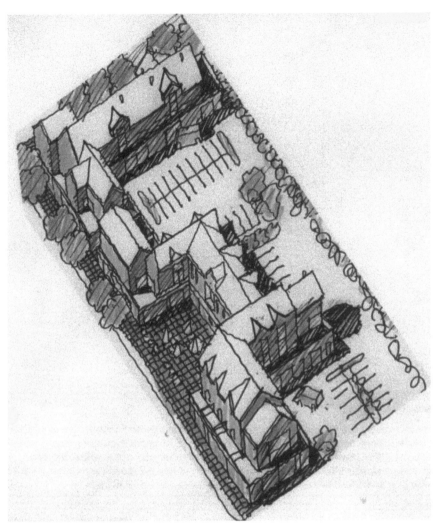

Figure 6.24. Edge opportunities: undulating edges. *Undulating edges can be continuous, linear, or broken, composed of right angles or curvilinear elements. A key principle is the consistent orientation to the pedestrian corridor and the varying setback that adds variety to the edge condition both functionally and visually. This sketch portrays a mixed-use two- to three-story building complex with perimeter at-grade retail and a key setback plaza (Sechelt, 2007).*

I cannot pass up the moveable or transient edge. The issue is actually quite serious in waterfront communities around the globe regarding view blockage. More and more common in waterfront tourism towns is the modern-day cruise ship, towering over the small town forms with eight- to 13-story ships above the waterline. Often they move in at night or early morning, disgorge their thousands of passengers and then slide off into the evening light. I have worked in Ketchikan, Alaska since 1976 BCS (Before Cruise Ships). The city rises up from the water to foothills and mountains after four to eight urban blocks. Views are abundant from the downtown waterfront to the west over Tongass Narrows, Clarence Strait, and the islands of the Inside Passage. The waterfront edge is fixed by docks, piers, and buildings,

water access

wetland view access

Figure 6.25. Edge opportunities: water as sensory edge. *The water–urban and water–natural edge conditions have many scales and levels of complexities, ranging from viewing platforms in industrial areas to public-access piers and beaches in downtown districts. The water edge is perhaps the most powerful and complex of all edge conditions. The edge is multi-faceted with water, transition zone (sand, rock, structure), and land edge (rip-rap, buildings, piers, etc.). The energy of the water is absorbed in the transition zone often with significant force or gentle touch. The cultural economic forces of cities, from traditional water-dependent industry to more contemporary tourism uses, have hardened and often obscured the urban waterfront. In water edge (1), an edge can permit access to and sensory exploration through touch of the water (Kenmore, 2010). In water edge (2), an edge can be enjoyed with the visual senses and separated from direct contact, as in the waterfront viewing platform (Sechelt, 2007).*

and, every day from early May to late October is transformed by transient 13 stories high by three-block-long moveable edges as represented by contemporary cruise ships.

Edges define space and space conversely influences the edges—particularly with the uses and human activities occurring within the contained space. Formal edges can contain and manage or direct the movements of large groups of people such as stadiums, the piazza leading into and fronting St. Peter's in Rome where thousands of people flow in, assemble, and flow out. The physical characteristics of these large containers often provide respite within the edges—shade and services— or are hard and smooth to facilitate a quick transmigration of large numbers of people from one space to another as in stadiums. Other activities may prefer a more playful edge strategy, where people gather, linger, socialize, and play, as in the outdoor edges around the perimeter of the Campo di Fiori in Rome—activities are influenced by the sun, shade, and nightfall along those edges. Edge characteristics respond directly to the CST matrix.

Finally, edges can be an integral part of *capture spaces* where they are designed to encourage lingering, pauses, and impulse activities: the contemporary shopping mall complete with entertainment on small and grand scales. Most shopping malls are formal structures with key principles of capture: anchor stores as destination attractions; corridors with highly visual and open façade edges facing the passing consumer, playful and attracting; limited access points to the outside; entertainment and food services; and above all—containment. Most conventional shopping malls have opaque exterior façade edges, with grand entries penetrating the solid edges—emphasizing the entries and beckoning the shopper to the interior containment space with transparent and porous commercial edges.

Corners

With the exception of the circle and the line or axis, unless broken or bent, most shapes have corners. They end a plane and may begin another, or break for an opening or passage. Corners can be dynamic or dull, leading to discovery or a disappointment.

I can turn a corner into an intimate courtyard or I can end up facing into a parking lot. How corners are treated is a part of the composition methodology. Because they are a stopping point or pause on a journey along a vertical plane, for example, they can elicit drama, suspense, surprise, security or danger, and anticipation. Because they represent a change in a composition, corners are a key feature in urban design.

Types of corners include:

- closed
- open
- dramatized or dancing (usually a vertical demarcation shape with movement from art-sculpture, contrasting shapes, etc.)
- corner opening
- curved
- transparent/translucent
- opaque
- connected (as in skyways or physical adjacency)
- soft and hard
- organic and manufactured
- deflecting
- anticipatory.

Surfaces

Surfaces are often overlooked in urban design as compositional features. Gordon Cullen (1961) appreciated and celebrated the textures and decoration of walls and walkways, from cobblestone roughness to walls of color and graphics. Surfaces activate vertical planes with color and stimulate patterns. In central Rome, not only the earthen colors of the walls add to the walking experience: the textures of additions, repairs, and whims of centuries of people adding character to the vertical and horizontal surfaces of the city enliven the vertical planes and hint at human stories, from graffiti to protruding classical sculptures along a wall or in a pasture with meandering cows (Sutra, Italy).

Contemporary surfaces can be bland, cold, and stark, offering little respite or interest to the pedestrian or passerby. Surface features can go beyond decoration—providing transparency, direction,

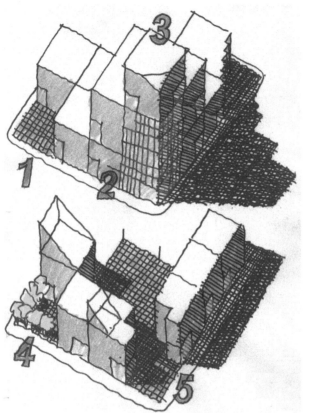

Figure 6.26. Corner opportunities.
Corner opportunities illustrates some of the many physical characteristics of corners from closed to anticipatory. Corners can be open and inviting with proper climate orientation (1); enclosed and transparent (2); highlighted or dramatized (3); transparent and soft (4); open and penetrating (5); and of course, closed.

Figure 6.27. Urban corners. *Urban corners summarize the many forms of corner features in urban contexts, from open and transparent to curved, dramatized, and opaque. Corners respond to pedestrian needs such as outdoor seating areas, safe and clear openings and entries, protected spaces such as indoor cafes with transparent edges, curved corners providing movement and direction around a corner, deflected corners again providing visual or physical movement, stepped, depressed, etc.*

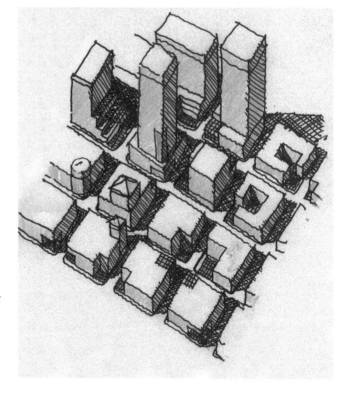

and orientation, softness in a hard urban environment with organic materials, pleasure and stimulus with art and crafts, and community information and signatures.

Surface features include:

- value with light to dark
- texture
- color
- porous to solid
- organic: soft and transparent or translucent
- manufactured: hard
- reflective
- informative
- moving: water features, reader boards, etc.
- audible: water cascades, music displays
- temperature sensitive: warm to cold
- uncertain.

Color is another aspect of urban composition overlooked and streamlined into neutral grays and monochromatic applications. *Color in Townscape* (Duttmann *et al.*, 1981) investigates color typology in townscape ranging from traditional usage to lively streets to case studies from around the world. Color can emote mood through color temperature (warm or cool), drama (muted or bright and intense).

An important ingredient with color is value, the relationship of light to dark, the way light is perceived on surfaces and the drama that relationships can create via contrast and mood—all through value. Value is discussed as a necessary ingredient in color usage in the arts more than in (urban) design. Placing light next to dark provokes a strong contrast; light to mid-light elicits a dispersed light effect; mid-light to dark can evoke a more muted environment. A few key and favorite references for color and value include *Color in Townscape* (Duttmann *et al.*, 1981), noted above, and *Painting Light and Shadow in Watercolor* (Lawrence, 1994).

Bibliography

Attoe, Wayne and Logan, Donn, 1989: *American Urban Architecture, Catalysts in the Design of Cities*: University of California Press, Berkley, CA.

Bettisworth, Charles and Kasprisin, Ron, 1982: "Tanana Valley Community College Master Plan": University of Alaska, Fairbanks, AK.

Capra, Fritjof, 1982: *The Turning Point*: Simon & Schuster, New York.

Ching, Francis D.K., 1979: *Architecture: Form, Space and Order*: Van Nostrand Reinhold, New York.

Cullen, Gordon, 1961: *Townscapes*: Reinhold Publishing, New York.

Duttmann, Martina, Schmuck, Friedrich, and Uhl, Johannes, 1981: *Color in Townscape*: W.H. Freeman & Company, San Francisco, CA.

Edgewood, City of, 1999: "Town Center Plan: Community Character and Land Use Study": Kasprisin Pettinari Design and Dennis Tate Associates, Langley, WA.

Kasprisin, Ron, 1999: *Design Media*: John Wiley & Sons, Inc., New York.

Kasprisin, Ron and Pettinari, James, 1995: *Visual Thinking for Architects and Designers*: John Wiley & Sons, Inc., New York.

Kenmore, City of, 2010: "City of Kenmore Open Space Opportunities: Making Connections": Kasprisin Pettinari Design, Langley, WA.

Ketchikan, City of, 1984: "Creek Street Historic District: Public Facilities Improvement Project": Kasprisin Hutnik Partnership with J.L. Pensiero and Associates/URS Engineers.

Lawrence, William B., 1994: *Painting Light and Shadow in Watercolor*: North Light Books, Cincinnati, OH.

Sechelt BC, District of, 2007: "Visions for Sechelt": John Talbot & Associates (Burnaby, BC) and Kasprisin Pettinari Design (Langley, WA).

Soja, Edward W., 1996: *Thirdspace*: Blackwell Publishers, Cambridge, MA.

Chapter 7

CONTEXT, PROGRAM, AND TYPOLOGIES

Context: the spatial container of reality

Context is more than "background" or setting as defined by most dictionaries. Unlike the backdrop on a theatrical stage, context is the theater itself, and the actors and audience as in Kabuki Theater (Eisenstein, 1949). Context is the community-container for reality (spatial, cultural, and ever-changing over time). The word is much used and abused in urban design and remains one of the most important aspects of design analysis. For analytical purposes, context is described by five dimensions for the container; each dimension has spatial manifestations:

1   bio-physical (local and regional)
2   jurisdictional
3   cultural
4   user: substantive and administrative
5   time/historic/event periods.

Bio-physical (local and regional)

Bio-physical is the biological underlayment of the spatial aspect of the context container: geology, soils, topography, water and land features, flora, fauna, the built form of humans and other animals (habitats), climate and solar orientations and the seasons affecting all of them. These are basic building blocks in every urban design analysis, providing key clues on the conditions and parameters facing the design process. This base information is critical to any design process and defines local identity through regional determinants.

In the early 1970s before *digital* graphic information systems (GIS) emerged in common use, I worked in Alaska's central region (greater Anchorage and surrounds) and the Fairbanks region (interior of state). Data for the design process were recorded on layers of mylar in plan form with pin-holes punched along the upper border. The holes matched a "pin-bar," a metal strip with raised metal dowels matching the holes in the mylar. Combinations of layers were then combined, coordinated by the pin-bar, and printed and analyzed regarding the commonalities and conflicts present in the comparisons—the non-digital version of GIS. These layers provided the basic "Monopoly board" for the design team: from moose and bear migration routes, to earthquake hazard zones, to forest types and extent, to human settlement patterns.

Whatever the analytical method, the bio-physical-spatial information sets the context and conditions for design interaction with the physical environment. Critical areas, habitats, forest recharge areas, and many more spatial conditions are identified for protection and conservation; areas susceptible to design intervention or alignment are made apparent for further analysis—the game board.

Jurisdictional

As in games like Monopoly (Parker Brothers/Waddingtons, 1935), you can land on a square only to find out someone else owns it. The jurisdictional aspects of urban meaning are critical forces in design decisions. For example, in any given small town in North America for a given block of land, the designer can discover the following:

*   local individual owners
*   land held in trusts (somewhat anonymous and difficult to work with)
*   corporate and real estate holdings (investment driven, similar to above)
*   out of state owners
*   public ownership (state, province, county, borough, city, town, village)
*   non-profits (housing corporations, historic trusts, native band/corporations)
*   short- and long-term leases (many food and department stores)
*   many more aspects of "ownership" or control.

In Alaska, for example, "public ownership" is not sufficient to describe land holdings because a vast array of federal and state agencies, municipalities, borough governments, and native corporations own and control significant land areas.

The issue of outright ownership versus short- and long-term leases deals directly with the time aspect of the CST trialectic. A major retail use with a five-year lease versus a 25-year lease is more susceptible to relocation, redevelopment, and uncertainty when strategizing about key downtown blocks in a 20-year redevelopment plan.

A basic and helpful task in setting the Monopoly board is a plan diagram that codes ownership types (public/private, local/out of state), percent of ownership and tenure (lease/own, tenure terms, etc.) as a start. In many ways it serves as the base layer for the CST matrix.

Cultural

The cultural layers consist of the social, economic, political, and historic aspects of urban meaning. We can fill pages of examples of cultural factors and each page can be represented by a diagram illustrating the spatial impacts and influences of these aspects. For example, in ethnically diverse communities, not only can the locations by urban block of ethnic groups be diagrammed but also their meeting places such as churches, clubs, organizations, and specialty businesses; the spatial relationships between social meeting places and home. This pattern begins to construct a spatial pattern of location and (implied) movement. These aspects are always changing as groups assimilate and redefine themselves.

One assignment I ask students to do that is transferable to larger scales and more complex communities is as follows:

*   Identify your housemates by gender and age.
*   If possible, interview them and construct a personality pattern matrix (Johnston, 1984/1986, 1991).
*   Record your housemates' activities during the evening after dinner (e.g. studying, television, music, computer games).

- Observe and record their selection of space and location within the house (one mate uses his/her bedroom with door closed; one mate uses the kitchen table; one mate carves out a corner of the living room).
- Describe the physical–sensory aspects of those spaces.
- Observe and record how each treats the space they occupy (one mate is insulated and out of view and hearing; one is at the kitchen table separated but within hearing range of household activities; one is in the living room corner with treats, music, pillows, and books—sharing the space with others).
- Compile an organizational diagram of how they are functioning in a given time–event period, i.e. 7pm to 10pm.
- Observe and record their interaction with their space, their mates, and mate-spaces.
- Compile a structural diagram of the house, locating primary activities by place, movement, and interactions over the time–event period.

This exercise accomplishes numerous objectives for emerging designers: observation, making connections between space design and behavior patterns, and visual portrayal (visual thinking) of CST factors. The point of the exercise is to connect cultural–personality patterns with the occupation and manipulation of space and its contents. Now take this assignment and apply the principles to a neighborhood or hamlet. They are transferable; be cautious using only digital methods and tools.

Designers are certainly not psychologists nor are they psychiatrists involved in environmental behavior analysis. In addition, they need a basic understanding of the connections between cultural patterns and spatial environments—thus the need for interdisciplinary teams for complex projects.

User

People and other animal species use the physical environment in various ways, sometimes in harmony and often in conflict or at least confrontations. Substantive users are the ones who actually live in, interact, and depend upon the physical environment for survival (all aspects of living). Administrative users are the ones who manage this environment and the two can often be far apart on intent and implementation. Understanding the agendas and influences of each is a necessary beginning to urban design analysis, as each impacts upon the built form in different ways. Bringing them together is a major design education task. Appendix II addresses the politics of design—engaging and working with people.

Time/historic/event periods

Time is a dimension that is a constant, in sync with gravity, marking the changes in the other CST dimensions; making current events soon historic and future anticipations soon to be reality, and history again. The changes in periods of time leave spatial imprints, especially changes emanating from human activity. These changes are important determinants or influencing factors for the design of human settlements and their reintegration with the natural environment.

Activities occur in time–event periods, periodicities (Johnston, 1991), that can be short and brief explosions or extended over time, depending upon interactions in the larger community context. They help designers mark and assess event impacts and eventually dissipate and change, transitioning into a new event period, making the CST connection.

The importance then of *program: what, how, how much, when.*

Program (need and opportunity)

A program is a set of coded instructions for activities and facilities based on want and need. They are coded according to the type and manner of application. Programming the television and DVD has certain symbols in code. In urban design, programming codes include specific physical elements and relationships related to the built form, coded by type of form (e.g. building and site configurations) and their underlying principles.

These principles emanate from the philosophical and cultural aspects of civilizations, leaving imprints on the spatial manifestations or outcomes of those civilizations. Program is at the heart of planning/design pre-design and implementation and is so often undervalued or understated in urban planning curricula. Even in new buzzword processes such as "form-based zoning," where land use is not a key factor in the determination of the form envelope (Form Based Code Institute, 2009), the massing is intended to contain buildings and open space. The type of building is determined by use, density, and orientation—essentially critical to deriving a realistic zoning form envelope. Any disregard for use and accompanying building typologies represented in the program is naïve at best. Consequently, programming sets the stage for design by specifying the *what, how much, and when* of community need, based upon community input.

Urban design is a bridging process between a more semi-abstract planning strategy and the emergent built form. As a part of the design process, the stated needs and wants or desires of the community—the specific instructions emanating from an analysis of urban meaning and functionality—are transformed into specific uses, the types of buildings, facilities and/or open space elements that are available to accommodate those uses, how they can be configured and staged, and how much quantity of each can fulfill the stated need. Without a meaningful program, the design process becomes a more difficult guessing game (as often occurs).

As is discussed in Chapter 9, the process of programming specifies a range of needs and wants that in effect define a "container" of issues for the designer, a container that is constantly redefined and changed. That range is characterized by two extremes or polarities and multiple sub-polarities within many aspects of the user-aspirations, the community *color wheel of opposite and complementary colors*. This is where the design process begins its true evolutionary path. This is the search for "thirdspace" (Soja, 1996), that unique and minimally compromising outcome that can only come from a dynamic process. Bridging polarities assists the designer in crafting spatial metaphors that encompass the essences of the polarities without separating, unifying, or blending compromises—more on that later. Programming then becomes the jumping-off point for content (as in story); that content is then brought into relationship with context; form options begin to emerge.

Form typology related to urban design

This section presented a dilemma for me as I began to enter the subject area of design typologies. All use–form types in architecture, landscape architecture, and engineering relate to and have urban design applications. Where to end? How far to go in depth? Too little information scratches the surface and too much becomes a technical manual.

I discussed this issue with planning and urban design students. Many, including practicing planners, did not understand typologies sufficiently to engage in or critique urban design compositions. Even in design review processes, this lack of understanding led experienced planners to focus on superficial issues, cosmetics, and detail not relevant to urban design decisions. As a result, I decided to provide a basic understanding of various typologies related to urban design with the understanding that each student has the responsibility of investigating and becoming familiar with the vast array of building use types in design.

This chapter sets out the basic types in building, open space, and urban design that have *significant applications to urban design composition*. Again, not an easy task. As a result, not all typologies are represented in this chapter due to space and time. I urge students to use this chapter as a beginning resource—to be added to and upgraded over time. As I discuss in this chapter, types are based on use–form principles of operation and function; principles change constantly as the CST matrix changes. The very nature of shopping centers is a prime example: they are evolving in use and form, and their typological characteristics change as they respond to consumer demands and competition, from shopping mall to town center to future hybrids.

Type represents coherence in use–form principles and can change at any given time in response to contextual demands of community. When their functional integrity is compromised or decreased, they do not contribute to a coherent development pattern.

Use–form relationships in design

In design, type represents organizational and structural principles or rules that are similar by application and not identical in either style or appearance. *Type* is not to be misconstrued with *model*—defining a copy or representation of an existing object that is repeated essentially *as is*. Type is inherent in space programming, representing an organization of spatial relationships representing housing, commercial and industrial uses, civic facilities, parking, environment, and other need factors. Type is also open to challenge depending upon the CST context; that is, type provides coherence between what worked in principle somewhere else and may be satisfactory in a new application. And type may not work without significant compromise, and is subsequently altered or redefined. Type is not universal. Thus, *challenging* type leads to a hybridization of conventional principles, seeking new and innovative applications based on the needs of context.

Labeling a land use zone as "medium-density residential", for example, is a statement of policy and program: use and quantity range. And the policy implies a range of building and site configuration types. Many planners do not understand these implications beyond the numbers. If "medium" refers to a range of eight to 16 residential units per acre, that is the amount of residences that can be accommodated with parking and open space in an acre, based on most community codes—and still vague as regards built form. There are specific building types that can accomplish this density within that range and they are different: attached and/or mixed-density buildings such as row-houses, townhouses, stacked flats, attached bungalows; and, in most cases, with some aspect of shared parking and shared open space. Cottage housing, often fixated on a stated market preference for "detached units," can accommodate up to eight detached units in an acre around a small courtyard with shared parking and minimal side-yard setbacks as small as 5 feet or 1.5 meters between buildings. The building and development types affect the number of units in a given area and are not ancillary to the planning process. To meet the requirements for more dense applications up to 16 units per acre, other building types are available that meet parking and open space requirements. Use, density, context, and typology are inherently linked.

Urban design can test the range of types in a given situation to determine the most appropriate for market, site "fit", and responsiveness to the larger context (adjacent and nearby). Accepting type is not a solution, merely a beginning.

The typologies of buildings, site configurations, and open space all have an underlying human dimension, a set of operating principles and characteristics.

Principle: typology is a convention, a continuing coherence of workability; and a set of organizational rules with an implied structural assemblage that defines the physical container of those principles. Type is a starting point, a guide, and is always subject to challenge, particularly if the coherence is disrupted or loses contextual consistency.

Building typologies

There are reference materials available for investigating and assessing building types for various uses and intensities, essential reading for planners and designers. These references amply describe and illustrate the types and their physical characteristics and requirements. The building types discussed in this chapter relate to an urban design context. Many of the typologies described here are useable in smaller cities and towns, the focus of my professional work.

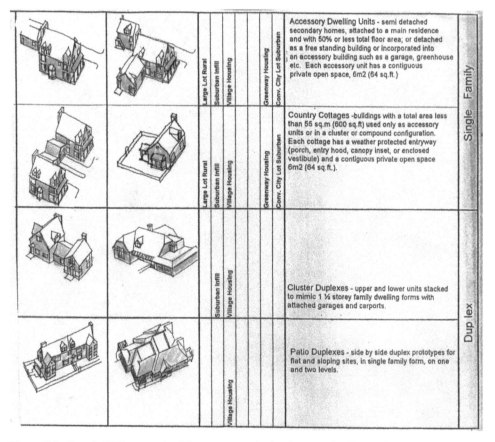

Figure 7.1. Campbell River matrix. *The matrix was developed to assist builders and citizens in understanding the scale, extent, and physical impacts of various building types for insertion into existing residential neighborhoods. The example is one of a number of posters that summarized the context type.*

Helping people understand the context-sensitive nature of design typologies can go a long way in improving the built form—as opposed to using a type just because the type worked somewhere else.

In "Campbell River Infill Housing Study" (1996), building types were identified as appropriate for specific neighborhoods within the city, based on existing and emergent built form, physical contexts/environments, scale, and design character. The appropriate types were displayed on a visual matrix for public information, providing residents and builders with a guide and choice of appropriate type utilization in an effort to increase urban design harmony within neighborhoods. Architectural features were not considered critical to the matrix.

Residential typologies

The following are examples of residential building types by density/intensity application. Their physical characteristics determine their relationship to site and context. For example, a double-loaded corridor residential building has stacked flats or units along a central corridor with access from the corridor. Exterior views are from the external wall. Based on these characteristics, each external elongated façade requires some form of open space (light, view, air) adjacent to the building usually requiring minimal setbacks between buildings and/or property lines and adjacent uses. Placing this type of building with one wall facing a bluff or another close building does not work. The typology has within its characteristics an emerging and implied contextual relationship. This may sound overly simple but I have witnessed too many well-intentioned planning students misuse building types through a lack of understanding of these built-in relational factors.

The following illustrations summarize many residential building types that are useful in urban design compositions, from urban infill applications to compact arrangements. They represent a sampling and are not universal. They require manipulation and hybridization in response to each applied context.

Residential building types in urban design applications

Housing can stand alone on large parcels, along waterways and beaches, and tucked away in verdant forests. Most housing occurs in groups, with levels of relationship forged by their placement. The configurations range from the double-loaded street corridor, to the row-house and townhouse linear arrangements, to clusters, to the more dense garden and high-rise complexes, and more. The types listed below are suitable for urban design applications.

There are many small or tiny houses that are suitable for infill in existing neighborhoods and/or in compact or cluster housing configurations. Lester Walker's *Tiny Houses* (1987) provides a fascinating range of historic tiny houses. I find many of these and their hybrids to be suitable beginnings for compact contemporary developments, particularly mixed-density applications.

- Single family detached house (one- to two-story bungalow, one-story ranch)
  - attached garage (front, side, rear)
  - detached garage (side, rear)
  - carport
- Single family attached houses
  - at garage walls
  - with arbors
  - at habitable walls usually one side (zero lot line)

- Cottage
    - small one story with optional loft
    - detached and attached
    - usually with shared parking
- Shotgun house
    - one-story rectangular structure, only one room wide
    - usually 12 feet (4 meters) to 15 feet (5 meters) wide
    - three or four rooms deep
    - straight central openings through all rooms
    - camelback variation has one second-story bedroom over kitchen
- Small cabin
    - one room plus sleeping attic
- Prefabricated house
    - many variations from stick-built to recycled shipping containers
- Guest house or studio outbuilding
    - one room with work space (studio)
    - semi-enclosed extensions optional
- Accessory/"mother-in-law" unit
    - over garage
    - attached to primary residence at common wall
    - separate cottage, cabin, or guest house to side or rear of main house
- Multiplex houses with separate entries and private open space
    - one and two story
    - attached garages or shared parking/carports
    - duplex
    - triplex to eight-plex
- Multiplex house (captain's house)
    - two to three stories
    - three to five units
    - single entry and foyer
    - shared open space (porch, yard)
    - shared parking (garage, carport)
    - usually situated on a corner lot with two street faces
- Row-house
    - one or two story attached common wall
    - individual entry and open space
- Townhouse/townhome
    - two-story units attached common wall
    - two-story unit above ground floor/sub-grade flat
    - two-story unit above ground floor retail/commercial (live/work)
- Townhouse with "mother-in-law" unit
    - one-story cottage attached at townhouse end wall(s)

- Stacked flats: garden homes
  – one-story units stacked vertically
  – single external entry/foyer
  – shared parking
  – shared open space
  – courtyard arrangements optional
- Stacked flats: corridor buildings
  – single-loaded corridor, one row of flats
  – entry from corridor, front or rear
  – double-loaded corridor, one row of flats each side of corridor
  – elevator buildings, usually four stories and higher
- Live/work mixed-use housing
  – residential above or behind commercial, office uses
  – larger upper decks for open space requirements
  – attached townhouse type or stacked flats
  – central parking and vehicle access/storage is common
  – landscape treatments in front yards
  – integrated into transition areas between single-use residential and non-residential uses
  – integrated into non-residential districts such as light industrial, general commercial
- Mixed-density housing compounds
  – farmsteads in rural areas (conserving open space)
  – urban compounds
  – various housing types within one cluster, attached and detached
  – shared open space
  – private open space per unit
  – shared parking
  – shared accessory buildings: studio, gardening, greenhouses, community use
- High-rise central core
  – square, cross, circular floor plans
  – central elevator core
  – form varies according to local/national codes
- High-rise connected cores
  – central core buildings connected above first floor (Access Trees: see Okamoto and Williams, 1969).

Many of these types are compatible with courtyard and centralized open space applications, from low- to high-density situations. The variations and hybrids are many and the above list provides the emerging designer with a place to start. How these types are manipulated to respond to context is the challenge.

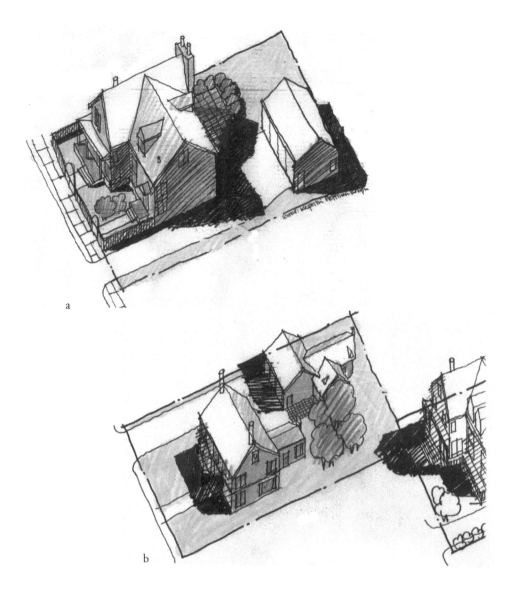

a

b

Figures 7.2 a–u. Residential building-type examples. *The following illustrations provide a sampling of the many variations of housing types and configurations available for low- to moderate-density context-sensitive applications. The principles of organization and structure for these types are key: connections to surrounding context, and building to open space and parking relationships. The first group, infill/mixed density, is suitable for infill and smaller lot developments. Mixed density refers to a group of residential buildings consisting of different building types (bungalow, cottage, townhouse, etc.). The second group, conservation design, is suitable for larger lot developments with significant open space features and is density neutral (no loss of density with increased open space requirements). The third group, medium to high density, illustrates basic building types as stand-alone and/or in cluster or courtyard configurations.*
Infill/mixed-density types:
(a) Attached duplex with individual entries, with one unit larger and/or setback from second unit
(b) "In-law" accessory unit above or attached to accessory building with small private yard

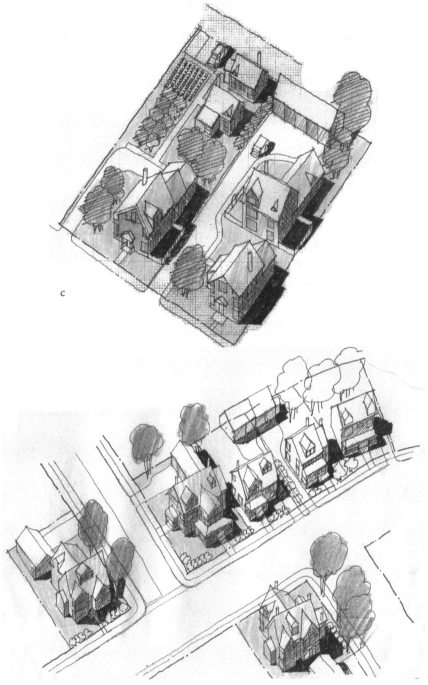

(c) Hamlet lot (three units) with mix of detached and attached units with shared driveway and individual entries and private yards
(d) Multiplex homes (single entry/foyer, three to five units—two plus two plus one) suitable for corner lots with two frontages, with shared parking/garage and shared open space. Can be developed as contemporary boarding house

(e) Courtyard housing with key units facing street, with individual entries, private and shared open space
(f) Panhandle cluster with shared driveways and small lots

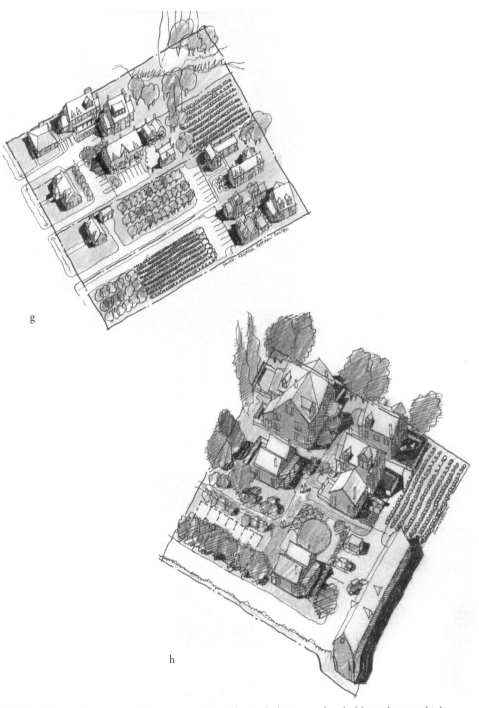

g

h

(g) Mixed-density linear clusters (long narrow lots) with attached cottages, detached bungalows, multiplex homes with private and shared open space
(h) Mixed-density farmsteads with detached bungalows, attached and detached cottages, duplexes, shared accessory buildings, private and shared yards

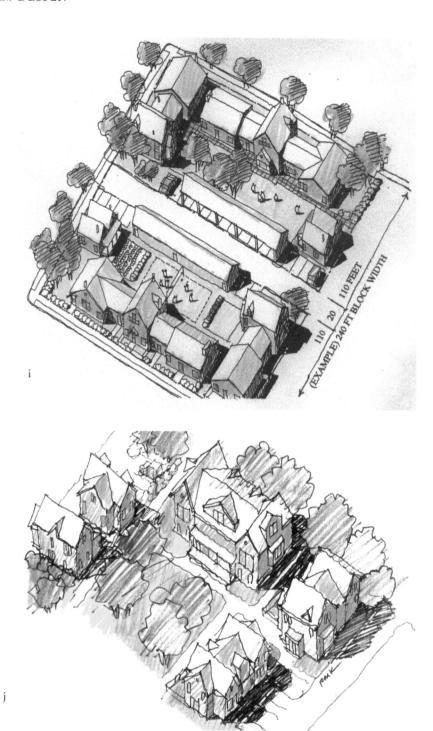

(i) *Small-scale urban infill complex with alley, private and shared yards, attached bungalows*
Conservation design:
(j) *Conservation hamlet with multiplex home, detached and attached bungalows clustered around common green*

k

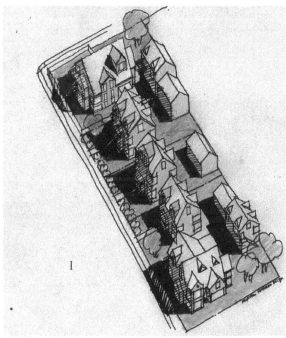

l

(k) Conservation design with small lot detached units above garage
(l) Repetition with variety, with single family detached homes and varying front yard setbacks

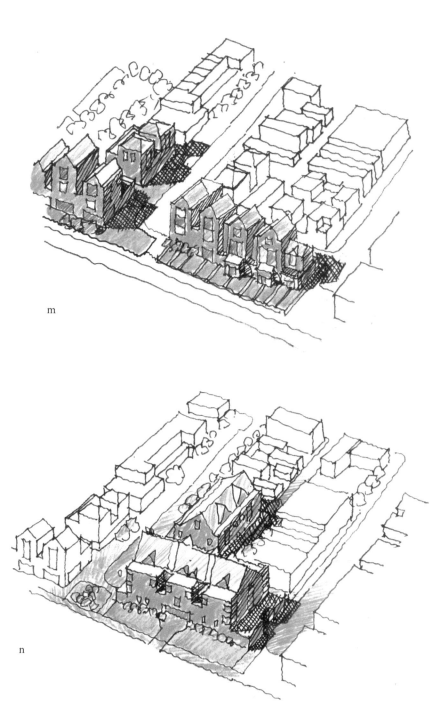

(m) Townhouse complex with diminished repetition through compositional variety along the streetscape
Medium- to high-density housing/mixed-use/live/work:
(n) Double-loaded corridor stacked flats above commercial with optional underground parking one or two way direction depending upon building width

(o) Stacked flats with single entry/foyer around courtyard; under-building parking at grade, one-half level and full level below grade
(p) Civic center and conservation design residential live/work units with central green area

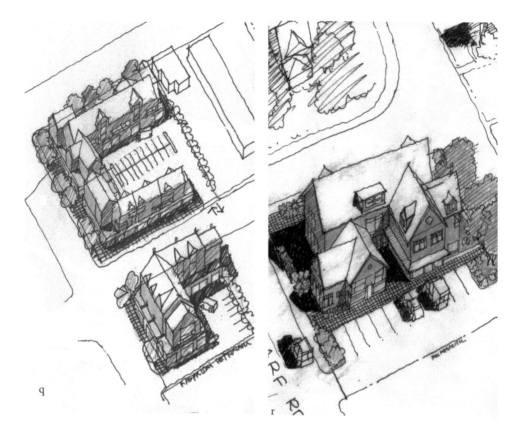

q

r

s

(q) Live/work housing as single family detached above work space and as attached units (row-townhouses, etc.)
(r) Other mixed-use residential and commercial types designed to fit into urban neighborhoods with side and/or rear yard parking, front yard landscaping, and residential-scale massing
(s) Mixed-use residential over retail/office designed to fit into urban neighborhood centers with strong pedestrian concourses, landscaping, and through connections to adjacent commercial and residential areas

124

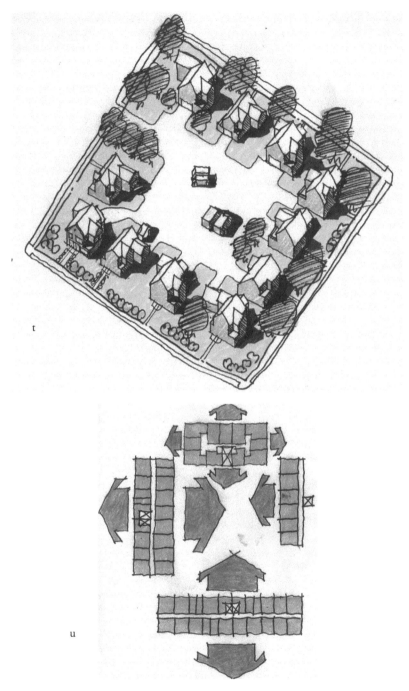

(t) Live/work with residential and light industry and/or wholesale commercial with additional working vehicle requirements: centralized vehicle storage and street-oriented landscaped yards and entries
(u) Types of residential buildings require different orientations for light, air, and views: double-loaded corridor has two longer façades; single-loaded corridor has one longer view façade; and stacked flats can have four different orientations.

Commercial building types in urban design applications

Downtown commercial blocks:

- urban scale
- small to medium city
- small town scale
- common characteristics:
  - zero setback
  - common wall
  - front entry
  - double-loaded (street/pedestrian) corridor
  - service to rear alley and/or front with designated time periods
  - parking in street and in shared lots/structures; also under building in larger urban structures
  - transparent street façades for pedestrian view
  - pedestrian amenities in public and private jurisdictions
  - open space setbacks or plazas for high-rise structures
  - alley access where feasible.

Scale and configuration of downtown blocks are key determinants for commercial building types. Block sizes can range from 200 feet square to large rectangular blocks, 300 feet by 600 feet, for example. Downtown commercial blocks function well in compact continuous and contiguous arrangements with strong pedestrian orientations along the street. Historic downtown configurations are characterized by individual entries, transparent façades, setback entries, and weather protection features such as marquees and canopies. New infill developments maintain the street frontage and orientation and may contain interior lobbies, courtyards with shops and entertainment/dining uses oriented toward the courtyard on one- and two-story balcony arrangements.

Smaller block sizes facilitate improved pedestrian flow throughout the downtown district. Larger block sizes are best served by mid-block pedestrian penetrations at grade and above and below grade depending on the physical contexts. Arcades through the blocks can provide protected pedestrian flows along retail corridors connecting one street to another. Without this through-block pedestrian feature, the use of the automobile can increase and pedestrian flow between blocks is lessened.

Many cold climate cities incorporate above-grade enclosed public skyways through key downtown blocks. These are pedestrian friendly and can degrade ground-level retail functionality by drawing consumers away from the street level activities.

Shopping mall:

- super block arrangement
- island configuration (building mass surrounded by surface parking and/or parking structures)
- limited peripheral development pads
- pedestrian concourse, enclosed or semi-enclosed
- major tenants with ancillary supporting tenants
- *capture* design with ancillary attraction uses: food courts, entertainment and dining, recreational facilities, amusement facilities

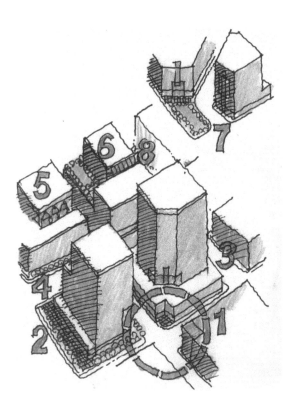

Figure 7.3. Downtown commercial typologies. *Light, air, nodes, and block size are key factors for livable downtowns. Downtown blocks have compositional and functional strength at key intersections (cross structure) (1) where buildings can be dramatized especially at their corner elements; setbacks provide pedestrian spaces with solar access and reduce the massing impacts of larger buildings (2); pedestal buildings reduce massing impacts of larger buildings and provide space for interior courts (3); building setbacks reduce mass and allow more light onto pedestrian areas (4); preservation of historic buildings and conservation of contextually significant groups of buildings strengthen cultural and physical identities within the changing downtown core (5); rooftop gardens and urban agriculture add softness to the cityscape, reduce impervious surfaces, and add a new compositional dimension to the urban scale (6); remnant or unusual spaces formed by changes in the street grid or other infrastructure can provide unique pauses and respites in the busy downtown (7); and mid-block pedestrian passages strengthen the connections between and among longer block grid patterns (8).*

Figure 7.4. Smaller downtown commercial typologies. *Small downtown districts require the same compact, continuous, and contiguous characteristics of larger downtowns. The shopping malls evolved from these older downtown compositions with contiguous retail commercial uses with transparent façades, encouraging pedestrian flow and impulse buying. Removing buildings in the linear block front results in missing teeth (ms), disrupting pedestrian flow and generating pedestrian–vehicular conflicts along the sidewalk areas. Parking (p) is best suited to the interior of the block and on the street. Small front yard setbacks can provide pedestrian pauses and amenities (ps). Corner features at key intersections (ce) can strengthen pedestrian orientation and reference.*

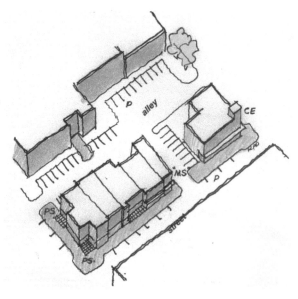

- pedestrian disconnect with public arterials and walkways
- parking quantities keyed to maximum consumer days
- opaque external walls surfaces.

Shopping plaza:

- usually one-sided or single-loaded commercial strip
- exterior pedestrian corridor along front façade
- surface parking in front setback
- delivery in rear and side setbacks
- minimal pedestrian amenities
- transparent external front façade.

Big-box:

- warehouse configuration with multiple interior functions
- island configuration
- primary entrance as opposed to linear multiple entrances
- surface parking in front setbacks
- delivery in rear and side setbacks
- minimal pedestrian amenities
- opaque external façades.

Shopping malls and plazas are remnants from the 1960s and have undergone morphological changes ranging from the early open concourse double-loaded corridor plaza to the enclosed mall with major retail anchors, capture spaces, and entertainment facilities. Many malls and plazas occupy between 25 and 30 percent of the site area, with the remaining land left in impervious surface parking lots. In response to competition from revitalized historic downtowns, big-box retail warehouse typologies, and consumer demands, the malls and plazas are changing into town centers and leisure centers.

Town centers are diverse in use, with civic, cultural, office, and residential uses combined with retail facilities. Open space is provided at key locations, reducing impervious surface conditions. Leisure centers are smaller types often close to larger malls. They provide leisure activities such as coffee shops, cafes, small dining/pubs, bookstores, and other smaller retail outlets and limited residential uses. They are gathering places within the larger, often suburban (less dense) commercial district.

As the shopping mall/plaza typology continues to change in response to competition and market, the opportunity for infill becomes feasible. They are existing land banks for future development. Connecting the numerous shopping malls and plazas that often concentrate in a district is the critical design challenge: lessening vehicular movements and increasing transit and pedestrian environments through compact development practices.

Big-box retail warehouses can be treated in the same fashion: reducing their mass with additive transformations; connecting the boxes to a local street pattern and open space focus; infilling the site with new mixed-use facilities and dispersed parking areas.

Town center (contemporary):

- mixed-use retail center augmented with civic functions (library, theater, misc.), offices, entertainment, residential

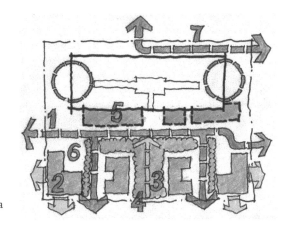

a

b

Figures 7.5 a and b. Shopping mall as emerging pattern. *Shopping malls are typically islands of enclosed commercial space arranged around a captive pedestrian-oriented core within a field of parking and hard surfaces. As they mature and evolve, key compositional relationships can be added to the existing complexes to make the mall compact and connect the larger complex to adjacent and nearby uses. These include as in (a): introduction of a local street network that can connect incrementally to adjacent redevelopment parcels and to the main thoroughfare (1); development of peripheral development that is oriented to the main thoroughfare, the new local street network, and adjacent development (2); a green open space that connects the modified mall to the main thoroughfare and acts as a centerpiece for pedestrian activities (3), providing a visual corridor to the interior of the complex (4); reducing the mass of the existing mall with breakouts of transparent vertical planes oriented toward the new local street network (5); small dispersed landscaped parking lots with strong pedestrian connecting paths (6); and, where feasible, combined or shared service roads and alleys (7). Figure (b) illustrates an older shopping mall with infill residential, office, transit, and open space facilities, transforming the older center into a new neighborhood.*

- pedestrian concourses, open and/or semi-enclosed
- smaller clustered parking lots
- peripheral commercial pads more common
- open space focal component: pedestrian gathering area, event space
- improved pedestrian amenities and connectivity: sidewalk hierarchy ranging from pedestrian concourses to protected walkways within parking clusters to connection to public walkways
- improved landscaping amenities.

The contemporary town center concept applies to historic downtown districts that have degraded due to competition from shopping malls and big-box facilities. They may not be able to compete as shopping centers with the loss of key uses such as food and department stores, hardware, and clothing stores. They can reinvent themselves as mixed-use town centers with the significant addition of downtown housing, civic and cultural facilities, and specialty retail stores.

Leisure center:

- smaller, mixed-use commercial complex: retail with coffee shops, cafes, bookstores, etc.

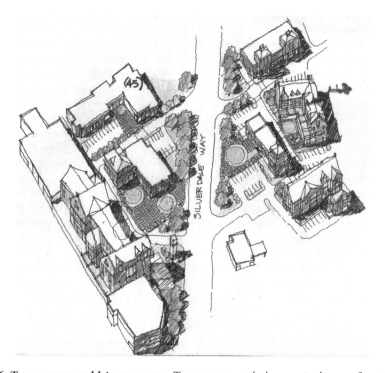

Figure 7.6. Town centers and leisure centers. *Town centers can be larger, mixed-use configurations with civic, cultural, commercial, office, and residential uses. They can be newly constructed on larger acreage or reconstructed shopping malls. Leisure centers are usually smaller configurations with specialty uses and consumer comfort amenities (cafes, coffee shops, bookstores, pubs, etc.). The illustration portrays two older shopping plazas, across a major arterial from one another, redeveloped as a dual town center/leisure center. Open space is coordinated to provide on-site pedestrian amenities and focal area as well as a combined open space downtown entry feature. Residential units are added to the rear of the site and new retail buildings are located close to and oriented toward the main thoroughfare and the existing development.*

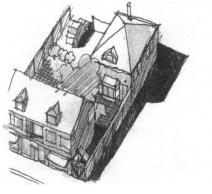

Figure 7.7. Mixed-use single site. *In smaller cities and towns, mixed-use infill on single sites can re-energize older downtowns with new residential uses that support older retail/commercial buildings.*

Mixed-use single site:

- residential and/or office over commercial or located to the rear of property with courtyard
- stacked flats or townhouses above commercial
- transparent front façade.

Live/work or shop/house mixed-use:

- stand-alone building or in attached and semi-attached clusters
- parking to rear, side, and/or interior compound
- landscape and/or pedestrian-oriented front setback
- transparent front façade.

Built form typologies exist that have transferability and/or can serve as a base for new development patterns. They can have unusual characteristics in their existing compositions that can add strength to new configurations. They can provide a departure from conventional typologies and contribute a local identity, scale, and signature. I have experimented with a number of hybrids in practice, particularly in rurban or edge communities where people want growth without using suburban dispersed typologies, thus the term *rurban*. Two of these are noted and illustrated below.

Hybrid types: I include a couple of examples of hybrid typologies that can be fashioned from types found throughout the built environment.

Crossroads mixed-use complex:

- cross-compositional structure road network, keyed to one intersection
- horizontal and vertical mixed-use combinations
- major pedestrian amenities in a compact development configuration
- "Main Street" orientation along crossroads
- open space focal area
- parking to side and/or rear and on-street
- pedestrian connectivity via paths and block penetrations.

The crossroads is a rural and semi-rural built form recognizable throughout Canada and the United States. Many developed around a general feed store, grocery store, service station with supporting residential buildings, possibly a grange or community hall all located at a single intersection. With highway widening projects, many of these crossroads configurations have been lost to the bulldozer.

Nursery complex:

- recycled and/or new semi-rural nursery compounds
- mixed building type: nursery buildings, greenhouses, accessory buildings (barns, sheds), hierarchy of residential buildings in associated compounds
- small clustered parking lots
- interior complex open pedestrian concourses, walkways
- mixed-use retail, general commercial, entertainment/dining, event facilities, residential.

The nursery complex originated from work in a semi-rural community for a new civic/town center in close proximity to an existing nursery. The nursery was to be phased out and the land sold for development. The nursery type generated concepts for a retail and civic center using many of the nursery forms.

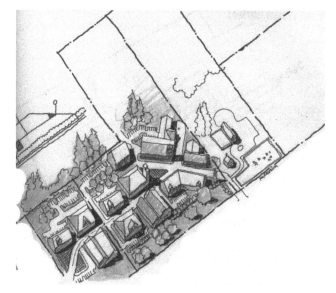

Figure 7.8. Crossroads hybrid. *Key features of the crossroads hybrid include a slow-moving local street parallel and connected to main thoroughfare. Crossroads have an intersecting street (oblique angle for more variety leading to rear lot parking); a small-scale pedestrian main street; dramatized corner elements on intersection buildings; small-scale pedestrian open spaces.*

Figure 7.9. Nursery hybrid.
A new city hall received an important site near the entry drive. Retail uses were located in arcade-type buildings, long and narrow with interconnecting openings not unlike a market building. A small number of residential buildings framed the entry and provided transition elements for adjacent planned residential areas. Gardens and pea patches intersperse the complex in the manner of a nursery, buffering dispersed parking areas.

Office building types in urban design applications

Office buildings present a wide range of building types for both specific uses that affect the building configuration to generic uses that require flexibility. For most applications, planners are advised to view office buildings more related to their structural/space-framing characteristics. For example, many office buildings are three-dimensional matrices based on the square or rectangular grid. Grid dimensions vary widely based on construction techniques and functions. Once the given grid is specified or understood for the function of the building, the three-dimensional matrix can be designed to take many shapes and configurations. In reality, barring excessive construction costs, office building shapes are quite *plastic* and pliable.

Types include:

- high-rise to medium-rise central core
- high-rise on pedestal or podium
- single or multiple entry double-loaded corridors
- single-loaded corridor
- interior courtyard
- stand alone with single entry
- mixed-use and live/work.

Configurations of office buildings range from downtown mixed-use and high-rise buildings to office parks, modeled after campus-type arrangements. Characteristics of office parks or campuses include:

- courtyard and quadrangle open space focal areas
- landscaped front setbacks
- parking in clusters to rear and/or side of complex
- pedestrian amenities.

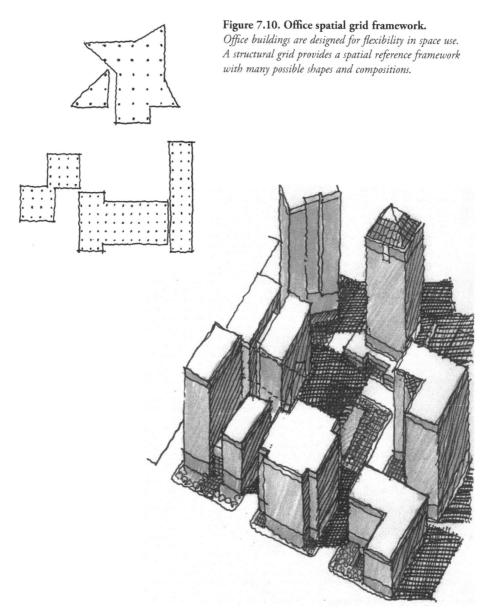

Figure 7.10. Office spatial grid framework.
Office buildings are designed for flexibility in space use.
A structural grid provides a spatial reference framework
with many possible shapes and compositions.

Figure 7.11. Office building variety. *Office building variety illustrates the shape and arrangement of typical urban downtown office buildings: high-rise, pedestal, stepped, "L," and "U" shaped and bridged. Many have interior courts up to four stories or more in height. Others have atriums on the upper level (often designated as public open space by code). The varieties are numerous. Many office building complexes are set on two-plus-story pedestals with retail commercial uses at the base and office functions above in towers. The pedestals can provide a continuous street frontage that responds to zero setback massing of surrounding buildings.*

Entry plazas are conventional requirements for high-rise office buildings due to the high vertical massing of tower structures. Buildings are set back with pedestrian amenities at grade and related levels (raised platforms or sunken plazas). Enclosed transparent interior open space amenities and green roof treatments are common for both aesthetics and economy (surface water treatment, insulation factors, reflectivity).

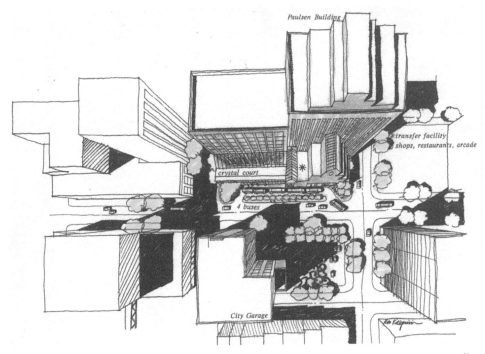

Figure 7.12. Office building as mixed-use transit hub. *The platforms or pedestals of urban center office buildings can serve multiple uses such as transit transfer facilities as in the illustration, light rail stations, museums, and other civic functions.*

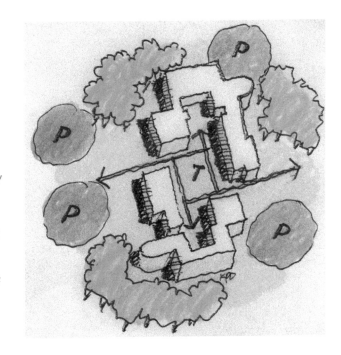

Figure 7.13. Office campus typology. *The campus typology is useful in structuring larger complexes of office buildings. Characteristics include quadrangle-type interconnected open spaces with smaller dispersed parking lots. Open space types are both formal as a setting for the buildings and informal as gathering and resting space for the office populations.*

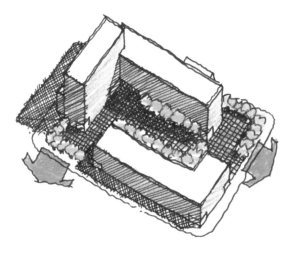

Figure 7.14. Office courtyard.
Common configurations for office buildings often include an interior courtyard with physical and visual access to the street at key points. This also provides air, light, and views for multiple façades.

Figures 7.15 a and b. Recycled office space. *The other extreme in office space from the downtown tower is the incubator office in recycled buildings. In many small communities, residential areas on the fringe of downtown fall into disrepair; non-residential uses encroach upon older neighborhoods. The residential street with sidewalks, landscaped front yards, parking to the rear and/or side provides excellent incubator office space for start-up businesses. In the illustrations, a mid-section was added to an existing house, connecting the house with the recycled garage augmented by a small court.*

a

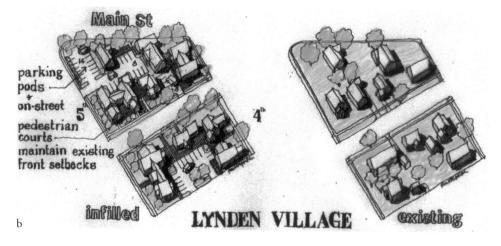

b

Institutional building typologies in urban design applications

Academic, research, medical, and other institutional building types are normally specific to the program needs of departments and specialties. This specificity requires a further level of analysis to determine a building- and site-specific space program. Generic office building types are often associated with institutional buildings as ancillary facilities. Many institutional building types occur in complexes such as office parks, campuses, and urban enclaves. I mention them here in that they can pose a significant catalyst for urban design development.

Open space types in urban design applications

Open space typologies are inherent in all aspects of urban design; and in many instances are organizing structures for urban compositions. They include and are not limited to the following:

- building setbacks and yards
- decks and patios
- streets, avenues, boulevards, and other rights of way
- "squares," courtyards, and plazas
- formal and monumental open space (hard and soft)
- hill climbs
- entrances and gateways
- eddies
- passive and active parks/recreational facilities
- solitude areas (preserves, meditation areas, quiet areas)
- festival areas:
    - outdoor music
    - the "bandstand" park
    - art/craft festival (closed street, parking lots, park areas)
- open, semi-open, and enclosed concourses
- recycled infrastructure (bridges, railroad rights of way, viaducts, etc.)
- gardens, pea patches, and urban agriculture
- roof gardens
- buildings acting as landscapes
- meadows and commons
- cultivated open space
- natural landscapes
- nursery and garden centers
- watersheds and bodies of water
- storm-water reuse areas
- view-sheds
- waterfronts:
    - natural
    - urban reclaimed
    - marinas and uplands

- public access facilities (viewing, promenades, trails)
- environmental art projects
- urban art spaces
- parking lots.

Selected examples

The following examples are a review of selected open space types in urban and community design. Some are conventional and others are hybrids. The basic principle still applies: types are useful as long as they respond to and are compatible with the specific context. If not, they can be used as starting points for hybrids and innovative approaches.

Streets, avenues, and boulevards (the axes)

- urban center/town center streets, avenues, boulevards, and associated planted areas
- sidewalks and promenades
- green streets
- disappearing streets
- urban malls and concourses
- shopping/market streets
- entertainment and event streets
- residential streets (from walkways and trails to gathering areas and people-streets) (see Jacobs, 1993).

Street types in North America for the most part are remnants from the post-war years and the 1960s, accommodating traffic flow with little or no relationship to surrounding land use. Fortunately, streets and streetscapes are now in a rapidly changing state, morphing from auto-dominated movement paths to multiple-use corridors of open space, pedestrian amenities, transit, bike, and car corridors to green streets with dry wells and no curbs. Manuals abound: City of Toronto Planning & Development, Ontario, *Streetscape Manual*, 1995; Regional Transportation Authority of Northeastern Illinois, *Developing Choices for the Future: The What, Why and How of Transit-Oriented Development*, 1995; Chicago Transit Authority (CTA), *Guidelines for Transit Supportive Development*, 1996; Oregon Department of Transportation, *Highway Design Manual*, 1996; Washington County Department of Land Use and Transportation, *Uniform Road Improvement Design Standards*, 1997; Province of Ontario, K. Greenberg, *Canada Alternative Development Standards: Making Choices Guideline*, 1995; Metro Regional Services, Portland OR, *Creating Livable Streets Handbook*, 1997, and many others.

Of the more innovative typologies emerging in North America, "green streets" and *the disappearing street* (Sechelt, 2007) offer the designer alternatives to the classic street right of way.

Community centers

Community centers are an emerging trend in neighborhood revitalization, in cooperative housing developments, and in larger-scale planned communities. They are an alternative to the highway-oriented shopping plaza and shopping mall as gathering places and community interactions. The range of uses

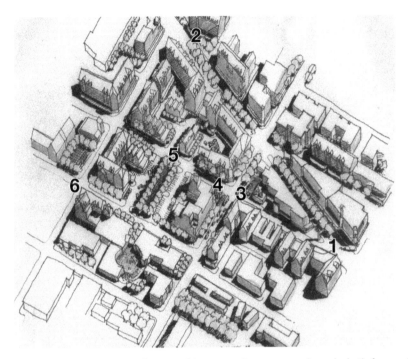

Figure 7.16. Composite open space diagram. *Many types of open space enliven the built form and provide passive and active space for people going about their daily tasks. Landscaped boulevards visually and audibly soften the impacts of major thoroughfares (1); street trees provide shade, color, and a softening agent to the hard streetscape and building façades (2); water features provide buffers to traffic noise and gentle movement for places of rest and pause (3); southerly facing corners provide opportunities to sit in the sun (4); promenades provide major pedestrian connections between high-activity blocks (5); south-facing courtyards provide space for outdoor dining and entertainment (6); formal activity spaces accommodate theater and music events (7).*

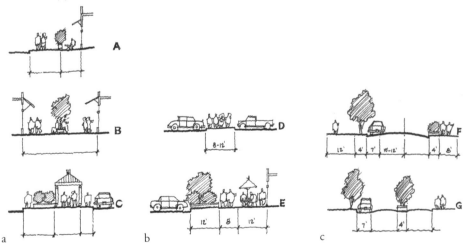

Figures 7.17 a, b, and c. Sidewalk types. *The following sections illustrate a hierarchy of sidewalk types often used in urban and town center developments. The widths are based on a three-feet or one-meter dimension for a pedestrian lane.*

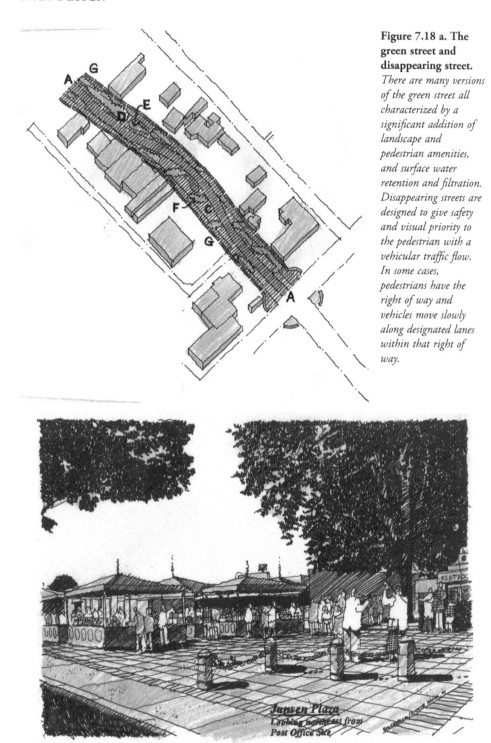

Figure 7.18 a. The green street and disappearing street. *There are many versions of the green street all characterized by a significant addition of landscape and pedestrian amenities, and surface water retention and filtration. Disappearing streets are designed to give safety and visual priority to the pedestrian with a vehicular traffic flow. In some cases, pedestrians have the right of way and vehicles move slowly along designated lanes within that right of way.*

Figure 7.18 b. Shopping/market streets. *Shopping and market streets serve multiple functions: moving traffic, accommodating pedestrians, and serving as open or semi-enclosed markets as in Jansen Plaza.*

Figure 7.19. Entertainment and event streets. *Entertainment and event streets are designed to accommodate street fairs, markets, musical celebrations, and many more activities. They are designed with wider widths, pedestrian-oriented surface materials, and space for display booths and citizen gatherings, as in Wharf Street Plaza.*

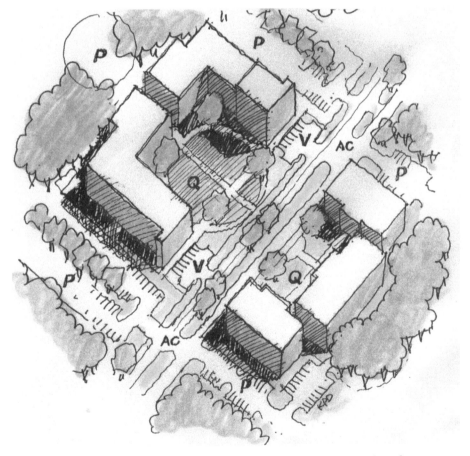

Figure 7.20. Campus quadrangles. *Office parks are often arranged in a campus-style configuration around courtyards and/or quadrangles. Parking is to the side and/or rear, with some exceptions for limited visitor parking in front setbacks near the main entry(s).*

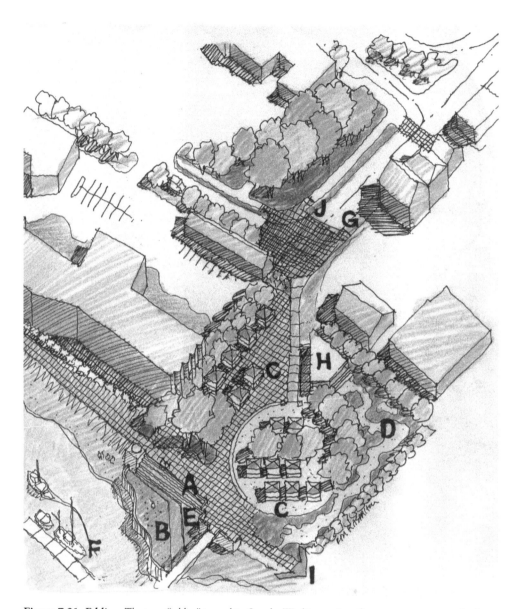

Figure 7.21. Eddies. *The term "eddies" is used in Seattle, Washington in reference to open space setbacks that act as resting areas for pedestrians as in (d). They can include landscaped passive areas or outdoor café-type uses.*

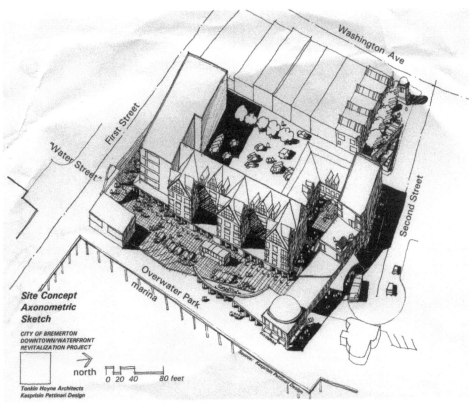

Figure 7.22. Hill climbs. *Hill climbs are a fascinating feature in communities with significant topographic changes between urban blocks. Seattle has the noted Pike Place Market Hill Climb connecting the market to the Elliot Bay waterfront. In Bremerton Hill Climb, the outdoor pedestrian street connection to uptown from the Puget Sound waterfront park and ferry terminal consists of both an outdoor stair climb and linear buildings with vertical assists. The hill climb is now flanked by a convention center, shops, and restaurants in Bremerton, Washington.*

depends upon the profile and needs of each community. Basic uses and principles of organization and structure include and are not limited to the following:

- limited retail uses such as small grocery/general store
- café or coffee shop
- community meeting spaces
- flexible smaller spaces for small-group meetings, classes
- day care
- community kitchen
- a variety of housing types including special needs, live/work
- civic uses including library connection, outreach learning center
- shared studio and craft spaces
- shared open space including passive and active areas, pea-patches or garden areas
- transit connection.

Figure 7.23. Environmental art.
Environmental artist Lorna Jordan[1] is internationally renowned for her landscape-as-art projects, ranging from pedestrian bridges crossing major highways to water filtration facilities designed as landscape art. This image portrays the Terraced Cascade in Scottsdale, Arizona, an environmental artwork and theater garden inspired by the marks that humans and water inscribe on the desert. Expressed as both miniature watershed and abstraction of the human body, the work provides a means for people to imagine their place within the larger Indian Bend Wash—a watershed with extreme conditions of drought and flooding. The work consists of a series of rib-like terraces and a vertebrae-like cascade is nestled into the hillside. Harvested storm water intermittently flows down the cascade into a mesquite bosque that offers shade and respite from the desert sun. The Cascade acts as a gateway to the park and is a part of a regional path system.

Figure 7.24. Urban sculpture: Century City Fountain. *Urban art plays a significant role in open space design. In recent years, glass artists such as John Luebtow[2] are producing work that is larger and space defining. Glass sculpture is no longer art in the landscape. The art is the landscape. John designed and assembled "Venus Vitae" ("Winds of Life") for the Century City Fountain in Los Angeles, Century Park East. The glass sculpture and water feature consists of 12 sheets of kiln-formed and etched glass delineating geometric shapes based on the kindergarten lessons of Frederich Froebel (1782–1852).*

Figure 7.25. Urban art as spatial composition: San Francisco Fountain. *In 1988, John Luebtow designed and assembled the San Francisco Fountain, 100 First at Mission Street, commissioned by Skidmore, Owens, and Merrill. It is composed of one-inch-thick slumped and etched glass, lighting, stainless steel anchoring, and support system with Urazuba granite, audio, and water movement. John's design intent was to create a visually passive, restful space with soft, wavy, undulating linear movement of the glass in harmony with the water's motion, direction, and flow.*

Figures 7.26 a and b (p. 146). Community centers. *The community center example organizes residential and community uses around a mixed-use building with small grocery store and café with classrooms to the rear and in the upper story, flanked by an outreach learning center with an arts and crafts shared studio. All uses are assembled around a courtyard open space structure with slow-moving lane for passenger drop-off and pick-up passing through the site.*

a

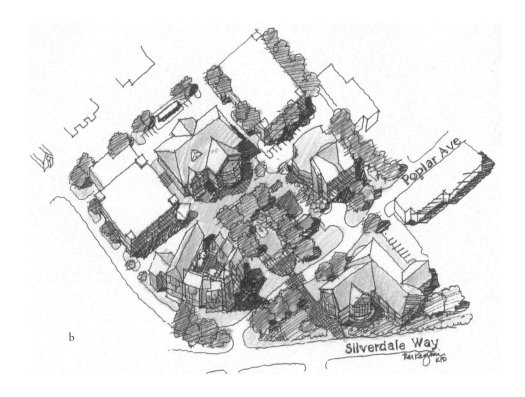

b

Poplar Ave

Silverdale Way

Figure 7.27. Civic–community centers. *In larger community districts such as downtowns, multiple neighborhood commercial centers, a more extensive form of community center can include and not be limited to the following: a theater auditorium, meeting rooms, studio and craft spaces, special needs housing (students, artists, etc.), a special school facility, an interpretive center, a branch library and outreach learning center, and a variety of open space, ranging from a sculpture part to quiet and group event spaces. (Lorna Jordan.)[1]*

Final thoughts on typology

(Urban design) typologies are components and parts of design composition, with principles developed from experiential function-based applications. They are not absolute as I have stated earlier. To use them indiscriminately can lead to compromise and cliché. Most designers, myself included, fall into this trap due to time and budget pressures, and an over-reliance upon professional precedents and conventions. Increasing the awareness of the compromise fallacies (unity, separation, 50/50 blending) is key to an exploration for more innovation in these function-based typologies, using them as a foundation for change through hybridity.

Gordon Cullen (1961) envisioned an "art of relationship that weaves together all the elements that go to create the environment: buildings, trees, nature, water, traffic, advertisements and so on" (p. 10). Cullen deviated from established typological analysis by not dictating (as by type) the shape of the town or environment; instead manipulating form as seen and experienced through the "faculty of sight," as seen in a series of "jerks or revelations," as one passes through the urban environment. He calls it *serial vision*. And I add: *sensual serial vision*. His work advocated for more discovery and perceptual connection of the senses to the urban environment. This sensual perception can be degraded or diluted in the over-use of typology for expedience and economy.

In the making of community compositions, the more urban designers identify the rich cultural, spatial, and historic/time factors inherent in community, the more discoveries and sensuality of place can occur. This richness requires a departure from, or less dependence upon, typology. You may wonder why I end the typology section with thoughts on contrast and conflict. Referring back to why we engage in urban design, I restate that urban design's chief role is to evolve the telling of the spatial story in meaning and function. The story requires freshness and is constructed of a combination of parts that have worked before and are relevant now, and new hybrids and notions that further advance the story, the spatial metaphor. These hybrids often emerge when we confront and engage the contrasts and conflicts in community interactions—not bypass or suppress them through easier methodologies. In the making of the story, as in the making of a watercolor painting, the principle of contrast, of creating drama with a juxtaposition of established type and experimental notions, is at the heart of design.

Like Sergei Eisenstein in *Film Form* (1949), Cullen appreciates the reaction of the mind to contrast (*conflict in form* for Eisenstein), to "the difference between things . . . through the drama of juxtaposition" (p. 11). In the powerful words of Eisenstein:

> Conflict as the fundamental principle for the existence of every art-work and art-form. For art [and design] is always in conflict:
>
> 1   According to its social mission [relationships in culture and meaning]
>
> 2   According to its nature [process of discovery and interpretation]
>
> 3   According to its methodology [making compositions that respond to complexity]
>
> . . . To form equitable views by stirring up contradictions within the spectator's mind, and to forge accurate intellectual concepts from the dynamic clash of opposing passions.
>
> (Eisenstein, 1949, p. 46).

I enjoy these passages because they remind me to make the effort to confront the underlying forces of form in search of innovative methods or strategies for composition in urban design—building on established and coherent typologies and not being trapped by typology.

Cullen's typologies of townscape are split into two elements: an "existing view" and an "emerging view" manipulating these two as a linking process to form relationships as a coherent drama of space. His three means of understanding or viewing the urban form are:

- *Optics:* the serial vision that recognizes the cognitive perception through visualization of environment (see also Arnheim, 1969).
- *Place:* most importantly, Cullen recognizes the body's "instinctive and continuous habit" of relating itself to the environment, a fact often forgotten in planning and design, and more than the human dimension, this habit of relating creates place!
- *Content:* for Cullen, this is an examination of the fabric of towns: color, texture, scale, style, character, personality, and uniqueness—all applying directly to the senses.

The concept of urban design typologies gets a lot more complex; becomes more than inventoried patterns of space; becomes in effect relationships manifested as and in space, *place* as opposed to *space*.

For many urban designers in the 1960s, including myself, we searched for ways to improve ourselves as architects and landscape architects through urban planning and urban design. The drawings of Gordon Cullen inspired us and carried with them the sensual view of urban form, perceiving that form with the senses. I urge the beginning designer to understand typologies for what they are: starting points, sets of principles that can meet the challenges of the CST matrix. And, points of departures as the CST matrix demands more and new principles of organization and assembly. I also urge emerging designers to set aside the digital graphic tools now dominant in design process for a pause. Revisit Cullen's works for a truly sensual experience (Cullen, 1961). Challenge yourself with Eisenstein's call for the discovery of dynamic outcomes or "thirdspace" (Soja, 1996) in the pursuit of the creative differences in community, often contrasting and conflicting in their spatial expressions.

Before leaving this section, two more approaches or ideologies presently infusing urban design with ideas and experimentation are critical for this discussion of typology: New Urbanism or neo-traditional design and creative or living systems design.

Neo-modernism: New Urbanism, as represented by the Congress of New Urbanism, is an outgrowth of (corporate) modernism, "constitut[ing] a genuine search for a secure and humane community . . . [or] a born-again nostalgia for a plethora of historical referents . . . deeply subversive of existing urbanization, with a tendency toward isolationism in the form of middle-class values and prices, green-field sites, and gated communities . . . driven by a fundamentally economic and political agenda" (Cuthbert, 2003).

As in all approaches, there is a range or polarity of value. New Urbanism has codified building type, urban design configurations, and street design into design packages attractive to many communities—solidified typology. This attraction also includes the realtor–financial sector based on many factors including single family detached marketability, nostalgia and thematic applications, and a formalized and predictive design structure.

Post-post-modernism (creative systems): Post-modernism may have opened the "anything goes" doors for designers but it still had not defined the other side of that proverbial coin—what next. Since the 1960s that other side has begun to emerge in philosophy, the environmental movement, in design and even business through an ecological process. I refer to that other side as integral design, where the "anything goes" approach refers to a freedom in design based on the creative energies in the cultural–spatial–temporal reality of living systems (community and the environment). The integral nature of that creative energy is the basis for experimentation in design. It interacts to form emerging spatial patterns of human communities—as coherent design, as accidental form, and as calamitous and degrading functioning rubble.

In describing this integral design, I use the term *creative systems* or *creative urbanism*. Others may use *neo-ecological, eco-systems, etc.* I definitely shy away from "sustainable" as I find the term vague—living systems are dynamic and can range from evolving to devolving and are not stable. Also there are two distinctly different approaches to the systems debate. More is discussed in Chapter 9 but as a prelude to examples of creative systems typology or lack thereof, let me distinguish between a number of views of "systems".

To paraphrase Ferguson (1975), *systems* represent a need for synthesizing and analyzing complexity seeking the most efficient solution to a problem through the establishment of an optimal relationship between resources expended and the results obtained; it is fundamentally a process of assessment and choice.

And/or, "The systems view looks at the world in terms of relationships and integration" (not unlike the definition above). However, instead of concentrating on basic building blocks or basic substances (typologies), "the systems approach emphasizes basic principles of organization ... (also) exhibited by social systems: 'Living form must be regarded as essentially an overt indicator of, or clue to, the dynamics of the underlying formative processes'" (Capra, 1982, pp. 266 and 267, respectively).

In Chapter 9, I discuss the concept of "urban meaning and functionality" as a form of this dynamic formative process that produces or manifests the form indicators we refer to as "urban form". For now, in typologies, I offer the following five principles:

1   Established typologies, like building blocks, are valid in direct proportion to their coherence with the emerging *urban meaning dynamic*.
2   Typologies form the basis for representing a valid functional organization that can be hybridized in direct proportion to the organization's deviance from coherence with the emerging urban meaning dynamic.
3   Most new hybrid forms can be assembled from principles within existing typologies.
4   Bridging between significant poles of difference (contrast and conflict) in urban meaning may require new emergent typologies.
5   New emergent typologies can meet significant resistance (fear) from established aspects of community (financial, marketing, development, construction, etc.) and require an interactive educational process for understanding, acceptance, and application.

Notes

1   Lorna Jordan (Seattle, WA) is a studio artist working in diverse contexts such as downtowns, parklands, ecological preserves, watersheds, buildings, and water reclamation plants. Lorna enjoys the collaborative process of working with diverse groups (designers, agencies, communities, and funders). She was the lead artist and designer on Terraced Cascade, Scottsdale, AZ (2006–2010) with Black & Veatch, Ten Eyck Landscape Architects, and GBtwo Landscape Architects. Lorna has received numerous awards for her artwork, including Place Design Award from *Places Journal* and the Environmental Design Research Association (EDRA) for Waterworks Garden; National Association of Counties Achievement Award (Broward County); Valley Forward Merit Award for Terraced Cascade and a national ASLA Planning Honor Award for Seattle's open space strategy, the Blue Ring, among many others. Lorna has her studio in the Fremont neighborhood in Seattle, WA.

2   John Gilbert Luebtow (Chatsworth, CA and Langley, WA) is an internationally renowned studio artist working in glass, metal, and ceramics. John has a Master of Fine Arts Degree in Glass from the University of California, Los Angeles; Master of Arts Degree in Ceramics from the University of California, Los Angeles; Bachelor of Arts Degree, California Lutheran College, Thousand Oaks, CA. He has over 160 articles published of his works and has received nearly 20 awards and honors for his work including: 2009 Presidential Who's Who; National Foundation For Advancement in the Arts "Teaching Recognition" (2000–2007); Outstanding Artists and Designers of the 20th Century (Cambridge, England (2000, 2003–2004)), and more. John has exhibited in over 175 exhibitions in galleries, museums, and universities around the world including: City of Napa, CA; Corning Museum, Corning, New York; Carnegie Museum, Oxnard, CA; Santa Monica Museum of Art; Louisville Art Museum, Louisville, KY, and many more.

Bibliography

Arendt, Randall, 1996: *Conservation Design for Subdivisions*: Island Press, Washington, DC.

Arnheim, Rudolph, 1969: *Visual Thinking: Critical Reading in Urban Design*: University of California Press, Berkeley, CA.

Campbell River, City of, 1996: "Campbell River Infill Housing Study": Campbell River, BC, printed by Kasprisin Pettinari Design, Langley, WA.

Capra, Fritjof, 1982: *The Turning Point*: Simon & Schuster, New York.

Cullen, Gordon, 1961: *Townscape*: Reinhold Publishing, New York.

Cuthbert, Alexander R. (ed.), 2003: *Designing Cities: Critical Readings in Urban Design*: Blackwell Publishers, Cambridge, MA.

Eisenstein, Sergei, 1949: *Film Form*: Harcourt, Brace & World, Inc., New York.

Ferguson, Francis, 1975: *Architecture, Cities and the Systems Approach*: George Braziller, New York.

Jacobs, Alan B., 1993: *Great Streets*: MIT Press, Cambridge, MA.

Johnston, Charles MD, 1984/1986: *The Creative Imperative*: Celestial Arts, Berkeley, CA.

Johnston, Charles MD, 1991: *Necessary Wisdom*: Celestial Arts, Berkeley, CA.

Okamoto, Rai Y. and Williams, Frank E., 1969: *Urban Design Manhattan (Regional Plan Association): A Studio Book*: The Viking Press, New York.

Parker Brothers, 1935: *Monopoly*: Waddingtons, A board game adapted and developed in 1935 from "The Landlords Game" by Quaker Elizabeth Magie.

Sechelt BC, District of, 2007: "Visions for Sechelt": John Talbot & Associates (Burnaby, BC) and Kasprisin Pettinari Design (Langley, WA).

Soja, Edward W., 1996: *Thirdspace*: Blackwell Publishers, Cambridge, MA.

Walker, Lester, 1987: *Tiny Houses*: The Overlook Press, Woodstock, NY.

Chapter 8

EXPERIMENTS IN COMPOSITION
THE BASIS FOR PLACE-MAKING

Graduate urban planning and design students contributed examples for this chapter, a portion of which are included, specifically Figures 8.5 through 8.11 and 8.13 through 8.18. They include: Christy Alexander, Eric Alskog, Ion Arai, Diana Benson, Nick Bond, Erica Huang, Hiroko Matsuno, Hannah Jane McIntosh, Eddie Hill, Rueben McKnight, Craig Montgomery, Davila Parker-Garcia, Jessica Stein, Zhi Wen Tan, Kenn Teng, Clay Harris Veka, Adam Webber, and Jason Woycke.

The urban design process is often referred to as "place-making," a form-based interpretation of urban meaning and urban functionality into spatial metaphors—sensory and sensual built environments that are considered special in the eyes and experience of the observer. The more aspects of *urban meaning and functionality* incorporated into the process, the more complex becomes the challenge of place-making. Integrating the rich stories of community with the compositional principles of art is a necessary and critical challenge for contemporary designers, and often overshadowed by the demands of economic and functional program requirements. Fashioning spatial compositions that respond to and structure this *urban meaning*, maintaining a compositional integrity within the complexity, begins the *art of urban design*. This is the place for playful exploration of design—using crafting methods.

Exploration leads to discovery. Crafting methods (drawing, model-making, cut-outs, etc.) all require a physical manipulation of materials into design compositions—a journey into the unknown, on the path that emerges only after each step into the unknown. This physical manipulation is critical to discovery as the process entails experimentation with both structured and known principles such as typologies and design conventions and unstructured and unknown or uncertain explorations where new principles emerge. Digital tools can supplement this process and I encourage students not to rely extensively on them as they reduce, in my experience as instructor and practitioner, the discovery process through pre-set structures and formats; and, most importantly, a disconnect of key crafting senses. I realize there is a great deal of opinion and debate surrounding digital vs. crafting methodologies in urban design processes. I leave that final decision to instructors and students, and can only urge students to engage their fears surrounding this physical sensory engagement and *play*.

This chapter describes exercises I use in my "Urban Design Composition" coursework at the University of Washington to prepare urban planning students for advanced urban design studios. Those students with design backgrounds also benefit by revisiting compositional principles. As I stated in the introduction, intelligence and motivation are not sufficient in themselves to engage in design, the making of place. Making *place* requires an understanding and experience with the elements and principles of composition as the foundation of making spatial metaphors.

The planning students enjoy these exercises and I hope the reader will as well. They are offered as a base for educators, designers, and lay people as hands-on experiments in composition. They are guides that in themselves are open to experimentation. I encourage instructors and students to challenge and change them—maintaining their underlying intent.

Design requires the immersion of the designer as a person into the process. Design is not antiseptic, devoid of feeling and opinion, personal values and passions; and, design requires a larger dedication to the needs and passions of the community and its environs—a very complex journey. Being able to identify and appreciate urban form as history is a start; and understanding historic morphology is not sufficient as a base for design as the CST matrix or context is less apparent. Learning how to play with the aspects of form is the other side of the learning equation.

Sequence of experiments: the exercises are designed to build skills, confidence, and an evolving understanding of the elements and principles of design composition with increasingly more complex applications. The sequence generally includes:

- the simple and abstract manipulation of the primary shapes in two dimensions
- using these preliminary exercises to add the vertical or "Y" axis dimension
- manipulation and experimentation with primary volumes
- assembling basic compositions in two and three dimensions
- constructing programmatic play-pieces: introducing *need*
- expanding program and site conditions to the compositional process
- experimenting with real-site applications of compositional relationships, adding the culture/space/time contextual matrix.

The exercises also experiment with theoretical concepts such as *merging, bridging polarities and remnants* as discussed in Chapter 9. The reader is encouraged to use these exercises as a guide to practice design-play and design skill-building.

Required skills: play always requires some form of hands-on manipulation of tools, objects, shapes, etc. No, not playing a computer game with your fingers or stylus. Play as in crafting (seeing, touching, turning, folding, cutting, messing-up, getting dirty)! Many of my planning students have little drawing experience and some trepidation at using their hands as opposed to their mouse or stylus. Consequently, many of the book's exercises use construction paper, tape, glue, and scissors as beginning tools (remember "kindergarten"), and makes the play accessible for most people. As a part of the exercises, I also introduce axonometric drawing and plan diagramming so that the play-skills can be expanded as the reader progresses to more complexity. Refer to Appendix I.

And remember, fear is a necessary ingredient in creativity (Webb, 1990); we all have some reticence in various degrees regarding art and design; we need to recognize and work through fear's manifestations. There is the key: when in doubt, when "circling the wagons" in reticence or uncertainty, sit down and begin to play—cut, tape, glue *anything* to get started. The rest of the process takes over and play begins. Have fun!

Examples of student work: I intentionally do not include many specific examples of each exercise in order to encourage a fresh approach for those who choose to play, rather than being influenced by the play of others. Examples are included in clusters throughout this chapter as guides and represent basic work from urban planning students. There is a learning curve that begins with a great deal of frustration and leads to a great deal of satisfaction and excitement.

Understanding and working with primary shapes

I summarize key aspects of composition as a reminder of the principles at work in the exercises. More detail is provided in previous chapters.

The flexibility of primary shapes (remember: shapes are physical elements and are the "nouns" of spatial language)

Principles at work

The following exercises ask the participant to explore the many different ways of expressing the primary shapes without losing their original identities. In other words, take them to the point of breaking to explore the many ways of adjusting their main elements and components (center, radii, perimeters, corners, edges, etc.).

EX1: Observation of primary shapes

Intent:

Increase your awareness and observation skills; increase your appreciation of geometry as shapes in the built environment.

Tools:

- Three-ring binder
- Camera.

Tasks:

1   Take a walk with your camera. Begin assembling photographic representations of the three primary shapes and their associated volumes (cube, sphere, line axis) in real life, from natural to manufactured human environments. A circle in nature, you ask? Yes, at least two versions of the circle exist: a circle as a tree in plan, uneven yet a circle altered by its environment—radiating out from a central point in growth rings, adjusting to light, neighboring trees, weather, etc.; the other version as the pure circle, equal radii and consistent circumference—a pure math.

2   Use examples that are found in human settlement patterns and collect them in your binder. For example, a Rose window in a church wall is a circular shape that is dominant. A gable roof end is a triangle (part of a square). A globe light bulb is a sphere. A paving pattern may be radial, part of a circle, emanating out from the craft-persons position. Be creative. Label each image. Look for the small within the large and continue to observe the geometry of nature (including the human manufactured world). Increase your observation skills and awareness of your surroundings.

EX2: Manipulating the primary shapes

Intent:

Learn the characteristics of the primary shapes and how to positively manipulate them to fit real contexts as they maintain their shape integrity or key characteristics.

Tools:

- Construction paper
- Scissors
- Tape, or paper glue (preferred)
- Axonometric drawing, depending upon your comfort level.

Tasks:

Using a circle, square, triangle, and line, each approximately four to six inches across or in length, construct the following:

1   Represent each shape in solid, void, and outline form.
2   Identify and articulate with, or on, paper the physical characteristics (elements and components) of each (i.e. a circle has a shape expressed by a perimeter, a center, a radius/diameter, a series of arcs, etc.). A line and an arc are sufficient to represent the circle, as is an arrow with starting point and arrow head. Glue and tape or draw the characteristics for each primary shape to another piece of colored construction paper for display. Do more than one version per shape to identify the many characteristics. This exercise is intended to improve your observation skills and identify those characteristics taken for granted and usually not observed and therefore not used by students in design complexity.
3   Using a pair of scissors, make cut-outs of each primary shape (circle, square [and triangle], line axis), four to six inches across. Use construction paper or some easy-to-cut cardboard stock. Manipulate each shape a minimum of three different ways to change the conventional shape (a solid square, for example) without losing the original identity, i.e. square.
4   Suggestion: use scissors or a sharp knife to cut into the shapes. For example, a square can be represented by four corner pieces; or four dots; or a triangle with one diagonal (of a square) and one floating corner, etc. Push the primary shapes to their breaking point yet don't break them (if you do break them, consider that a positive learning exercise). A circle can be represented simply by an arrow and a center point (radius). Do as many of these as you can. This is a basic and valuable exercise.

EX3: Recognizing compositions in the real world

As you did for basic shapes, begin this section with more observation of the geometry in the real world. On your walks, look for more complex arrangements of shapes in two- and three-dimensional compositions. Focus on the mixture or combinations of shapes, the actions (repetition, variety, etc.) that energize those shape combinations, and the use of light to dark relationships, (i.e. value) that creates drama and attention within them.

Intent:

Increase your awareness of basic compositions within the built environment: what works, what seems awkward, what appears complicated.

Tools:

•   Three-ring binder
•   Camera
•   Walking shoes
•   Curiosity.

Tasks:

1   Select an area for observation such as a block in downtown or an older commercial center near home.

2   As you walk along, look for compositions in the architecture that contain elements and relationships mentioned above.

3   What to look for:
   –   *Mixed shapes* can be a circle within a square or rectangle (door?); half circles within a triangle (gable roof with scallop shingles?); diamonds within a grid (pavement patterns?).
   –   *Spatial actions* can be the grid containing the diamonds above; the line or axis separating or connecting two spheres (barbells?); a radial burst with lighting elements along each burst, and so on.
   –   *Value contrasts* can be the black and white on a banner; a strong shadow pattern falling on a light surface; the softness of light on a statue with flowing robes.

4   Do contour sketches or photograph your observations.

5   Record and place in binder.

EX4: Making two-dimensional compositions

Intent:

Experiment with simple compositions using the primary shapes and manipulating those shapes to increase the complexity of the arrangements.

Tools:

•   Scissors
•   Construction paper
•   Paper glue
•   Cutting board
•   Cutting knife (optional)
•   Safety awareness (always cut away from yourself and keep your fingers out of the way!)
•   Axonometric drawing option.

Tasks:

1   Suggestion: make at least two two-dimensional compositions.

2   Use a sheet of construction paper as a base for each; or, you can put the construction paper on a piece of illustration board or foam core for more stability.

3   For the first composition, using only a circle and a square approximately four to six inches across, make three compositions by integrating the two shapes together, three different times (manipulate shapes as per early exercises); for example, a hollow circle within a solid square or a part of a circle (a pie shape) and four corners of the square—experimentation is necessary and beneficial.

4   For the second composition, using a circle, square, triangle, and line as axis, make three different compositions, manipulating shapes as desired (use only the following angles for the axis—0/90, 0/180, 45/45, 30/60):
   –   The axis is the key spatial action tool (line becomes connector); the axis can be straight (0/180), bent, curved, etc. and can be the organizing principle for other shapes. Remember: principles are rules of conduct that aid in organizing shapes into a coherent (form) relationship.
   –   Use at least the following organizing principles: repetition, repetition with variety, gradation, and be aware of others.

5   Make a copy of your design to write on and describe in notation form what organizing principles are used to form the composition.

6   Place in binder.

EX5: Adding the vertical dimension

Intent:

Experiment with three-dimensional design by adding a vertical dimension to two-dimensional compositions.

Tools:

- Construction paper pad, medium to stiff (stiffer the better)
- Scissors
- Stick glue, paste glue, or frosted tape
- Toothpicks (optional: about a dozen)
- Four or more straws (optional)
- A piece of cardboard or stiff backing material about 11 x 11 inches up to 17 inches as a base.

Tasks:

1   Again, use construction paper or a stiffer tag/poster board; as a prelude to the three-dimensional construction, expand on your two-dimensional compositions in the previous exercise, using modifications of a square, circle, and axis.

2   Make sure that all the shapes are in some form of relationship based on the principles of composition (repetition, repetition with variety, rhythm, gradation, etc.) and use one of the basic compositional structures (grid, circle, radial burst, triangle, etc.).

3   Review the types of vertical and angular or tilted planes (Ching, 1979).

4   Assess your two-dimensional composition and experiment/play with the addition of vertical planes (above and below your basic grade or horizontal plane) to define three-dimensional spaces within your composition.

5   Feel free to add above-/below-grade horizontal planes (roof, sunken plaza, etc.) to reinforce your ideas of enclosure with the vertical planes.

6   Use straight, curved, tilted, etc.—be as expressive as you can for this exercise.

7   Do at least two versions for practice; do not hesitate to play and redo based on your observations and reflections.

What to look for:

- Do your shapes still relate to one another or do they just float on the paper?
- Does your axis act as connector, movement channel?
- Are your primary shapes still recognizable in the composition?
- Can you identify an overall compositional structure within the composition?
- Is there any drama resulting from the combination of vertical and horizontal planes?

EX6a: Constructing the basic volumes

Principles:

Modify basic solid forms to create more complex shapes without losing the "parent" form. This is similar to the very first two-dimensional exercise: modifying the square and circle where the "parent" is still visible as the form is manipulated.

Remember: the cube has a center and eight corners, two diagonals, and can be broken down into smaller grids of squares and cubes; the pyramid is found within the cube; the sphere has a center, radii, arcs, diameters, and circumferences; the axis can have width and depth as well as be solid or broken.

Intent:

Familiarize yourself with the basic volumes through the crafting process (cut-out or drawing).

Tools:

- Construction paper or tag board (any board/paper stiffer than construction paper but not as thick as illustration board)
- Scissors
- Paper glue sticks or tape
- Soft pencil
- Triangle or straight edge.

Tasks:

1   Using approximately a four-inch to six-inch base, construct two pyramids; two cubes; two spheres all the same base size (spheres are four or six inches in diameter).
2   Suggestion: for pyramids, draw a six-inch square on the paper. Extend out from the center of each side a perpendicular line of the same length. Connect the end of that perpendicular line to the two corners; do the same for each extended line. Cut out the "star" and crease the line where each triangle meets the base square, fold to the center and glue.
3   Suggestion: for a cube, lay out the base square and draw four more squares of the same size extending from each side of the base. Cut, crease, and fold together. Cut the top square and glue on.
4   Suggestion: for a sphere, you can cut a number of circles, using a four- or six-inch diameter, then cut a slit in each circle to the center and splice together. Or cut out a circle, notch each quadrant line with scissors, cut out four half circles, and notch those. Fit together.
5   Actually constructing these solids increases the thinking with the senses or cognitive perception and is not busy work!

EX6b: Manipulating the volumes

For each set of volumes, manipulate them in at least two different ways to break them down without losing their physical characteristics. For example, the cube can have one entire square plane removed and it is still a cube; cut the corners off at 45-degree angles and it is still a cube; cut circular holes into two or more square planes and it is still a square. Use your imagination and actually try to make the solid go away—yes, you have gone too far and now you know where that is!

This is an important exercise as it portrays the many variations of the base solids. Why? The solid can be manipulated to respond to or fit into a complex physical context and still hold its geometric (and mathematical) integrity.

EX6c: Combining manipulated volumes

Now, for each of the above constructions, add another element or two to each to increase the complexity. For example, to the pyramid, take a solid square equal to the pyramid's base; cut another square (or circle) void or window within that square; slip it down over the top of the pyramid until if finds its resting point. You can also take a cube, cut a circle in the bottom, and slide it over the top of the pyramid or vice versa.

Overlay or superimpose one primary shape and/or volume onto another to get a third and distinct form. You can use planes and/or volumes for the additive. You can also take away from a volume (i.e. the cube) to insert another into it.

Remember: placing nouns–objects as shapes on a spatially referenced base map, for example, only locates those objects in space. (In writing, the noun is used to describe a thing; and in design the object is used to describe a form, element, or shape—a similar application). Demonstrating and visualizing the relational interactions between and among those objects and the underlying physical context on the base is the real communication!

Reminder:

Elements are nouns–objects–shapes:

- circles/spheres including pie shapes
- squares/cubes including triangular shapes
- lines/axes.

Principles are verbs–actions–connections that establish relationships between and among elements:

- *gradation:* variations in light, color, texture, sound, even smell
- *repetition:* a recurring shape or pattern of shapes in a design
- *repetition with variety:* a recurring shape or pattern of shapes that can change sizes, value, texture, etc. in alternating sequences
- *variety:* one composition that has varied shapes composing it, not necessarily the same shape
- *alternation:* a recurring shape or pattern of shapes that have a specific rhythm to their repetition, such as ababab/b aabbaa b/ababbababababab
- *dominance:* you decide and highlight: the largest, the loudest, the alpha, the whitest/darkest, etc.
- *patterning:* an arrangement of form with at least two repetitions, possibly indicating a change or emergent pattern.

Compositional structures

Principles:

From the circle, square, and line a variety of compositional assembling forces or frameworks emerge as structuring devices, referred to as *compositional structures*. They are hybrids of the circle and square, sphere and cube; and bring together, construct, and assemble various organizational parts, elements, and relationships into spatial constructs or compositions. Remember that *organizations* are relationships of uses, activities, etc. not assembled into a specific form or spatial composition. Form results from a connection among relationships among the organizations, the structuring of those organizations, and the crafting process. This pre-dates and provides the underlayment to "form-based" design and zoning applications now currently popular.

Goldstein (1989) offers a solid base for these explorations and includes 16 compositional structures. Other variations and hybrids are possible. This experimentation series is an important step in understanding and playing with rational means of making form. As situations and physical contexts become more and more complex, these hybrids can serve the designer well in fashioning order within this complexity.

Compositional structures:

- Bridge
- Cantilever
- Centrally placed object
- Circle
- Curvilinear dominant
- Diagonal
- Diamond
- Even spread
- Grid
- Horizontal
- L-shape
- Radial burst
- Triangle
- Two centers
- Vertical.

Tools:

- Construction paper
- Paper glue
- Scissors and cutting knife
- Soft pencil
- Corrugated paper
- Triangle
- Axonometric drawings.

EX7a: Compositional structures in plan

Intent:

Familiarize yourself with each of the 16 compositional structures, understanding the basic "parents" (circle, square, and line) and the offspring hybrids associated with each—by crafting not memorization.

Tools:

Same.

Tasks:

1   For each compositional structure, in plan form, around four inch maximum per side, construct or draw the structure and highlight its major components. For example, a circle may be cut out of paper and the radii, one diameter and an arc or two can be highlighted. Construct a number of variations per structure to familiarize yourself with the myriad variations that are possible.
2   Take a photograph of each or make a bond copy (color is not important).

EX7b: Adding the third dimension to compositional structures

Tasks:

1   On the original or a drawing copy if available, add vertical elements to a number of selected compositional structures to transform them from two-dimensional shapes into three-dimensional assembling forces. Use vertical lines, planes, and even voids.
2   For example, take the circle and add vertical elements around the perimeter, a circle defining a framework for vertical elements, becoming a third and distinct composition.
3   Often, the circle can be understated or invisible and still remain apparent or active in the composition.

These exercises experiment with the cube, axis, and sphere as volumetric compositional structures, each exerting a dominant influence on the overall design: organizing and assembling the spatial metaphor.

Experiments in the transformations of form

Principles:

Through artistic experience and history, a number of methods to transform or change a form or composition have emerged that are useful in architecture, landscape architecture, and urban design: adding shapes and volumes, subtracting shapes and volumes, and changing the dimensions of the original. The original form or composition can be altered to expand yet retain key elements of its original parentage (cube, for example); or the original form can be changed into a different and distinct outcome from the original.

•   Additive
•   Subtractive
•   Dimensional.

I add to these three the following: merging and bridging. With merging, two or more forms and/or compositions are brought together in a way that crafts new forms at the melding of the originals, while maintaining original aspects of each. With bridging, two differing or conflicting forms or compositions are brought together in compositional consensus where the key characteristics or integrity of each still remains. In both cases, the originals are not completely *blended* to form a third mono-form; instead it results in a *thirdspace* that is different and retains key aspects of the originals.

- Merging
- Bridging (polarities)
    - direct assimilation vs.
    - remnants.

Bridging is also a part of a larger urban design methodology of making connections: between transit to development centers, past to present, downtown to waterfront, etc. "Remnants" is a methodology that James Pettinari and I have been experimenting with as a way of bridging past to present and future patterns, among other connections.

EX8a: Additive transformational actions

Principles:

Transforming form and composition in urban design is a constant and complex process, with form (as design) constantly interacting with, pressured by, and responding to the realities of urban meaning and functionality. The challenge is to change the physical characteristics of shapes and volumes with transformational actions that maintain design integrity in relation to those interactions.

Tasks:

1   Select a base solid: cube, pyramid, or sphere with a four- to six-inch base.
2   Select another solid and add it to the base solid.
3   How? Here are some examples:
    a   To a cube, add a smaller cube to one of the surface planes.
    b   Or add one smaller cube to each vertical face plane.
    c   Or wrap one smaller cube (or more) around one of the four bottom corners of the base solid.
    d   To a pyramid, add a cube to the top of the pyramid.
    e   Or set the pyramid on top of a cube.
    f   Or superimpose the pyramid with a cube where part of the cube is absorbed into the pyramid.
    g   To a sphere, insert a pyramid tip down into the sphere.
    h   Or insert the sphere into a cube.
4   Try at least three of four of these to loosen up and experiment.

EX8b: Subtractive transformational actions

Principles:

Change a form by subtracting parts from the original without losing the parent identity. This is useful when manipulating a form to respond to a contextual situation and the retention of the original form-identity is desired.

Tasks:

1   Select a base volume: cube, pyramid, sphere, axis.
2   Carve out another, smaller volume from the base volume.
3   In reality, the subtracted volume responds in form to contextual conditions.
4   Some examples:
    a   To a cube, subtract a smaller cube from one to four of the bottom corners (they can all be different size cubes as well—repetition with variety).
    b   To a pyramid, cut off the top one-third of the pyramid and turn the subtractive form over and stick it into the remaining base solid.
    c   Or cut off one or more of the pyramid corners.
    d   Option: use the subtractive forms as additives in a new design with the base volume (see Chapter 6, Figures 6.4 a and b).
    e   Play is the operative word! Many people are new to this form of spatial thinking and it takes effort and attention.

In form-based or compositional structure massing diagrams, the location of outdoor courts and setbacks can be carved out of the massing envelope as subtractive elements with solar orientation and repetition pattern.

EX8c: Changing dimensions

Principles:

A form can be changed by simply altering one of its dimensions (length, width, height, circumference, radius, etc.). Increase or decrease one edge of a cube and reconnect the corners; make the entire cube smaller or larger; make one half of the cube smaller or larger; or make two opposing face planes smaller than the rest, reconnecting the corners. This is an obvious transforming action with buildings and is also useful in urban design. For example, altering the dimensions of a street grid, or reducing the width of a street right of way are all ways to transform shapes by dimensional changes. And they all have consequences: if I reduce the width of a street, I may lose a lane of on-street parking.

Tasks:

1   Using your axonometric drawing, experiment with dimensional changes to each of the following: cube, pyramid, sphere, and axis (as channel).

2   First, draw the original base solid at approximately four-inch dimensions on base.

3   Using overlays with tracing paper, change one or more dimensions and redraw the resulting form.

4   Do a final trace of the finished form.

5   Try the same exercise.

Urban design applications:

• *Open space design:* repeating the same pattern and changing the dimensions of the basic form(s) in that pattern. Building massing design: alter the dimensions of building mass components to establish modulation along with repetition and variety, based on contextual conditions.

• *Street grid design:* changing the dimensions of a street grid; this changes the number and type of residential parcels that are accommodated on the block, in turn affecting the building typology for those parcels.

The density and physical characteristics of residential street grids and associated blocks and parcels can be greatly influenced by the dimensional changes for those grids. By changing a street grid from 300 feet in length, say, six 50-feet wide parcels, to 600 feet with six parcels, alters both walkability and building characteristic. The smaller block and parcels may provide bungalow-type residential buildings; the larger block and parcels may encourage larger residences and front-facing garages.

EX9: Additive/subtractive compositions

I use this exercise and others like it, always tweaking them, in my "Urban Design Composition" course. For the reader, the exercise can be used as an experiment or merely as an example of assembling a composition using the additive and subtractive transformational actions.

Tasks:

Compose an urban block development scheme with office building masses that respond to the following:

• each other (three volumes: twelve, eight, and four stories in height)
• repetition with variety
• additive and subtractive transformations
• solar orientation
• streetscape sensitivity
• adjacent context
• human scale.

Context:

The physical situation for this assignment is a downtown block with the following conditions:

• Scale: 1 inch = 20 feet.
• Base size: 11 x 17 inches or thereabouts for physical model (suggest using corrugated cardboard for base).

- North–south is oriented to a 17-inch length, east–west to a 11-inch width, and indicate a north arrow on model or drawing.
- A historic church is across the street from the southwest site quadrant.
- An existing park is across the street from the northeast site quadrant.
- Existing office buildings with zero feet front setbacks fill the remaining adjacent quadrants.
- Base buildings have square floor plates comprised as cube components, essentially a three-dimensional cube matrix.
- There are three buildings on the block.
- You may use as many cubes as you desire (you set the cube dimensions).
- You may use axes, pyramids, spheres as per your preference in the final design.

EX10: Merging transformational actions

Principles:

Merging is a transformational action that occurs in the edge or periphery space of a form or composition. A form or larger composition can be changed by merging parts into adjacent forms, compositions, and even adjacent voids as a soft or disappearing edge. Merging is a key *relational action* useful in the integration of two or more forms. A key principle in merging: the *parent* forms are still recognizable, with their original identities, in the final outcome, merging to form a new shape (offspring) at and in the edge or peripheral space between and among the original forms. Merging can reinforce and dramatically hold together the larger composition by strengthening the physical relationships between and among basic shapes and volumes.

Merging can take various forms:

- interlocking with hard edges
- blending with soft edges
- creating variety with a combination of hard and soft edges
- intermixing with smaller combined parts of the original forms.

This is a dynamic exercise in that there are many unpredictable results from the merging process. This exercise can be done with either an axonometric drawing type, a plan diagram, or three-dimensional cut-outs with construction paper or tag board.

Tasks:

1   Prepare two squares, each scored with a grid (make the two grids different in either size and/or color or value).
2   Break off smaller squares as individuals and clusters from the parent grids and intermingle, forming a transitional or peripheral zone between the two squares.
3   Play with the intermingling and experiment with various integral compositions.
4   If the grids were on a physical context, a site with topographical or building features, the transition zone must respond to that underlying context.

Urban design application examples:

- Relating a new development to an existing built form pattern along the edge or periphery zone.
- Relating two or more differing new developments (use, typology, intensities) along the edge zone.
- Relating two or more developments to a natural or significant built feature.

EX11: Merging composition: a residential community

Again, the reader can use this as either a study example or an exercise for experimentation (and fun).

Principles:

Using merging as a transformational action, particularly subtractive actions for the larger buildings and additive for the smaller buildings, relate the two larger buildings with a merged transition area including open space and the accessory uses.

Context:

Residential units can fit in a 20-foot cube as two-story units, in a 30-foot cube as the same but larger, or as two townhouses side by side.

All units and in particular the interior units of the larger buildings require light and air access. The mixed uses can be a part of the larger buildings or integrated into the merged transition and are readily identifiable. One hundred and twenty parking spaces are required on site with each space at 8 x 18 feet.

Site is 220 x 400 feet urban block with the following conditions:

- relatively flat
- office park on western boundary
- older two-story stacked flat residential development on northern boundary
- older single family houses being converted to general commercial on the east side
- wetland and marsh area on southern boundary
- begin with two buildings on the site, one 12 cubes high by four cubes wide with a 20-foot cube side; the second with eight cubes high by six cubes wide with a 30-foot cube side.
- suggested scale: 1 inch = 20 feet no smaller and 1 inch = 30 feet is OK.

Tasks:

1   Draw a ghost frame (grid, triangles, circles, etc. your choice) on the base.
2   Draw a grid per specs on the parent volumes in an axonometric drawing; you can also do it in paper with scissors, with wood blocks, or with foam cut-outs.
3   Do conceptual sketching in plan to begin the process for big pattern ideas.
4   Find a starting point: where are the larger cubes in relation to off-site conditions? How do these cubes relate to orientation and to one another? Where is a suitable transition area?

EX12: Bridging polarities

Principles:

Bridging polarities is a multi-dimensional process of connecting two opposing, significantly differing, or conflicting extents of a relationship. The process is used in psychiatry (Johnston, 1984/1986) and is derived from creative systems theory. I use the methods in public involvement processes with group relational issues: workshops, design charrettes, and conferences. In design, *bridging* is used as both a spatial connection action and as a spatial composition distinctly different from the elements being connected, yet encompassing key aspects or integrities of each (polarity). Part of the objective of this process and methodology is to move beyond the two polarities and explore new compositions consisting of a new construct that avoids compromise between the polarities.

The polarity–relationship framework (composed of multiple sets of polarities) can exist as interactions between relationships in existing spatial contexts (disagreements regarding the use of open space funds in a neighborhood, for example); differing concepts and ideas or approaches (maintaining industrial uses or developing tourist facilities on an urban waterfront); and differing and often conflicting probable spatial outcomes to a compositional problem. A simple example of a polarity–relationship framework is the color wheel: a framework (circle) comprising at least 12 color entities or identities in relationships with adjacent (analogous) and opposing colors, blue and orange, yellow and purple, red and green. Remember: polarities in the color wheel are composed from the three basic primaries—red, yellow, and blue. Pick one (red) and what is left is a combination of the remaining two (yellow and blue) or green. Blue leaves us red and yellow (orange) and so on.

For a bridging dynamic or transformation, the color wheel or circular structure establishes opposites along each diameter, creating color opposites (often referred to as complements) that, when placed in close proximity to one another in a painting composition, provide a heightened dramatic stimulus (a complement) for the larger composition, usually at or near the center of interest or focus. They work in harmony with the other elements and principles of the larger composition and maintain their original integrities. Essentially they are completing the whole: always complementing the remaining primary and secondary colors of the color wheel not present in their mixture (red to green, blue to orange, and yellow to purple).

In the larger design process, I often find it useful to identify the opposite or polarity of notions or concepts generated during the exploration phase. Why? First, identifying the polarity requires an understanding of the basic concept and puts that concept into a larger "container" or perspective. Second, identifying the polarity requires the designer to turn the initial concept inside out; and in turn, often reveals new directions or approaches.

The color wheel expresses both the parent identities of the color/light relationship (red, yellow, and blue), the secondary and tertiary relationships of analogous connections (red plus yellow equals orange, blue plus yellow equals green, and red plus blue equals purple), and the opposing color relationships (red to green, yellow to purple, and blue to orange). And the opposing relationships can be complementary and are used as such in two-dimensional arts as the polarities are bridged and brought together (in close proximity) yet not mixed.

The same approach can be used for the spatial elements and principles in a composition as exhibited in the following experiments.

Bridging as a literal connection:

- pedestrian bridge
- park over freeway
- building(s) over freeway.

Bridging as a metaphorical connection:

- environmental art structure that channels water and moves people across a divide (freeway, river, etc.).

Bridging as a thirdspace connection.

- transit center used as connection between a downtown core and a waterfront, separated by a highway (see Appendix I, Figure A.1)
- a historic remnant pattern (railroad line) reconstructed as multi-modal (bike, trolley, pedestrian) corridor as a past to present bridging action.

Tasks:

1   Begin with a circle and a square, each four inches minimum in diameter/width.
2   Craft six different compositions that combine them without losing their identities and integrity. In *merging*, the two initial shapes were broken down and integrated at their edges, a form of bridging. In this exercise, fashion a distinctly new and different composition with the initial shapes as integral parts of the composition and not dominant. Does the final composition represent a new and different outcome and incorporate the two initial shapes?

EX13: Bridging polarities with remnants

Principles:

Remnants are parts or pieces of historic patterns that are obsolete or inactive. They can consist of natural features such as a forest recharge area minimized and made dysfunctional by residential subdivision development, or wetlands that have been filled beyond their ability to absorb and filter water. They can consist of infrastructure remnants such as abandoned railroad lines and corridors, historic street patterns, viaduct rights of way and more. And they can consist of building structures used for specific industrial or manufacturing purposes long obsolete. These remnants are historic artifacts, physical elements in the landscape with little or no contemporary purpose. And they can be used as actions or devices to bridge the past to the emerging future ... by using them as foundations in a new development framework, with new purpose.

Intent:

Identify, conserve, and rejuvenate a historic pattern or object into a contemporary urban design pattern, where the historic pattern forms the basis for the emerging design.

Tasks:

This is not easy, and takes research and investigation to implement. I use past projects as a basis for example exercises that can be replicated or used as a guide for local exercises.

Landscape remnants as bridges. Often overlooked in land development projects are the remnant wood lots or partial forested areas that occupy a site and surrounding area. With some investigation, many of these wood lots can be identified as remaining parts of a larger forest that provided historic water recharge areas and protected habitat area. Many developments may maintain portions of these wood lots as decorative or buffer elements in the overall master plan design. This applies to wetlands, creek corridors, watersheds, prairies, etc. Other options include:

1   Identify and map the original extent of the historic forest (in a rural and non-manipulated state)
2   Identify and map the original or historic water recharge or discharge areas as well as can be accomplished with historic records
3   Assuming that "restoration" is not feasible, use the existing remnants and the historic ghost print of the forest as a basis for an open space network within proposed development; where the remnant parent may form the basis for an open space pattern for residential development that bridges past and present
4   Assuming that restoration of the historic bio-function of the forest is not feasible, explore a partial reconstruction through bio-fields, new appropriate tree plantings, and other pervious surface treatments within the historic pattern.

Building configurations as remnant bridges. In rural or exurban areas, development pressure can result in the loss of historic building configurations such as small crossroad and road house complexes and farm complexes including houses, barns, and other outbuildings and their clustering patterns. Opportunities for bridging are numerous both in the retention and rejuvenation of buildings and the contextual clustering patterns. Remember: this concept is not about preserving a historic artifact. The intent is to incorporate the remnant into an emerging contemporary pattern with renewed vitality.

Spatial reference systems

Principles:

Spatial reference systems are compositional structures that are used to provide a reference and orientation base to more complex compositions. I call them *ghost or transparent structures* because in many cases they are not visible to the naked eye, underlying or hidden in the larger spatial construct. They are an important foundation for beginning designers in that they enable more complex assemblies to occur within a clear order.

In urban design, spatial patterns are often adopted as policy implemented by others over an extended time-frame. Change comes with the many hands that implement the design framework. Given a firm reference structure or framework, the original, underlying, and organizing urban design principles can withstand incremental changes over time.

For beginning designers, the circle, square, and axis provide the starting points, expanded by the sphere, cube, and channel/ribbon, etc. Remember the early exercises of manipulating the primary shapes:

circle, square, and line. Using a grid, for example, the designer can provide a horizontal matrix for reference and order as an organic and "free-flowing" shape emerges to the eye.

Here are starting structures for spatial reference systems:

- grid
- circle
- grid with circles
- grid with triangles
- grid and axis
- diamond grid.

EX14a: Transparent grid

Tools:

- Construction paper package
- Glue
- Scissors
- Graph paper
  or
- Grid paper with felt-tip pens
- Tracing paper.

Tasks:

1 Playfully craft an organic, curvilinear, or free-flowing vertical plane(s) by overlaying it onto a grid.
2 Locate the curving plane on key intersecting points on the base grid. Remember that the main grid can be broken down into smaller grids to increase the variety of reference points and consequently tighter curves. In this example, the grid is composed of one-inch squares on an 8 x 10-inch base.
3 When the vertical plane is composed, rotate the base to 30/60 and elevate the verticals in an axonometric drawing at numerous points along the plane.
4 Eliminate the underlying grid by tracing over, or if in construction paper, relocate to a clean sheet of paper.

EX14b: Transparent circle

Tools:

See EX14a.

Tasks:

1 Playfully craft a series of right-angle (square components) forms onto a circular ghost structure.
2 Break the circle ghost structure into smaller circles for more variety.

3   Seek a complex composition, creating spaces that relate to one another and the larger pattern.

4   Use a one-inch square grid as a starting point.

5   Graph paper ranging from 8 x 10 inches to 11 x 17 inches.

6   Rotate the plan 30/60 degrees and raise verticals in an axonometric drawing.

7   Eliminate the underlying circle structure by tracing or transferring the paper sculpture to a clean sheet.

EX14c: Three-dimensional transparent matrixes

Principles (matrices and orbs):

The principle of a spatial reference system can be expanded to volumetric applications, either grid or circle components. This method is useful for designers in envisioning ideas in three dimensions, using axonometric drawing, as the designer works from plan to volume and back and forth again. As the plan is changed, the volume changes as well; and the reference system maintains a rational reference structure in place.

Tools:

Variable:

•   Block of modeling clay, scored in grid on all faces
•   Legos or similar toy set using modules
•   Blocks, wood, or plastic
•   Axonometric drawing process (my preference).

The best materials are ones that can be broken down in smaller dimensions than the original grid.

Tasks:

1   Begin with a three-dimensional spatial reference structure, a grid matrix in this example. Carve out a form that is different from the grid (the grid is not obvious in final form) that still relates to the matrix.

2   In this case the matrix is a cube composed of multiple grids, and smaller grids within the larger.

3   This exercise can bring into play a number of the transformational actions discussed earlier: additive, subtractive, dimensional, merging, and bridging.

4   Another variation is to begin with the matrix, establish a base plan concept, and begin to expand the plan in three dimensions.

The grid matrix is a useful tool for beginning designers in that a flexible framework provides a guide for "carving out" a design massing that satisfies both CST program requirements and responds to site and adjacent contextual constraints. The design process is one of experimentation and discovery when working in three dimensions. I work with freehand axonometric drawings over the grid, exploring ways to integrate the emerging design with site challenges.

Typology exercises

Building types are forms and arrangements of buildings that represent organizational relationships of use, density, and intensity. The organizational relationships are relatively constant and their physical assembly can vary according to context and other program determinants. Types can be viewed as principles of organizational relationships with variable forms whereas models are organizational relationships in replicated or repeated forms.

These exercises are designed to assist the non-designer in understanding the importance and utilization of urban design/building types in specific contexts. These types, by their organizational requirements, have an *appropriateness of application* factor; and are context-scale sensitive. That simply means that they cannot be applied everywhere, in any physical situation. For example, if a site in a low-density residential area is allocated for 30 housing units where the units can be accommodated by a low–medium-density design application, two-story attached and detached buildings, a multiple-story building with 30 units may be inappropriate for the site context. I say "may be" as there are always exceptions given a contextual rationale. The numbers may work but the site appropriateness does not work. A double-loaded corridor residential building (flats on each floor arranged along a central corridor for access) works if both exterior lengths, the exterior orientations, have access to light and air. When arranging these types on a site, orientation to a freeway or bluff or blank wall for one side is not appropriate or sound design composition (even if the building "fits").

I have observed planning students arrange land use "blobs" of housing units in situations that are not appropriate either for function or quality of life. They don't understand the types and their organizational relationships (internally and externally).

Templates for design. Again, typologies are only as valid as their integral relationship with the physical context of urban meaning. They are guides, starting points, ingredients in a recipe that form a basis of experimentation, exploration, and hybridization; they are not to be accepted as absolute, nor taken out of context and used as models or copies, a common practice in development and design. Many smaller communities "cut and paste" design guidelines from other communities due to staff shortage and budget shortfalls. These guidelines often include development typologies and result in spatial outcomes such as "dormer-ville" and "generic Bavarian"[1] where borrowed clichés abound and thematic design is a mish-mash of inaccurate fantasies. I chuckle when I remember Professor Pat Goeters (Notre Dame, 1966) telling us students that if one wanted a historic theme, copy it exactly or don't attempt it at all! Of course, he did not even want it copied but the point was well made. Historic themes are models, replicas, historic memories not necessarily suitable for contemporary use; and they may have compositional principles that can be distilled into hybrid typologies, providing bridges from past form patterns to contemporary patterns.[2]

In design, I find templates of typologies to be very useful in exploring site development potential, quickly and accurately. A template is a pattern tool that I use as a starting point. For example, given density and market aspirations for a given site by a client or as part of a community's design guideline testing process, say, 12 units per acre, I draw up a *number of configuration options* on an acre square at a desired scale using building, open space, and parking types that can accommodate the project program (see Figures 8.1 through 8.4). With a number of these templates available, I explore site concepts, testing both the template selections and their fit to the site context. And yes, this can be done digitally and I can do it faster and more effectively by *crafting*, thinking through the process visually with hand, eye, and drawing tools. The drawings are ready and suitable for client meetings. These are simple examples representing many variations.

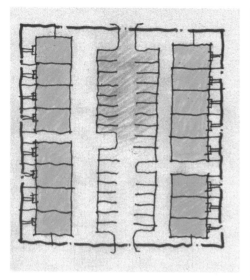

Figure 8.1. Template townhouse acre. *Construct a one-acre or hectare-sized parcel and "fit" the appropriate building, parking, and open space requirements on the site with appropriate typologies as a starting point, particularly for master plan design.*

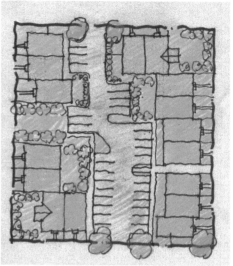

Figure 8.2. Townhouse design from template. *The template provides a starting point for design manipulation of the site program elements, resulting in context-sensitive design concepts.*

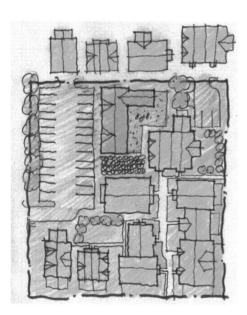

Figure 8.3. Farmstead template. *A mixed-density concept with variable building typologies used as a starting point for context-sensitive design concepts.*

Figure 8.4. Office campus quad template. *There can be many variations of templates based on the program requirements for use, size, site, etc.*

At a given place in the process, as ideas in plan begin to mature or gel, I can even switch to an axonometric template that can be combined with other similarly oriented templates at the same scale and compose more complex development scenarios. The templates begin to change and evolve into hybrids as the design process evolves with additional exploration and meaning–functionality analysis.

EX15a: Courtyard housing (low density)

Intent:

Let us begin simply by using single family detached housing types (bungalow) and arrange them around a courtyard. This is a historic development configuration typology now often referred to as "cottage housing" or courtyard housing. Most building codes will specify the front, side, and rear yard setbacks, commonly 20 feet, 12 feet, and 25 feet respectively. An option you can use here is an eight-foot deep front fenced yard facing a common courtyard, ten-feet side yard setback, and eight-feet rear yard setback to common parking.

Tasks:

1   Set a scale at one inch = 20 feet for an acre site.
2   Assume a 30-feet wide courtyard.
3   Parking spaces are 8 x 18 feet.
4   Access drive is 20 feet in width.
5   Suggestion: make a template on graph paper of at least two different configuration bungalow-type houses, one detached and two attached.
6   Using either construction paper cut-outs or tracing over the templates on graph paper, arrange as many units on site as you can with the required parking.
7   Part of your task is to research the floor plates or footprints of bungalow-type residential buildings.
8   As you do this exercise, ask yourself if you would be content living in your composition.

There are many variations to this compositional exercise. Mix the combinations of attached and detached and feel free to vary setbacks as long as you adhere to the minimum required.

EX15b: Townhouse cluster

Components:

Do the same exercise using townhouses with the following characteristics:

*   units can range from 16 x 28 feet to 24 x 36 feet; suggestion: do two sizes for variety
*   a maximum of four units attached
*   research the characteristics of townhouses
*   prepare templates on graph paper
*   same parking requirements
*   same front yard setbacks
*   be creative on common open space or courtyard
*   one-acre site.

Again, many variations are possible. Remember that the primary orientation on a townhouse (common side walls) is the front façade and side façade for corner or end units.

EX15c: Farmstead cluster (mixed density)

Intent:

Investigate, identify, and apply a variety of residential building types to a specific cluster on a one-acre parcel; anticipated density: 10 to 12 units.

Components:

- one-acre-square parcel
- one multiplex home with single entry, foyer, and five residential units (two units on the first and second floors each and one unit on the third floor)
- two to four single family attached one-story cottages
- two detached single family bungalows
- one shared garage or car port
- individual yards per building
- common shared yard(s) per cluster
- common building or studio.

Tasks:

1   Determine scale of design for 20 x 30-inch paper size maximum.
2   Research and draw templates of building type footprints.
3   Draw templates of parking lot/car port footprints, and/or cut out templates from construction paper, and . . .
4   Play and do not stop at first attempt—build from that first effort!

EX15d: Research office park campus style with housing

Intent:

Investigate, identify, and apply office building typologies to a campus development typology. What is a campus typology? Hint: campus!

Components:

- five-acre-square parcel
- four types of office research buildings to fit
- clustered shared parking areas, one space per 1,100 square feet of office space
- parking spaces are 8 x 18 feet
- access drives are 25 feet wide

- open space
- shared for entire complex
- shared for complex segments
- other housing
- garden stacked flat units in four-story buildings; dense configuration associated with 50 percent of office buildings; a mixture of townhouses is permissible
- north arrow and graphic scale
- scale to fit 20 x 30 board maximum.

Tasks:

1   Research and draw at least two different office building typology footprints; remember that the structural bays of the buildings are key characteristics and are flexible as a grid structure.
2   Use the campus quadrangle-type open space as a structuring and organizing form.
3   Composition wants to be dense and urban.

EX15e: High-rise office complex

Intent:

Investigate various types of high-rise office buildings and the plaza or open space relationships at ground level; prepare a site plan of four towers in a design relationship.

Components:

- four high-rise buildings, at least three with different heights and footprints based on your office building type investigations; heights are not critical to exercise
- plaza open space components associated with each building
- assume underground parking and two access points (ramps)
- reflect some street pattern with downtown core street widths
- historic church with 20-feet front yard setback is across the street at northeast corner
- existing six-story office building with zero setback across street to north for full length of block
- townhouse complex along west block with units facing the street
- vacant land to south earmarked for civic complex with outdoor event space along the street side
- consider views and light orientation for each building
- show north arrow and graphic scale
- suggested block size: 330 x 660
- scale to fit no larger than 18 x 24 base.

Tasks:

1   Research and draw templates for office building types, again focusing on the structural bays.
2   Be aware of how each building relates to the others (views, light).
3   Be aware of how each building relates to off-site conditions.

4   Important: this exercise requires a design composition that responds to both on-site conditions and off-site contextual influences.

5   Play in either construction paper/tag board mode or axonometric drawings.

EX15f: Ceremonial center/civic center

Intent:

Have fun and experiment as this has many interpretations and variations. The intent is to enable you to loosen up and play with a larger-scale, more formal composition.

Components:

- circular event hall with 20,000 seat capacity
- demarcation (high rent or prominent) office complex
- landscape forms for large-scale public events
- landscape elements (used to define space as opposed to occupying space as decoration)
- exhibition hall(s)
- entertainment/food complex
- strong pedestrian movement patterns
- elevated tramway
- parking facilities/structures
- housing is an option not required
- other as you see fit
- large site, essentially a four-block urban scale with each block at approximately 300 x 300 with streets in a 60-foot-wide row.
- scale to fit on a 24 x 30 board maximum.

Tasks:

1   Research and draw templates of the various components.

2   Review professional design magazines for examples of the building types to familiarize yourself with their size and functions.

3   Do some fieldwork to visit similar building types in your area.

4   What compositional structures can organize and assemble the many pieces of this puzzle?

5   Use construction paper cut-outs or templates and axonometric drawings to study the ideas.

6   Complete a rough draft, view and assess the composition, and ask yourself in what ways it can be improved.

Increasing complexity: urban design projects

This section provides examples of real-site projects for end of quarter/semester group work. As time is a factor, with possibly two to three weeks to complete their work, I have students join together to construct a three-dimensional study model with corrugated cardboard or chipboard. Students cut out physical program elements (housing, commercial, etc.) by building type. Each student is asked to prepare ahead of time a number of design strategies. In class, students use the cut-outs to *play* on the model with various compositions that meet program criteria. As each student assembles and discusses his or her concept(s), the model is photographed for further analysis. Other students are urged to participate with constructive comments regarding each construction.

The following examples can be used as guides for design composition exercises. Most of these projects are completed as a part of the composition course and not a design studio where more time is available for a more complete design.

EX16: Kitsap Mall infill design

Background and intent:

Kitsap Mall is a regional shopping mall in an unincorporated portion of Kitsap County, north of Bremerton, Washington on the Kitsap Peninsula in Puget Sound, west of Seattle. The mall is surrounded by a composite of smaller shopping malls and plazas in super-block formations all served by wide boulevards; it is not pedestrian friendly.

Typical for many regional shopping malls, the complex is an enclosed concourse typology with large anchor stores, such as department stores, at key locations. Large parking areas surround the building complex on all sides with minimal peripheral development. The complex is a single-use development (commercial retail) under four separate ownerships.

Tasks:

1   *Background materials:* as a team, assemble base maps and other general site information.
2   *Space-use program:* prepare a space-use program (what, how much, and generalized organizational relationships) prior to beginning the design process. Students can act as a team for the program definition.
3   *Model:* working as a team, decide on a base scale; construct a three-dimensional cardboard study model for everyone's use, including the key buildings to remain and perimeter off-site buildings, not to exceed a 36 x 48 inches overall base size, if possible (4 x 6 feet maximum). Use corrugated cardboard for background or context buildings. Exaggerating building heights is permitted within reason (improves photographic record and shadow effects from floodlights). When doing the base model, an option is to make a print of the base map and glue the print to the cardboard base with liquid adhesive. Use the base to locate and size buildings; roads are provided on the print.
    a   In this example, for time efficiency, the mall building model was constructed without a roof and highlighted all interior pedestrian concourses, courtyards, and entries.
    b   All pedestrian areas are displaced as orange tag-board or alternative with small grid drawn on the tag-board for major courtyards and gathering areas.
    c   Natural or planted areas are in green paper.
4   *Building components:* building components identified by the team as major additives:
    a   retail shops
    b   department stores (existing)
    c   office buildings: 400,000 square feet, two to eight stories in height (85 feet maximum)

d   performance theater

e   library: 40,000 square feet

f   new restaurants and entertainment facilities

g   residential population to be determined with units arranged in both separate and related "neighborhood hamlets" as a part of the mixed use of the larger complex; residential buildings can include:

      i   townhouses and townhouses over flats

      ii   garden units (common entry lobby)

      iii   double-loaded corridor with parking underneath

      iv   tower with lobby and central core

h   parking areas

      i   surface lots

      ii   parking decks

i   interior site transit stop locations

j   clearly defined pedestrian and bicycle routes

      i   major open space features and recreational facilities including passive and active areas such as: basketball courts, tennis courts, athletic club with enclosed swimming pool, dog run-area, passive parks, and festival spaces

k   a major semi-public open space to be located at the southern site area

l   mall concourse is to be connected to major arterials

      i   mall complex must remain with some manipulation thus the reason for showing existing concourse and building masses

      ii   if you have a good argument for adding anything else, make it.

5   *Products:* students provide the following: digital images of final design concepts; a written assessment for each scheme describing main compositional concepts and design principles; a massing perspective traced from the aerial oblique images of the concept models.

Project examples sequence

The following images provide a brief view of a progressive sequence in compositional design for students of planning and urban design. Not all exercises are illustrated as I encourage readers to explore and play on their own initiative without being influenced by other student examples. This sequence represents student work ranging from basic shape and volume manipulation to advanced studio applications based on the compositional studies. The following examples include student work from both the Kitsap Mall and Seattle Viaduct: Uncovering Seattle studios.

The exercises are constantly being upgraded and altered as students explore and question the process. The sequence of exercises assists students with little or no design background education in accessing and engaging the urban design process, melding meaning and functionality with compositional order.

Many students contributed work for the book and a few examples are provided. I am acknowledging a few among many who helped expand and test the learning sequence in design composition.

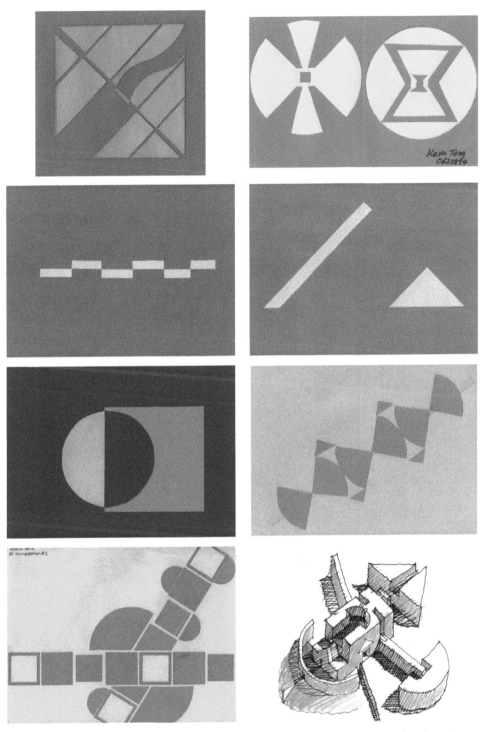

Figures 8.5–8.18. *The sequence of images provides a brief example of the learning process from basic shape and volume identification and manipulation to advanced culture/space/time program modeling to advanced urban compositional order in complex contexts.*

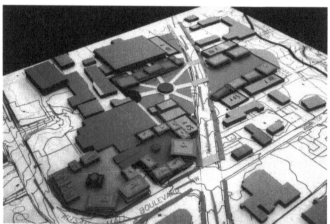

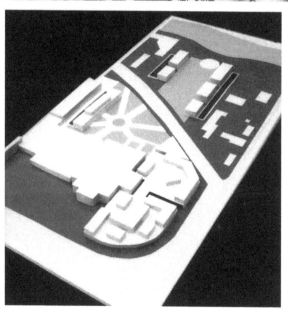

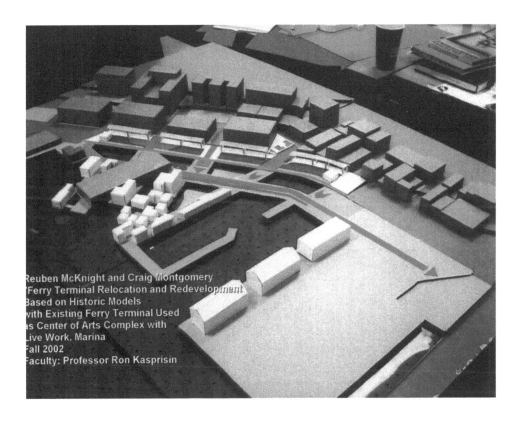

Reuben McKnight and Craig Montgomery
Ferry Terminal Relocation and Redevelopment
Based on Historic Models
with Existing Ferry Terminal Used
as Center of Arts Complex with
Live Work, Marina
Fall 2002
Faculty: Professor Ron Kasprisin

A HOME ON A HILL

Housing joins the
Pike Place Market + Seattle Aquarium

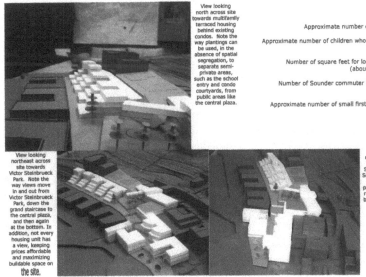

View looking north across site towards multifamily terraced housing behind existing condos. Note the way plantings can be used, in the absence of spatial segregation, to separate semi-private areas, such as the school entry and condo courtyards, from public areas like the central plaza.

View looking northeast across site towards Victor Steinbrueck Park. Note the way views move in and out from Victor Steinbrueck Park, down the grand staircase to the central plaza, and then again at the bottom. In addition, not every housing unit has a view, keeping prices affordable and maximizing buildable space on the site.

VITAL STATISTICS

Approximate number of housing units on site: 300 units

Approximate number of children who could attend the school: 500-800 children

Number of square feet for local grocery: 15,000-20,000 sq. ft. (about the size of a Trader Joes Market)

Number of Sounder commuter trains stopping at station per day: 10,000-14,000 daily trips

Approximate number of small first floor retail spaces: 15-20 spaces

View looking north across site towards Victor Steinbrueck Park. Southern exposure is maximized, particularly for the row houses in the bottom right hand corner.

DETAILS

181

A Walk Through History
Discovering Seattle's Natural and Human Past

Transformation of the
Natural Landscape

The right-hand side of this perspective photo tells Seattle's natural history. The higher terrain is lush with native vegetation and evergreens. Descending from the trees to the water represents the advancement of time. The terrain is transformed -- the hills are logged and the terrain is sluffed into Elliott Bay (represented here by the rocks).

Prior to being filled with Denny Hill soil and city refuse, Seattle's Elliott Bay waterfront was largely mud flats and tidal pools. *A Walk Through History* recommends restoring part of the waterfront to its native state, as shown in the below perspective.

During the first decades of the twentieth century, new settlers to Seattle undertook a mammoth construction project known as the Denny Regrade. One of Seattle's many hills, Denny Hill, was effectively hosed-down and washed into Elliott Bay.

The hillocks in the above perspective mimic the Denny Regrade mounds seen in the photo. These hillocks were the intermediary phase of "construction".

Notes

1   In 1986, KPD prepared a "Phase II Waterfront and Downtown Plan" for Poulsbo, WA in Puget Sound, west of Seattle. The community previously adopted a "Norwegian" theme for downtown façades. Very little if any semblance of Norwegian architectural character or details were present in the thematic adaptation to Poulsbo. In a public meeting and in sketches and diagrams, I offered examples of Bergen, Norway as a guide for new façade treatments if that is what the community truly desired. Those suggestions were not implemented and the continuing result is what I refer to as "generic Bavarian," a compilation of undocumented non-historic clichés.

2   I, like other designers (Arendt, 1994), have experimented with rural development typologies that cluster residential development and conserve significant portions of the landscape without using conventional suburban cluster typologies (parking in the middle surrounded by one or perhaps two residential types at most). Principles of historic farmsteads, as illustrated in the graphic above, can have use in contemporary design as new hybrids: clusters of diverse housing types around common open space, shared parking, shared outbuildings and private space for each residence. Subsequently, the historic dairy farm model becomes a new and relevant rural cluster typology.

Bibliography

Arendt, Randall, 1994: *Rural By Design: Maintaining Small Town Character.* American Planning Association, Chicago, IL.

Ching, Francis D.K., 1979: *Architecture: Form, Space and Order.* Van Nostrand Reinhold, New York.

Goldstein, Nathan, 1989: *Design and Composition.* Prentice Hall, Inc., Englewood Cliffs, NJ.

Johnston, Charles MD, 1984/1986: *The Creative Imperative.* Celestial Arts, Berkeley, CA.

Johnston, Charles MD, 1991: *Necessary Wisdom.* Celestial Arts, Berkeley, CA.

Webb, Frank, 1990: *Webb on Watercolor.* North Light Books, Cincinnati, OH.

Chapter 9

THEORETICAL CONSIDERATIONS

The composition of complexity

This chapter provides a base for the rationale of design—identifying and telling the story rather than applying set typologies that may not be appropriate for the specific context. Hence the reference to *creative urbanism*. I am not trying to start a new movement in design, merely to explore and expand the many factors of urban life or urban meaning that are critical to and influence design process, methodologies, and outcomes. Essentially, I am exploring new methodologies to deal with the complexities of urban meaning and functionality as they are formed by the interaction of culture, space, and time. This part is a discussion, a dialogue of directions and relationships I have seen emerging over the last 42 years of practice and 21 years of teaching in urban design. I believe strongly in the need to experiment with new methods in order to address the complexity of urban reality.

Theory is a set of well-developed concepts related through statements or expressions of relationship, which together constitute an integrated framework that can be used to explain or predict phenomena (Strauss and Corbin, 1998, p. 15). These *concepts* are generalized ideas or abstract notions, not formulae, and are therefore *speculative* based on conclusions resulting from observations of unusual or emerging occurrences in communities and their larger civilizations. Theory provides the practice of urban design with principles and statements of relationships that guide process and outcome. They are not absolute and are functions of the workings of civilizations, their arts, science, and philosophies. And they are constantly changing.

Theory is only as good as its application to reality and does not exist in an academic vacuum. Theory evolves from the dynamics of the multiple dimensions of reality, responding to emerging patterns, and in turn is altered and changed by those patterns as they mature. Urban design provides a set of tests as physical constructs within those patterns and their community contexts. Urban design also requires caution regarding new and populist yet potentially vague notions such as green design and sustainable design. If these and other similar terms are used separately from an ecological process, I argue they are disjointed and misleading.

This chapter explores principles that I have experimented with in practice and in academia that follow from patterns emerging from the day-to-day experiences of Pacific Northwest, Alaskan, and Canadian communities in relation to design issues. These patterns emanate from the larger actions of society, including art and science, and can be translated into guides for experimentation in urban design (and the process of public involvement in planning and design: see Appendix II). The theory discussed here is a foundation for experimentation, not a manifesto. The creativity of the researcher/designer is an essential ingredient to the process (Sandelowski, 1995). And along with that creativity is *fear,* a necessary ingredient in creativity, and overcoming fear in a creative process is a part of the larger design procedure (Webb, 1990).

There are many starting points for this theoretical dialogue. I begin with a skeleton framework of terms and ideas that are later woven together in a series of design principles and suggested methodologies.

Uncertainty in complexity

As a designer, I am influenced by ecologically based principles and an interdisciplinary approach to the living systems within community. Eco-design can only emanate from an eco-process, not one that simply comprises eco-hardware or eco-products. That process by the very interactive nature of living systems is characterized by an uncertainty in outcome. Embracing this uncertainty is a beginning step in a community design process.

Grounded theory

Grounded theory is based on (qualitative) observation more than on deduction; where the theory, by procedure, is allowed to emerge from the data, forming realities not before envisioned. "Qualitative evaluation inquiry draws on both the critical and creative thinking—both the science and the art of analysis" (Patton, 1990, p. 434). We shall see this established and reinforced in the writings of Fritjof Capra (1982), Charles Johnston (1984/1986), Edward Soja (1996), and others referred to in this chapter. Critical to our journey is emergence of form and composition from an exploration of the complexities of urban meaning and functionality, striving to set aside the tendency to compromise and predetermine outcomes.

Principles of uncertainty

Grounded theory and its procedures also lead us to what I refer to as the *principles of uncertainty*, a key starting point for (urban) design and the politics of design. Principles include:

* having aspirations without goals (ends that one strives to attain (*Webster's Dictionary*, 1975))
* being open to multiple possibilities, including polarities or the significant differences between and among possibilities as a way to establish the relevant container for dialogue and/or design
* generating a list of options as probabilities, not outcomes
* experimenting with diverse and multiple paths of design expression such as art, music, and sculpture to stimulate thinking
* exploring nonlinear forms of thinking using multi-layered parts and polarities analysis, non-compromise testing, and cliché circumvention
* keeping the process healthy (maintaining the integrity of the dynamic energy of the process—keeping it fresh and vital)
* expanding methodology to deal with complexity—not reducing methodology for ease of application
* engaging in *play*!
* a journey without goals as the awareness of a design that *does not exist* prior to the creative process
* there are many answers—(there is no "one," there is no 50/50 as in goal planning).

The complexity matrix (CST)

Design context or reality: CST and the n-dimensional matrix
This is a big concept and for our purposes I define it as the basic context and essence of community/ civilization that can be described as a relational trialectic of *culture, space, and time (history)* referred to

in this book as the CST matrix (Soja, 1996). The trialectic expands to complex dimensions contained in an n-dimensional matrix (Kaku, 1994) with multiple smaller realities or systems, each with elements and principles manifesting CST in relational emergent patterns. The bottom line: reality may have dozens of dimensions in addition to x, y, z, t all reflected or masked in the complexity of community. We cannot address them all and we need to forge new methods to be aware of their existence in order to improve our interdisciplinary design efforts.

Let us explore the concept of the n-dimensional matrix, a concept in physics expressed by Kaku that pushes our concepts of reality and urban meaning beyond known space. This matrix is not concentric and responds to and simultaneously changes context.

Context is not synonymous with background or setting as in a stage set. Context is a keyword in contemporary planning and design and is misused constantly. The State and Provincial Highway departments use "context-sensitive" design to express an emerging appreciation for the surrounding community's complexity, a positive sign. Redefining context in urban design (and related engineering components) begins our journey to develop more capable methods for composing urban form in complex situations. Context is reality; and reality again is expressed as a trialectic of culture, space, and time. In culture are the key disciplines of physics, biology, and others in an ecological interdisciplinary relationship.

Culture

Culture is the core of the CST trialectic, representing the patterned behavior of peoples over time in space. Culture can be established or traditional, transitional, emergent as in Soja's focus on Los Angeles (1996 and 2000). The needs, demands, characteristics, and expressions of culture all contribute to a complexity of context that cannot be ignored or bottom-lined. Simple methods are no longer sufficient to deal with this complexity. And since *design* is a function of culture, it needs to change and adjust as culture changes. Design remains the making of composition where product decisions are required. This process is both personal and public/private and results in incremental contributions to changes in reality. This is not about diminishing the designer's role but greatly expanding the complexity and responsibility of that role.

Principle: reality is fundamentally creative, reorganizing and restructuring itself based on the interactions of these formative forces of culture, space, and time; as a function of the physical world, it will do whatever is necessary to survive.

Principle: reality comprises nested and related containers or cells of CST interactions both coherent for periods of time and changing over time (as in the matrix).

Principle: structural changes in a living system such as community and neighborhoods occur from within not from without; they are influenced by external influences.

Principle: reality is analyzed in terms of interdependent parts or smaller systems—not independent pieces. Again, the trialectic of CST—culture, space, and time (history)—are interconnected both locally and non-locally.

Principle: individual events in a community do not always have a well-defined cause as they may be influenced by non-local causes interacting with local processes.

Space

Space is the emerging, pausing, and receding outcome or physical manifestation of cultural–contextual interactions in time. Space is more than a container or enclosure for human behavior—imprinted by culture-in-context and reflecting that culture-context in turn.

Space is sometimes accidental, expedient, and intentional or designed, characterized by physical elements such as shapes and volumes that are activated by principles of organization and assembly. At some point in time, space results from a creative system: manufactured, delivered, and assembled. Space is real, not abstract, and consists of *perceived space* (through the senses and accustomed spatial practice), *conceived space* as a representation of space (design), and *lived space*. And *thirdspace* can be found in the margins (Soja, 1996).

Space as *place* is an assembled metaphor for urban meaning and functionality in real, often raw, contexts. The metaphors range from compromised space to meaningful *place*—from spaces of dominance and power to those on the periphery and at times resistant to the dominant spaces. To forge meaningful metaphors requires a discovery process of the creative capacity of community interpreted through design.

Principle: every human action has a spatial outcome and manifestation.

This seems obvious and is often overlooked in planning analysis. Reflect upon your daily actions and record the spatial environs or influences related to those actions.

Principle: space emerges in a built or impacted form, pauses, and recedes into obsolescence or obscurity.

Space is an emergent phenomenon as the human actions (and those of related life forms) generate and manipulate the spatial environment, from the ant hill to the skyscraper and gated community. All spatial compositions are held accountable to the reality of physics and biology: they grow, pause, or sustain for a brief time, and degrade, collapse, and reconfigure. Space is emergent with the polarity of descendant.

Principle: space as outcome is uncertain even though intended.

Space as intentional construct is affected by the act of making and the act of being a part of reality or context. Context absorbs and interacts with the intentional space and changes the space in both qualitative and quantitative ways.

Principle: space has three critical phases—being made as physical composition, being tested in and by reality or context, and being changed by that testing: thus the uncertainty.

Assuming that a design is complete when constructed and made a part of the urban form can be shortsighted and misleading. Nothing remains the same, as context or reality is encountered.

Principle: space is influenced by location in the matrix:

- center: stable, static
- periphery: less stable, resistant, dynamic
- adjacent: in tension or agreement
- remote: detached or disengaged
- nearby: associative.

The CST matrix of community affects the nature of space and the dynamics or capacity of that space to be creative. In the social districts or containers of urban community, the established centers are stable and dominant. They are static and lacking in an ability to change and be creative relevant to society. "Space is fundamental in every exercise of power" (Soja, 1996)—from land use to design standards to zoning. And the power is often at the center—dominant. The interaction of cells or parts within the CST matrix is influenced by the intensity of interaction among parts as they emanate away from the center. Various relationships exist, with levels of intensity of interaction ranging from analogous compatibility to tension to contrast and conflict. The further out toward the periphery, the more internal demand for change and the more creative the forces for change.

Principle: space has meta-dimensions—unknown and uncertain contributions.

Returning to Kaku, the n-dimensional matrix of reality reminds us that all influences and forces upon the design-context are not known. Recognizing the larger dimensions and their unknown nature can prepare us for uncertain actions and events. This is not an abstract concept, as every relationship and interaction in community manifests outcomes not anticipated or predictable. We can identify probabilities as we go through the emergent composition-making and testing process. Nothing more and nothing less.

Principle: individual events in a community do not always have a well-defined cause as they may be influenced by non-local causes interacting with local processes.

Structural change occurs from within systems. And, the (human and community) systems are a part of a much larger system, ranging from adequate community context, to regional context, to planetary-biosphere, to universal. Respect for the larger dimensions of the n-dimensional matrix can be both humbling and informative.

This is a perspective emanating from practice and academia, from practical problem-solving to reflection and introspection. These principles require the designer to separate process from goals and predictive methodologies. These principles require an exploration process that is interdisciplinary, uncertain with paths of discovery—pursuing non-predictive outcomes, outcomes that do not exist until they emerge from the creative process. They all require an organized and structured composition—rational not regimented.

Consequently, space is inherent in culture and time, carrying meaning and function in a coherent pattern, and changing and being manipulated by the forces of culture and time. New patterns emerge, remnant patterns linger, requiring connections or bridging devices to the future.

Time

Time is a measurement of reality that contains moments of occurrence and event periods or periodicities that frame human actions. As an ever-changing measurement, time frames the emergence, pausing, and receding of all human actions. This creates and erases spatial patterns in the changing landscape. Form takes material in the making process and releases that material in its breakdown, all within an event period. The design of cities consists of time-relative statements of space–culture relationships, organizing and structuring realities.

Principle: history is knowledge expressed by artifacts and spatial patterns.

Past events are expressed in elements and patterns left over in the built form. They have physical presence and may or may not have current relevance. They can be preserved as physical monument, as cultural reminder or celebration, or incorporated into an emergent new pattern with new meaning and function.

Principle: current time represents emergent not static spatial patterns.

All current time events are emergent, pausing and descendant. The pausing state is a short-lived period of alignment and coherence soon to be affected by the interactions of context. The point is that all (spatial) relationships based on their CST matrix are in flux.

Principle: future time is uncertain, containing probabilities not predictions, goals, or guarantees.

Nested realities

Nested realities are the parts of a community that have sufficient creative capacities to survive on a given scale, not capable of being broken down further unless into unrelated pieces; understanding that they are again connected to and incorporated into larger parts. They can be referred to as "containers," "watersheds," "minor systems," "adequate contexts," "formative processes," and others. I will use "living parts" and "nested realities" to refer to these within the CST or n-dimensional matrix.

Principle: nested realities are ongoing community systems that exhibit actions of creative self-organization and self-structure. The designer is an integral part of, and translator and interpreter within, this self-forming process.

Creative capacity

Creative capacity consists of the resources and energy level within a community or living part necessary for that community to effect change (from within).

- Major structural changes for most living parts or communities occur from within, not from exterior forces, depending on the level of creative capacity for success.
- Physical symptoms of decay or decline in communities such as vacant or dilapidated buildings, increases in crime, etc. can be indicators for a decline in the community's ability to creatively redefine and reinvent itself.

Principle: components of reality do seek consistency with one another and with themselves. Reality is creative and will do what is necessary to survive. And reality is an n-dimensional matrix of interactive parts and as such requires an overall consistency of the various parts in order to have a structure. Communities undergo a process of self-maintenance that can be identified and reinforced or strengthened. Most healthy communities have a large number of options for interacting with their environment and produce feedback mechanisms, positive and negative, to indicate the quality of that health. Observing the amplification of certain deviations in the community is a feedback mechanism. For example, the emergence of the big-box retail outlets was an amplification of the shopping center patterns, deviating from the conventional shopping mall in both marketing strategy and spatial construct (warehouse). Another classic example involving shopping centers and the self-organizing nature of communities (positive and negative) is the small American town that zone land along the highway for commercial/shopping center/big-box uses, and then stress about the decline of the historic downtown miles away from the highway. Pushing one or more of the variables of the system to their extreme values creates stress on one or more parts, and facilitates adaptation in others. However, from a larger view, the fluctuations causing the stress are indeed outside influences and can stimulate the community and its historic downtown to adapt, change, and be creative. The community leaders had other options for making positive changes from within given a larger view.

Polarities

Each reality or living part of community has boundaries. These are hard and soft (i.e., established and entrenched or solid) or boundaries that are emergent, receding, porous, fragile, etc. Key aspects of such boundaries, as evident in the hard/soft metaphor, are their polarities—the opposite extremes of a reality as defined by the CST interrelationships. A color wheel is an example of a relationship among three primary entities and the opposites they create within the wheel. Pick one color, a primary or a secondary: blue, for example. What remain of the triad primaries, yellow plus red, establish the opposite color—orange. Yellow to purple and red to green. Polarities occur within physical characteristics (light to dark) and within cultures (politics of the left and right). As we pursue design methods in complex realities, these polarities offer an array of design explorations. Bridging these polarities in design is discussed later in the chapter.

Polarities exist within every human action and dialogue and are consequently a part of the design process. Any meeting of a group of people can be represented by the polarities found in the extreme viewpoints in the group. They can be minor contrasts and in serious conflict. As people discuss wants and needs within the urban meaning and functionality matrix, divergent and opposing views and spatial notions of those needs emerge.

Design and complexity

Creativity

Creativity is an exploratory process and methodology, borne of a crafting process that is both process and product in concert. Creativity has a beginning, a middle, an end, and a beginning.

- Characteristics of creativity are passion, motivation, fear, awareness:
  - Creativity as process is both linear and cyclical.
  - Creativity as product is both real and incremental, emergent and receding.
  - Creativity is conceived, developed, placed in context, tested by and through context, changed as a result, then "completed" yet emergent and receding.
  - A major function of urban design is to perform an "architectural/urban design test" within a crafting process relative to a real context.
- Creativity is a dialogue that explores "known space" in order to reach and change the boundaries of that space, entering and defining new emergent spaces in a community.
- Creativity is non-compromising:
  - Creativity resists "oneness" where all ideas and options are compressed into one solution or idea.
  - Creativity resists "separation" where conflicting ideas or polarities are encased as separate entities.
  - Creativity resists "blending" or 50/50 resolutions where one half of each position is combined and the other halves are discounted.
  - Creativity thrives in non-goal driven processes.
- Creativity is non-idealistic, where ideals are predetermined outcomes that can have a role in testing innovation.
- Creativity is a meta-determinant where the outcome is uncertain and based in the process.
- Creativity is coherent where it does not ignore what works, and what can be carried forward.

For the designer, creative capacity goes beyond drawing well, making attractive compositions, designing proportional buildings—these are necessary competencies to explore known space and not necessarily creative actions.

Perception of reality through design

Our comprehension of reality is affected by the reality of sensory experience and the media of its representation (Arnheim, 1969). The media of representation relies on:

- perceptual concepts
- intellectual concepts
- where visual media are more perceptual

- where verbal media are more intellectual
- both are needed in the comprehension.

Perception

Perception involves the imposition (placing within the mind) of a network of concepts (basic patterns) derived from sensory raw material (observed and recorded through the senses).

Concepts

Concepts are "congealed generalities" (Arnheim, 1969) or semi-abstract patterns whose nature depends on the media generating them. See also *Representations of Place* (Bosselman, 1998).

Design concepts lead to the building or constructing of a story, a spatial metaphor, by deriving a composition of organized shapes, values, and colors with various patterns organized into structural relationships, as well as producing a sense of a story by using a spatial vocabulary with textual descriptions that evoke mental images. Transforming concepts into spatial stories is an act of cognition that combines the complexities of perceived reality (substance) and the conceptual structure of media (form). The conceptual stage is the early cognitive process of reference and orientation, and conceptualizes significant items and builds from them.

In this book, the crafting process is held in high esteem as a path to evolving the spatial story. Non-objective visual art or ornament or the precision of technical imagery risks losing their relevance to what we can see and touch and therefore conceptualize as design patterns. The intricacy of detailed argumentation or a narrative account (including hard data from computers) may lose its structure of guiding forces and thereby interfere with its intelligibility. Remember: verbal expressions are sequential, logical trains of thought. Spatial expressions are more simultaneous, reluctant sequential translations (Arnheim, 1969).

An overview approach

Years ago in a painting workshop with Eric Weigardt, AWS, after having taught watercolor painting for ten years, I frustratedly told him that I had a crisis of approach. Being knowledgeable about the many ways to approach watercolor painting I now found myself at a point of indecision: where to start, what sequence or strategy to use? My knowledge was getting in the way of my playful process. Eric's answer to me was simple: begin where you are most comfortable at the time and proceed outward. Needless to say, his advice worked.

Approaching the composition of complexity from the perspective of urban design is in many ways similar to the frustration noted above. The approach I am comfortable with is finding an area and scale where I can begin engaging the multiplicity of methods and ideas in a workable container or nested reality. Consequently, the following overview is just that, not a menu or linear instruction booklet, but design actions in a workable sequence (that can be altered and hybridized)—a strategy.

Context for overview

Community context as culture, space, and time. Starting points:

- Recognize the emerging questions and issues within the community context.
- Identify a general context of urban meaning, which I refer to as an adequate context within a larger influencing context; i.e. the creek shed within the larger watershed, both active living parts

nested within one another. The adequate context is based on an analysis of short to intermediate influencing CST factors.

Parts/CST analysis

- Construct a "parts analysis" (Johnston, 1984/1986) for the adequate context that specifies the CST matrix through field analysis, interactive public involvement processes, and other interdisciplinary input. This includes:
    - identifying the cultural (social, economic, political) components of the context
    - describing the spatial characteristics or manifestations and outcomes associated with those components
    - identifying the historic patterns leading up to these manifestations and the time periods associated with their present existence (the CST matrix begins to expand).

Principle: "parts" = creative patterning, principles of creative organization.

Principle: every perception of pattern is a perception of order—look for patterns and interlocking patterns in complex structures.

Polarities analysis

- Identify the polarities (usually sets of . . .) within the adequate context to establish temporary boundaries for manageable analysis; imagine a group of neighborhood people engaged in a discussion on a community vision: following observation and interview methods, the two most opposing viewpoints can be identified (remodel the old school for a community hall, versus tear it down for a new basketball arena), polarities for smaller viewpoint clusters (use the school as a senior center versus a teen billiards hall)—the color wheel of at least three polarity sets (red/green, blue/orange, yellow/purple).
- Measure the tension within the group and the range of difference among the participants.
- Identify the critical positions and principles of each polarity.

Bridging polarities

- Bridge those polarities with a compromise test—identifying "oneness," "separatist," and "50/50" resolution fallacies:
    - There is no "one" answer to any challenge, integration is not oneness.
    - Separating components avoids integration.
    - 50/50 asks each to give up critical parts.
- Explore through dialogue and design testing the options and alternative directions available within the polarities.
- Interlocking polarities? Without compromise?
- Merging essences of polarities?
- Remnants as bridges from past to present/future.
- Seeking thirdspace.

Principle: form is associated with the process of interactive opposites or polarities fluctuating through maximum and minimum values in community.

Principle: constructive and deconstructive notions and concepts are existent in every polarity, providing clues as to the emergent patterns of the meaning and functionality of community.

Principle: the polarities in the emergent patterns of community, coherent and conflictive program elements, and principles necessary for adequate design testing processes.

Seeking thirdspace

- Seek a third and distinctly different outcome that moves the dialogue beyond the initially held polarities to encompass key elements of each pole with minimum compromise—thirdspace (Soja, 1996).[1]

The thirdspace notion initially seems abstract and unattainable and cannot be determined prematurely nor through a goal-driven process. Thirdspace as design emerges from the larger creative process, not as a solution embedded in the process but as a new reality emanating from the workings of process, which in design is the crafting process.

How does the designer make form with these abstractions?

Seeking thirdspace in design through design

As designers, we are educated and trained to make things. Our task is to translate ideas and notions into physical spatial constructs, spatial metaphors, translations of urban meaning and functionality. As we engage with more complexity in our pursuit of urban meaning, the design potential and creative capacitance are expanded, not reduced or limited. Here are some initial principles for investigation in design.

Principle: form is an overall indicator and translator of the vigorous change within communities resulting from underlying or inherent interactions within the CST trialectic.

Principle: all properties of community (CST) are understood by the designer as principles closely related to the methods of observation—that basic structures of the spatial reality are determined by the way we look at the world—that the patterns of the community are reflections of patterns of our (designer) minds.

This startles some of my students! The principle represents a caution as to the power of design (and its misuse). We have a responsibility in our observation of reality to strip away as many clichés, styles, ideals, and conventions as possible as we engage the design process. This is not easy or perfect and is a sobering benchmark for integrity in the observation and documentation of context. This is recognition that we are an integral part of every design–investigative process.

Principle: buildings and other physical elements of the city are vigorous patterns of activity which have a spatial aspect, a time aspect (beginning and ending), and a cultural (use) aspect that all contribute to the emergent and receding vigor of those building elements.

If we set up a camera in front of a public space (buildings and courtyard, for example) and record (observe) the change to that space from use, weather, material aging, etc. the *building as living entity in the larger pattern* becomes evident. It appears as object in space with mass and style. And yet, there are product-processes defining space, changing space, being changed by that space and inseparable from it.

Principle: spatial elements in composition and their activities cannot be separated and are simply different aspects of the same space-time context.

Conflict (or the positive use of polarities)

Sergei Eisenstein (*Film Form*, 1949), pursued a dialectic (logical argumentation) approach to design (film form, in his case). His approach within the framework of this book and the thirdspace approach of Soja and others maintains its strength and application. In his words,

The projection of the dialectic system of things into the brain, into creating abstractly, into the process of thinking, yields: dialectic methods of thinking; dialectic materialism—Philosophy.

The projection of the same system of things while creating concretely, while giving form, yields: Art.

The foundation for this philosophy is a dynamic concept of things:

Being—as a constant evolution from the interaction of two contradictory opposites.

Synthesis—arising from the opposition of thesis and antithesis.

. . . In the realm of art this dialectic principle of dynamics is embodied in

CONFLICT

As the fundamental principle for the existence of every art-work and art-form.

For art is always conflict:

1   According to its social mission because it is art's task to make manifest the contradictions of Being (to form equitable views by stirring up contradictions within the spectator's mind, and to forge accurate intellectual concepts from the dynamic clash of opposing passions).

2   According to its nature because its nature is a conflict between natural existence and creative tendency. Between organic inertia and purposeful initiative.

3   According to its methodology.

(Eisenstein, 1949, pp. 45–48).

I was struck and energized by Eisenstein's writings when I was in architecture school in 1966. That energy continues to this day as I fold into these thoughts the concepts of polarities in community and its design. Polarities, as two contrary qualities or powers, define the extents of urban meaning; they form the containers for the ongoing contrasts and conflicts in community, some benign and others significantly contentious. Art and design benefit from recognition and engagement with this polarity in the methods of design. That is what we are exploring in the composition of complexity.

Bringing design and complexity together

Again, design is a process of uncertainty, exploration, discovery, play, a rational interpretation of meaning and functionality. Design explores this complexity and makes and influences form and compositional decisions in our human settlements.

Design is to make things (for people and the planet)—not simply a topic to talk about "what ifs . . .".

A framework for continuing dialogue: the composition of complexity

Consider the following framework for integrating design and complexity:

Contextual CST matrix identification and assessment

Through planning and urban studies and established methodologies, the CST matrix is defined and analyzed: identifying relationships between and among the bio-physical, cultural, historic aspects of community. Within this analysis relationships and patterns are identified in spatial terms with spatial diagrams as:

- historic patterns remaining in or having significant imprint on the spatial/cultural landscape
- remnant potential patterns that have existing spatial components in the built form
- coherent and ongoing patterns that continue to function and meet current and possible meaning and functionality requirements
- emergent cultural/spatial patterns as hybrids, uncertain and/or unusual phenomena.

Current CST: "parts" analysis in the adequate context
This phase results in a "parts" analysis of cultural/spatial relationships within an adequate context, i.e. a spatial container representing local, nearby, and associative contextual influences. This consists of:

- organizational relationships at each scale ladder level within an adequate context
- current and emergent structural relationships assembling those organizations
- identification of emergent patterns emanating from the analysis
- represented in relational spatial diagrams.

Coherence and polarity analysis
In this phase, both coherence and polarity are investigated as a means of discovering notions that can be effective in integrating the coherent patterns and the polarities into a third and distinctly different outcome:

- The coherent patterns can be built form typologies, represented as elements and principles that continue to contribute to the CST matrix meaning and functionality requirements.
- They are represented in spatial diagrams.
- Polarities and clusters of polarities are identified as cultural/spatial elements and principles.
- They are assessed regarding event-periods of time where feasible.

Bridging polarities: designing for the dynamic periphery
The principles within the polarities are evaluated and discussed through design explorations. This is the phase in pursuit of thirdspace, the third and distinct outcome(s) that can encompass key principles of the original polarities (or affect their evolution). Polarity bridging and design testing can include:

- designing for each polarity in each cluster as an exploration: assume every polarity is an option
- designing for emergent patterns that are in alignment with the larger community CST matrix, i.e., they have significant coherence
- design insertion of catalyst elements, principles, and relationships into the CST matrix
- placing design interventions into the CST matrix to change strategies, remove serious dysfunctions
- re-energizing creative capacity within the community to enable self-restructuring
- identifying and representing cultural/space program development at multiple scales, including unresolved polarity requirements.

Conceptual compositional directions

Design compositions are emergent culture/space/time relationships that emanate through designer and community from the phases above. Time-frames for design are increased as the analysis and design testing require more effort and exploration due to the complexity generated by the CST matrix in context.

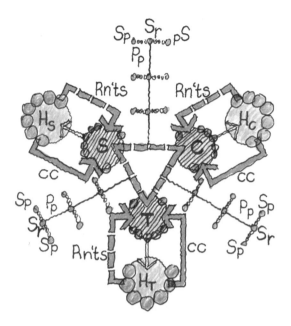

Figure 9.1. CST design complexity diagram. *Culture, space, and time are necessary integral parts of the design process for community. Not one, not two, but all three are a part of any analysis, thus increasing complexity. As space and culture, space and time, and culture and time are explored and assessed, relationships between and among the forces of CST are identified as significant relationships (Sr) and significant polarities (Sp). Each level of polarities (scale relevant: regional, metropolitan, city, district, neighborhood, etc.). Within each level, space-program elements are identified including those within the significant polarities for testing. The larger view also assesses the historic aspect of the CST forces (Hs, Hc, Ht) for coherent or continuing contributions (CC) to the meaning and functionality of community; and those remnants (Rn'ts) that exist and may have potential for reinvention into and as a critical part of contemporary emergent design compositions.*

The design spatial program elements and principles become a part of the larger process matrix (Chapter 1). Design composition experimentation and exploration begin at many stages as the program matrix and the interactions of the spatial relationships progress. Each polarity within the polarity clusters provides a range of program relationships, from minimally contrasting coherent relationships to maximum value conflicts. The tendency to stop prematurely in the process and make something can be overpowering. Staying with the process and exploring as much complexity as possible in time and budget constraints is an important challenge for the designer and can lead to rich and meaningful compositions in the built form. Playing polarity program aspects against one another can be a creative process that unlocks unforeseen spatial composition opportunity. This is not an easy task and requires many hands such as interdisciplinary teams to increase the quality of community design. The urban designer becomes the design guide or manager during this process, both interpreting input from various disciplines as compositional concepts and coordinating design input from other design team members.

Urban design compositions will be tested and challenged by reality. Making compositional decisions prematurely can lead to a protective mentality, forcing a predetermined or fixated design through the CST process rather than allowing the composition to emerge from that process. As I reflect back on my watercolor painting experiences, when I began to work with watercolor and the elements, principles and actions associated with watercolor's physical characteristics (water, evaporation, movement, transparency and luminosity, etc.), my work began to improve. I replaced control and management with a playful interaction with the medium and I found a new excitement and new discoveries not anticipated. I find this similar pattern in urban design—less certainty of outcome and more richness in the outcome.

In the final assessment, design exploration leads to the discovery of notions and concepts previously unformed in the matrix. The value of design as a spatial thinking process in relationship to the cultural and time/historic aspects of community is critical to forming meaningful and functioning human settlements.

Note

1   In public involvement processes, I utilize a spatial matrix/layered round-table methodology to assist in identifying starting points and directions with minimal compromise. In fact, a facilitator is renamed "referee" with the task of bringing discussions back on course from compromise-veering trends. The discussions usually begin with the key questions and issues (previously identified) discussed at a larger influence scale, with each succeeding discussion narrowing the scale down to the critical "adequate context." Following each scale level discussion, participants are asked to boldly print the top three conclusions from the dialogue on large note cards. These are placed on a wall to begin an emerging matrix that expands as the dialogue continues in scale-descending rounds. At key point(s) during the round-table discussions, facilitators review and summarize the emerging matrix, followed by a summation round-table dialogue. The critical principle at work (and not always successful) is the emerging pattern within the matrix. This pattern can *loosen the grip* of participants from initial agendas, positions, polarities, and focus their energies on what the matrix is beginning to communicate. In most instances, key aspects of participant agendas are inclusive in the matrix and those that may be "flamboyant," "outrageous," or "fanciful" often wither away under their own incongruities with the larger matrix. The process results in a final discussion regarding the matrix, not the initial agendas, and the directions and innovations that have hopefully emerged from the matrix. In some cases, given more time and a design charrette or intensive format, a design team interprets portions of the emerging matrix for the participants in architectural/urban design tests with axonometric/section and perspective drawings. This is highly effective in that the relationships between process and product are clearly advanced and the dialogue is perceived in a more real spatial context.

Bibliography

Arnheim, Rudolph, 1969: *Visual Thinking*: University of California Press, Berkeley, CA.

Bosselman, Peter, 1998: *Representations of Place: Reality and Realism in City Design*: University of California Press, Berkeley, CA.

Capra, Fritjof, 1982: *The Turning Point*: Simon & Schuster, New York.

Eisenstein, Sergei, 1949: *Film Form*: Harcourt, Brace & World, Inc., New York.

Johnston, Charles MD, 1984/1986: *The Creative Imperative*: Celestial Arts, Berkeley, CA.

Johnston, Charles MD, 1991: *Necessary Wisdom*: Celestial Arts, Berkeley, CA.

Kaku, Michio, 1994: *Hyperspace: A Scientific Odyssey through Parallel Universes, Time Warps and the Tenth Dimension*: Oxford University Press, Oxford, UK.

Patton, M.Q., 1990: *Qualitative Evaluation and Research Methods*: Sage Publications, Newbury Park, CA.

Sandelowski, M., 1995: "Aesthetics of Qualitative Research": *Image*, 27, 205–209.

Soja, Edward W., 1996: *Thirdspace*: Blackwell Publishers, Cambridge, MA.

Soja, Edward W., 2000: *Postmetropolis*: Blackwell Publishers, Cambridge, MA.

Strauss, Anselm and Corbin, Juliet, 1998: *Basics of Qualitative Research*: Sage Publications, Thousand Oaks, CA.

Webb, Frank, 1990: *Webb on Watercolor*: North Light Books, Cincinnati, OH.

Webster's New World Dictionary, Second Concise Edition, 1975: William Collins & World Publishing Co., Inc.

Weigardt, Eric, Ocean Park, WA, Watercolor Artist, Member: American Watercolor Society.

APPENDIX I
DRAWING TYPES FOR URBAN DESIGN

Principles at work

Before we get further into composition exercises, we need to better understand the visual/spatial symbols and the language they express of exploration in design. These symbols and language can be both crafted and digitized. Their principles are common to both scribing methods. I emphasize in this book the quickness and effectiveness of crafted methods for design exploration.

Drawing is a method of transcribing and conveying (as in writing, speaking, playing music, etc.) the language of design, *and is not a compositional or design product*! Drawing is a visual conveyance of spatial thinking consisting of symbols (alphabet) and meaningful expressions or relationships of space in graphic constructs (sentences and paragraphs, etc.). I refer to the drawing process as visual thinking. You do not need to be an architect or artist to "talk visually and spatially" with some very basic methodology. For non-designers, the basic types of visual constructs or communication, from my perspective, are:

- axonometric drawing
- diagrams (plan and 3D)
- contour drawing
- section drawing
- model-making
- perspective short-cuts and digital assists (options).

Short-cut variations of perspectives (qualitative drawings) are options and not critical in this context. They are primarily qualitative and have value in portraying physical relationships in a more realistic physical context. The other methods are both qualitative and quantitative, providing the designer with more flexibility in design composition and analysis.

The axonometric drawing, a form of paraline drawing where lines that are parallel in plan and elevation remain parallel in the axonometric, is a vital and easy method to learn and use. Before proceeding with other exercises in composition, the participant is encouraged to practice and become familiar with basic axonometric drawings. I have included as many short-cuts as possible to make your journey manageable and effective. There is distortion in most axonometric drawing types but this is negligible in the design composition process.

Essentially, axonometric and contour drawing processes enable you to sketch and manipulate design forms quickly and effectively, illustrating three planes of objects without perspective distortion. Let's get started.

Axonometric drawing

Tools:

- Adjustable triangle
- Straight edge (T-square, parallel bar or Mayline)
- Pens
- Flimsy trace
- Vellum grid paper, architectural or engineering.

Tasks:

1   *Axonometric (paraline) drawing:*
   - *Intent:* construct a cube, a pyramid, a sphere, and a rectangular solid (4 x 4 x 6 inches).
   - Do each form twice, first as a solid form and second as a void (two drawings per volume).
   - Make drawings about six inches in dimension per side; easier to work on than smaller dimensions.
   - *Make a plan and elevation of each first;* or have resource material of each at the desired scale (see expository note: plan/elevation this page).
   - Orient the plan to either a 30/60 or 60/30 angle from the base 0–180 horizontal (see expository note: 30/60 angle this page).
   - Showing all of your construction lines, elevate all verticals from each corner of the plan on a draft sheet of tracing paper (hint: use centers as well as corners to help "see"); if they are perpendicular to the 0–180 horizontal, maintain their 90-degree orientation.
   - Measure the heights on each vertical (from elevation).
   - Connect the upper heights, corner to corner, keeping lines that are parallel in plan and in elevation also parallel in the axonometric, include all construction lines (use colored pencils if desired); on a building with a pitched roof, draw the base box first, then find the center line of the ridge as it intersects the top of the box and measure the ridge or gable height from the intersect, then connect the ridge point to the outer and upper corners of the box.
   - Trace in freehand (your hand, not a software program!) in fiber tip pen onto quality tracing paper (transparent); do not use flimsy tracing paper as it is fragile and not suited for certain reproduction processes.
   - Do not use erasures; use the tracing paper overlays.
2   *Axonometric (paraline) drawing void:*
   - *Intent:* reverse the process and represent the volume as a negative shape or void.
   - *Cube:* construct a smaller cube within a larger cube; or drop a cube into a two-dimensional and larger horizontal plane.
   - *Sphere:* construct a sphere into a larger cube using center point and at least two diameter crosses.
   - *Pyramid:* same, using key corner points.
   - *Axis:* cut a channel into a two-dimensional horizontal plane.

Diagrams (plan and 3D)

Diagrams are semi-real graphic representations that can utilize various types of drawings: plan, section, axonometric, and perspective. They dramatize or summarize ideas, information, and analysis, filtering out information not relevant for that analysis or scale. Diagrams are best communicated with reference and orientation information such as direction, scale, and sufficient notes.

I use diagrams in summarizing the big patterns in design analysis; or key factors in contextual analysis. They provide an excellent format for presenting and discussing ideas and information in workshops, meetings, and design charrettes. They also provide the designer with an assessment tool: as data are analyzed and synthesized, the diagram is used as a means of prioritizing and focusing information on a contextual drawing such as a base plan.

Intent:

Represent the core ideas, issues, relationships, and data analysis in a spatially referenced and oriented base, filtering out unneeded detail. The diagram represents, in most cases, the major patterns of organization and structure, from site evaluation to space program organizations to the structural assemblies of those organizations in a physical context.

Diagrams related to built environment design have the following characteristics:

- spatially referenced and oriented orthographic base information, usually in plan diagram; also applicable with axonometric drawings and perspectives
- a clear and consistent symbol alphabet that is category-consistent and scale-relevant. The symbol alphabet has conventions as well as ample room for innovation by the designer. Conventions include:
  - color for uses and activities (red: commercial, etc.)
  - line weights for hierarchy of shapes (light line for background objects such as curbs, topography and heavier lines for building shapes; in many cases, the higher an object is off of the ground plane the heavier the line weight)
  - north compass orientation
  - graphic scale (mandatory) where scale is used
  - shadows, when used, accurately portraying vertical heights as opposed to darker outlines for pseudo-shadows.

Consistency principles include:
  - same symbol for one category
  - dimensional hierarchy for symbols according to the importance of objects within the category; for example, an asterisk can be used for commercial centers with the largest representing a regional shopping mall and the smallest representing a neighborhood retail center
  - same color palette for specific uses and activities; with color variations within that color palette based on hierarchy of use intensities
  - symbol consistency: I make a template for symbols (arrows, dashes, asterisks, circles, etc.) and trace them so that they are consistent and not distracting to the information being communicated.

Plan drawing

Basic to the architect, engineer, and landscape architect, the plan drawing is a straight-down right-angle view of a horizontal plane, illustrating relationships on that plane (house plan, office layout, block parcels, etc.). The plan is an orthographic and quantitative graphic vital for standard reference and measurement. A *conventional* scale[1] is assigned to the drawing for measurement purposes and is always represented in graphic mode as well as numbers so that the scale can be determined regardless of the plan's enlargement or reduction in size and therefore in scale. A plan is also a horizontal section where the section line cuts the vertical "view" at standard altitudes. In a house plan, the horizontal section is "cut" four feet above the floor, meaning that all walls are four feet high maximum from floor to the cut. Why? So that windows and door openings can be observed in the cut (vertical) walls. A city scale plan can have a designated horizontal cut line depending upon the information to be expressed. For example, an altitude of 50 feet can be established to cut through all vertical objects 51 feet or more in height from the base horizontal plane.

Contour drawing

Intent:

Draw only what you see, not what you think you see (analysis). A contour drawing consists of the edges, outlines, or contours of shapes in a composition or view. Within this view are outer edges of major shapes (a person) and interior shapes comprising that person's clothes and the light patterns following on all shapes within that person's form. This requires you to be a more focused observer of what you see!

This technique requires practice, and anyone can do contour drawing. Let me repeat that: *anyone can do contour drawing*. It requires focus and observation of the reality of an object and shapes within the object. If you find yourself drifting, drawing too quickly, you most likely have stopped observing and have switched into a memory mode, essentially drawing from memory—you have zoned out! *Refocus!*

Drawing on the Right Side of the Brain (Edwards, 1979) does an excellent job of explaining the background and techniques involved in contour drawing. Your personal library collection will thank you. Practice both the pure contour drawing (no peeking at the paper or drawing in process—train the eye to observe) and modified contour drawing, where you go back and forth from object observed to paper and drawing—back and forth, no memorizing.

Principles and tasks:

- Use drawing tools that have less friction with the drawing surface such as soft pencils (HB to 4B, felt-tip pens, Conte pencils); avoid any drawing tool that will scratch or drag on or into the paper as it will slow your movement down (ball-point and metal fine-tip pens are not helpful as they drag and gouge).
- Once you place your tool on the paper, do not lift it off; yes, keep it on the paper and do not hesitate to retrace your steps by going back and forth (this is a sketch not a masterpiece).
- In modified contour drawing, establish a frame of view for yourself by using a view finder (3 x 5-inch window cut out or the back of a writing table, for example) with half and quarter points marked on the window edge; and, like a camera lens, look through the window to establish the extent of the composition you desire to draw.

- Find a place (or places) along the window where a major shape (or shapes) meets the edge.
- Begin to draw what you see from that edge, looking at what the contour is doing (up/down, angle, curve, length estimated via window frame).
- I like to draw the major shapes in first to determine the overall composition within the view window before going back into the smaller contour shapes.
- Sometimes I enlarge my window if I incorrectly estimate the proportions within the original frame—it is okay, you can do that!
- Look for light shapes (soft—dotted, hard—line), pattern edges, all contours.

Suggested practice: every day:

- two one-minute contour drawings, assess if you are actually looking or memorizing
- two three-minute contour drawings, same assessment
- two five-minute contour drawings.

What to look for:

- Smooth lines usually indicate lack of focus and too much speed—slow down.
- Cartoon-like images indicate memorization of image, minimal observation.
- Keeping eyes on paper (drawing) for extended periods indicates memorization of image, no observation.
- You are better off looking at the object being drawn than looking at the drawing because the practice is in the observation and attention to contour characteristics.

Section drawing

Intent:

Section drawings are orthographic views, straight on or perpendicular to the viewer, similar to elevations. They are familiar drawing types for architects and landscape architects, are key vertical relationship tools for urban designers and planners, and are worth summarizing. Sections have three major components:

1. All vertical and horizontal planes that are actually cut through along the section line are highlighted with a heavier line weight or double line thickness or color.
2. All remaining vertical and horizontal planes *not* cut through remain in elevation and are a lighter, less dramatic line weight.
3. In most cases, sufficient background physical context (key buildings, adjacent buildings, etc.) is provided for viewer reference and orientation.

Process for sections:

1. *Plan map and reference elevations and/or photos:* you choose where you want to cut through the horizontal planes on a plan base map, to study for yourself or show observers a certain view of the vertical/horizontal/sloped relationships; have reference elevation drawings and/or photos for reference to the vertical elements.

2   *Cut/reference line:* draw a line on your reference plan, preferably at the same scale, through the site plan where you want the cut, making that line in plan the "bottom" of a view plane or window (as if you were looking straight down on the plan and see the top edge of a pane of glass representing the cut); this line is like cutting the plan along this line with a skill saw and removing everything in front of that cut on your side; it no longer exists in this analysis, revealing everything along the cut line and beyond it—going away from you into the distance on that topography elevation.

3   *Direction of cut/view:* indicate on your plan and cut line which way you want the view to be seen; draw a circle at each end of your cut line in plan, then draw a triangle or arrow on the outside of that circle (see Ron) indicating the direction of the view (so that someone else looking at the plan knows both the cut line location and the direction of the cut view); then use the inside of the circle to reference what the section is and where the section can be found in a larger set of drawings; for example, "B–B, A-12" says that this is section B–B (one B on each end of cut line in plan) that can be found on sheet A-12.

4   *Cut all vertical and horizontal planes on cut line:* as if I take a saw to a three-dimensional model, I cut vertically from top to bottom everything that is along that line or view window, as high up or down as is necessary to define the "adequate context"; I am cutting through both vertical and horizontal planes.

5   *Relationships:* the section cut illustrates vertical and horizontal relationships.

6   *No depth:* has no depth, no vanishing parallel lines (paraline drawing: all lines that are parallel in plan and elevation remain parallel); this is why, if looking straight on at a cube (90 degrees or perpendicular) I see only the front vertical plane and not the top or sides.

7   *Existential parts:* discard any and all plan and elevation information behind the cut line (behind your nose if it is pressed against the view plane window).

8   *Tracing paper:* put a clean sheet of trace (flimsy or if rich, vellum) over the plan drawing (with cut line and cut direction facing away from you) and tape down.

9   *Trace cut line/grade elevation:* trace over the cut line with your parallel rule or T-square and make that line your reference line at the grade or flat elevation level matching the topography along the cut line; if that varies from one part of cut line to another, you are simply drawing a graph with the x-axis up or down along the horizontal y-axis.

10   *Raise the cut verticals:* using your T-square and a triangle, raise up the verticals along the cut line according to their scaled heights from resource materials (elevation drawings and photographs).

11   *Raise other reference verticals:* raise up all other vertical planes that are beyond the cut line in your line of sight (one foot and outward to your adequate context distance); for example, if I wanted to show a church on the next block in the distant view of the cut, I can put that church elevation in as a significant reference item in a lighter line than the sectional cut lines; and/or if there is a hill or ridge in the distance I might put that in as reference as well, remembering to measure its vertical height from the base contour or elevation that it begins on—if a 30-foot-high fir tree is in a ravine in the distance and the base of the ravine is 20 feet below my reference cut line elevation, I will only see ten feet of tree.

12   *Darker cut lines:* all vertical and horizontal plane elements/lines/masses that are *on the cut line* are now made darker (heavier line width) or in some cases hollow line (not used here) than any and all vertical and horizontal plane lines *not on the cut line. Repeat: make the horizontal and vertical planes actually on the cut line more dramatic (darker, thicker) than any other elevation line;* we do not draw in the cut window panes along our cut line as they are usually too narrow for planning purposes (you will see them included in architectural detail sections).

13 *Context info:* for context info, include other site information that is in the direction of your cut view but not along the section or cut line. Treat as elevation: bring all planes in your view down to your horizontal (0–180) line perpendicular to you (your T-square), regardless of the orientation of the object in plan; in other words, you only see the portions of objects that are directly in your perpendicular view. If a cube is tilted from you at a 30/60 angle, you will see one side shorter than the other, not unlike an axon.

14 Once you bring all planes and their corners to you at right angles, measure their height and scale off the verticals from the corner points of the planes, *and from the elevation or contours that they are sitting on as the fir tree example above.* For sloped roofs tilted away from you other than 0–180, just find the high and low points and connect the dots.

Remember:

• can show elevations within sections
• always has a directional view
• view and the buzz saw cut are always noted on plan for reference of observer
• site sections are better with background elevation context as part of section
• line quality is critical to section: draw in all other data in finer line than sectional cuts so that cuts stand out
• shadows and depth: as in plan and elevation, shadows in section can be effective to indicate depth (cast usually at 45 degrees)
• shadows are cast on vertical planes only and are used to indicate setbacks in buildings and other detail.

Model-making

Intent:

Three-dimensional crafted models, made by hand, are key tools in exploring and evaluating spatial relationships because they reveal to the designer, through the crafting process, aspects of spatial relationship often not observed in orthographic representations. Study models, like diagrams, can begin with semi-realistic shapes representing larger patterns of composition with minimal detail, if any, maturing to a more sophisticated composition as the design evolves.

Model types that I frequently use and advocate with students are as follows:

• cardboard massing models for larger site compositions
• use and quantity designation on model components, useful during model gaming sessions and as models are photographically recorded
• base map reproductions to provide a physical context base with scale
• cardboard or chipboard topographic layers where appropriate
• chipboard or tag-board study models of building massing with color contrasts for existing (gray) and proposed (white) additions to the composition
• color additives for pedestrian areas, roads, water, and other components important to larger pattern recognition.

Figure AI.1. Plan diagram. *The plan drawing is referred to as a base map when the plan contains basic graphic reference and orientation information. Additional information can be added to further advance the level of analysis and the "base map" is always retained as an original reference source.*

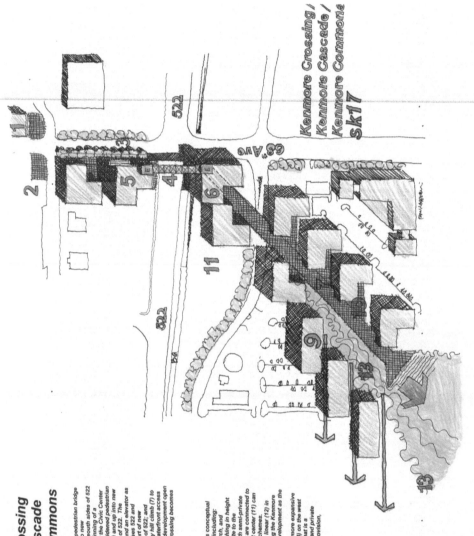

Kenmore Crossing /
Kenmore Cascade /
Kenmore Commons

sk17

Kenmore Crossing
Kenmore Cascade
Kenmore Commons

Highway 522 is crossed with a pedestrian bridge with elevators incorporated into new development on the north and south sides of 522 at 68th Ave NE. This is the beginning of a pedestrian spine that begins at the Civic Center (1) and Town Center (2), with widened pedestrian sidewalks down 68th Ave NE (3) and up into new development on the north side of 522. The bridge (4), accessed by stairs and an elevator as part of new building (5), crosses 522 and transforms into an enclosed part of new buildings (6) on the south side of 522; and cascades into a open-air grassy hill climb (7) to Lake Washington and public waterfront access as a part of public and private development open space provisions. Kenmore Crossing becomes Kenmore Cascade (8).

The illustrations portray various conceptual options for further discussion, including:
1. A progressive office, research, and residential complex diminishing in height from the north part of the site to the waterfront area (9), each with semi-private open space courts (10) that are connected to Kenmore Cascade; a transit center (11) can be incorporated into both schemes.
2. Another option that is more linear (12) in nature forming a street along the Kenmore Cascade with mixed use development as the spine of a larger complex.
3. A third variation portrays a more expansive sloping park open space (13) on the west side of Kenmore Cascade that is a combination of public park and private development open space provision, Kenmore Commons (13).

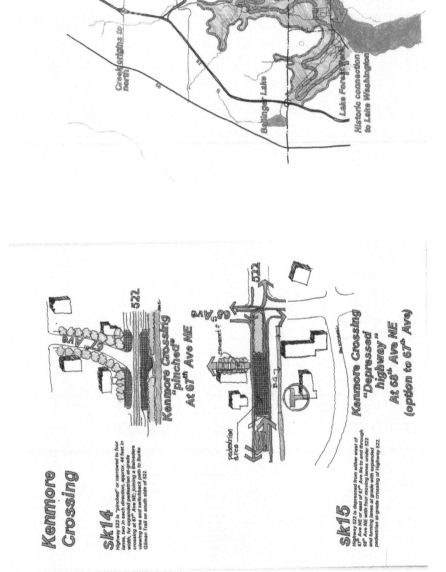

Figure AI.2. Plan diagram. *These plan diagrams are used to depict broad concepts and principles in urban design. The first represents manipulations of a highway to improve pedestrian crossing, using simple graphic symbols; and the second represents the larger land form patterns surrounding the emerging downtown core of the community.*

Figure AI.3. Building section. *Line value is used to graphically portray the vertical elements being cut through (as with a skill saw!). The cut planes are darker or bolder in relationship to the vertical and horizontal elements and planes not cut. Window openings are left blank or drawn with very light lines in comparison to the darker, bolder cut lines of the vertical wall planes and horizontal floor planes. All elements seen behind the cut line or in the distant view are indicated by a lighter line, thus the importance of the sectional view.*

Figure AI.4. Site section. *The site section utilizes the same principles as the building section. Based on the cut line decision through the site and the direction of the view, the section illustrates the cut ground plane and sub-grade features (underground parking, utilities, etc.) and above-grade natural and building features. The lighter value lines are maintained for all features in elevation and the darker and bolder lines are used for vertical and horizontal planes that are cut through (ground, walls, floors, parking lots, streets, water features, etc.) only along the cut line.*

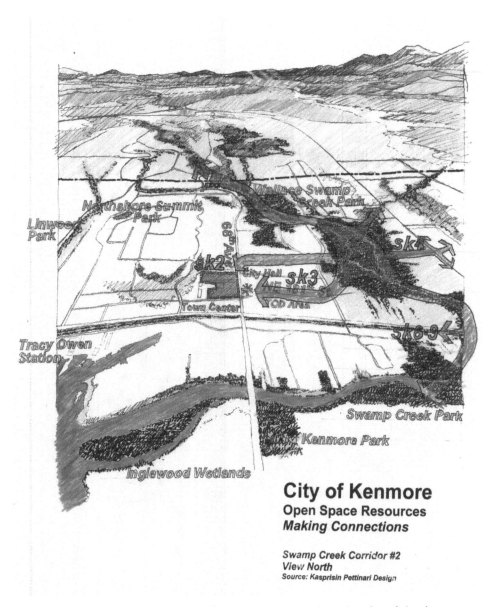

City of Kenmore
Open Space Resources
Making Connections

Swamp Creek Corridor #2
View North
Source: Kasprisin Pettinari Design

Figure AI.5. Aerial perspective diagram. *The aerial perspective can be used in place of plan diagrams where contextual images can strengthen the message. The example portrays the Cascade Mountains in the distant north-east with the major creeksheds and river-slough highlighted along with potential connections to major centers.*

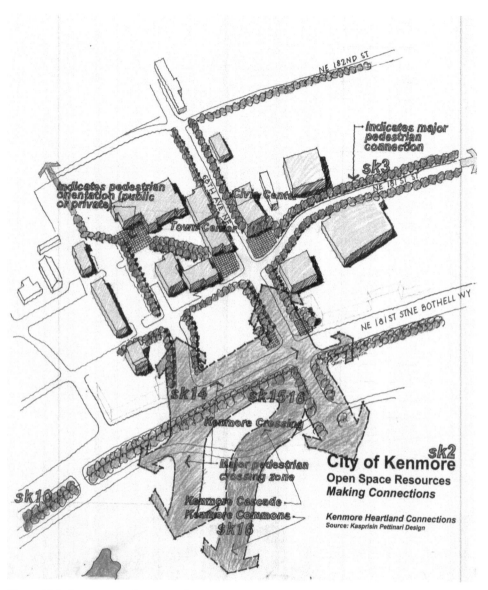

Figure AI.6. Axonometric diagram. *The axonometric view provides an aerial-like view of the emerging town and civic center and the potential pedestrian connections to other open space resources. Just enough contextual information is provided without overloading the graphic image with unnecessary detail.*

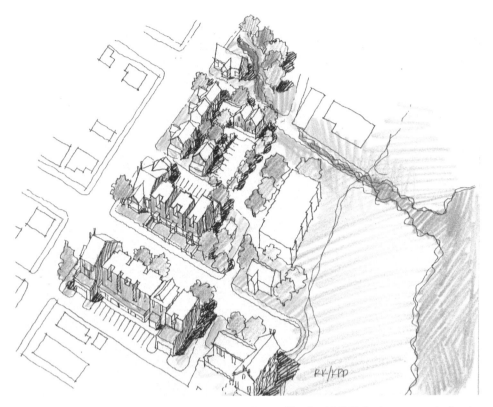

Figure AI.7. Axonometric drawing. *In "Downtown Design Handbook" (2006), the axonometric drawing was used extensively to portray the overall design intent of design guidelines. The axonometric drawings were reproduced and used as diagrams as well. Notice the orientation of the plan (30/60 or 60/30) and the basic requirement that all vertical lines are perpendicular to the 0–180-degree reference line—they are not slanted as can happen if the plan is not rotated. This slanting effect is confusing for most lay observers.*

Note

1   In the use of graphic information systems (GIS), many planners assign plan maps with non-conventional scales, causing problems of measurement for others involved in the process. The non-conventional scale can be used to measure data as calculated through the GIS program but cannot be used for measurement when using standard hand scales and other measuring devices (that are not going to cease in utilization because of computer technology). For example, when doing a downtown design, a standard scale based on the engineering (standard) scale can range from 10 increments in an inch to 60 increments in one inch per the engineering scale. These conventional scales are useful in fieldwork, team design work, workshops, etc. for hard copy plotted maps. Many GIS maps are plotted out in non-conventional scales: one inch equals 462 feet, for example, and is little use to the team, client, or process.

Bibliography

Edwards, Betty, 1979: *Drawing on the Right Side of the Brain:* Houghton Mifflin Co., J.P. Tarcher, Los Angeles, CA.

Kenmore, City of, 2010: "City of Kenmore Open Space Opportunities: Making Connections": Kasprisin Pettinari Design, Langley, WA.

Kitsap County Department of Community Development/Kasprisin Pettinari Design (Langley, WA), 2006: "Downtown Design Handbook": Silverdale, WA.

Sechelt BC, District of, 2007: "Visions for Sechelt": John Talbot & Associates (Burnaby, BC) and Kasprisin Pettinari Design (Langley, WA).

APPENDIX II
WORKING WITH PEOPLE: THE POLITICS
OF URBAN DESIGN

Introduction

I include this section as vital to engage the CST matrix, the basis for urban design. Without a quality interaction with people, a separation exists between why we design and the form that emanates from the design process. Working with people is an art that requires preparation, openness, genuine interaction, and personality.

As design professionals, our core mission is to plan and design with and for people, not machines. We at times forget that mission as we become immersed in policy, quantitative analysis and computer simulations, and of course form-making. Most of us recognize people as key ingredients in what we do and continually find ways and terms to minimally engage or evade the good folk of cities and towns: designing for "quality of life," applying "context-sensitive" design, designing "people-friendly" environments, and of course *planning* for "sustainability" (an oxymoron). All *slang* phrases. Most professionals are traumatized by the very thought of working with people, experiencing forms of fear or reticence at the very thought of "presenting" at public meetings. We spend more time laying down paper trails and going through the motions with hand-holding/feel-good exercises and techniques than really engaging community. A harsh statement, and, in my 42 plus years of experience, accurate.

Working with people is an inherent and necessary action for all aspects of community planning, design, and engineering. Best intentions are often short-circuited because of fears, tight budgets, shortened time-frames, arrogance, and ignorance. Design is a function of culture and culture represents the patterns of human behavior over time. Working with people is a necessary ingredient in the culture/space/time matrix. More often than not, public input is lacking or poorly engaged and the degree of compromise to design resolutions increases dramatically—and therein lies a critical issue for design: reducing or eliminating compromise.

Principles for working with people: compromise in design (a major source or contributor of design pollution or dilution) can be greatly reduced or made minimally significant by an interactive public process:

- with aspirations not predetermined outcomes (requires planning without goals)
- with dynamic processes (creative) that begin with and cherish uncertainty
- structured for consistent and coherent public participation
- refereed with compromise awareness techniques
- increasing the intrinsic value of community dialogue by use of representational media

- interdisciplinary collaboration
- with longer time durations of interactive involvement (and adequate budgets).

Let's explore this cluster of principles with examples, reflections, and recommended actions.

A personal awakening: the urban renewal experience

As a young architect–urban planner fresh from graduate school in the late 1960s, I was sent by a large architectural–engineering–planning firm to a small town approximately 20 miles from Boston. I was assigned as the project urban designer working with the redevelopment authority and the community to develop a downtown redevelopment plan and strategy through the urban renewal process.

I pursued a Master in Urban Planning degree in order to become a more community-oriented architect and went to the town thinking that I was there to better improve the community. I discovered the hard way that my dedication to architecture, fascination with design, and dedication to planning were problems waiting to surface (in relation to the community).

I lived with a family politically connected to both the local redevelopment board and state legislature. I reveled in the layers of politics: Democrats fighting amongst themselves (French, Italians, Irish, and Greeks primarily) and all uniting to fight the minority Republicans of the time. At the local watering hole, the mayor's table was always reserved and set for "pols" and guests, like our design team members. For young designers, the atmosphere was heady and politically charged. I was convinced that the downtown design plan in process through our hands was serving the "public." "Public" in reality meant presenting our progress to citizens and business leaders, not engaging them in a quality manner.

Of particular concern to me in later years was the realization that I and my young colleagues walked the streets doing "building condition assessment" surveys and made decisions based on future design potential rather than on the nature of the existing context and community value. The predetermined design drove key decisions too early in the process. Playing with space is playing with power.

And of course, when the design proposal, complete with elaborate drawings, a 10 x 4 foot model, etc. were approved by the redevelopment board, the team took the final design to the public for approval . . . and as I stood there listening to objection after emotional objection, the sweat ran down my back and I experienced my first serious fear of failure. It took me a while to figure out why; projects were implemented that were more in keeping with the personal pleasure of design than with the concerns and needs of the meaning and functionality of the community. The functionality was there in large part and not the meaning.

A fun side-story tells a lot about the underlying politics of design, from a different board room perspective: one day, after the team's basic design was established, which included removal of part of the main street and the local bank building (a handsome brick and stone turn-of-the-century structure), I joined the local politicians at the mayor's restaurant table where drinks were ordered and lined up for this young planner. I knew I had a meeting with the board of directors for the local bank at 2 p.m. that day but my colleagues around the table urged me to relax and enjoy. Needless to say the martinis flowed at lunch.

At 2 p.m. I met with the bank board. I stood up and my tongue must have been four inches wide because the only thing that came out of me was some garbled gibberish. They of course were all in on the "show the kid a lesson." High-backed chairs laughed and clapped at my spectacle. Needless to say, the politics of design had spoken; the plans were changed and the bank building and others reappeared in the final scheme—a positive design action in retrospect. And while the lesson was provided by the power structure of the community, it also translated to the homeowners and others who were impacted by our "good intentions."

The project was eventually significantly compromised (possibly for the better I must add) with a major realignment of the street pattern, improved parking, retention of the historic context, and removal of the new super-block scheme we young designers thought improved the community. Compromise is still what it is—concessions—something midway between two positions. There was a design opportunity and principles in the basic design that were lost in the bravado of young designers convinced of their importance to the community and their *ownership* of the design process.

There are many similar stories of well-intentioned design processes that through ignorance or arrogance missed an opportunity due to a lack of public engagement. In fairness, engaging the public can be fraught with tension and conflict, from the attendees with special financial interests, the dedicated activist or advocate unable to see the larger perspective, the attendee seeking "stage-time" in order to run for political office, and on and on. Then there are the concerned citizens, many of whom are interested, dedicated to the improvement of their community, and lacking in information regarding context, history, and design process.

Working with people becomes a multi-task process:

- co-informing and co-educating
- co-authors and co-owners of the process
- co-participants in the path of creative uncertainty, the emergent design
- co-evaluators of built form: the designer from outside and the participant from within.

Key principles and approaches

Before proceeding with case studies on interactive approaches to working with people, I want to connect applied public participatory practice to a theory base: *creative systems.* (See detailed discussions in Chapter 9.)

Theory and practice exist in relationship, not as separate endeavors. Theoretical considerations constitute reflections on unusual relational patterns observed and experienced in the field. They are considered or assessed with regard to the wider philosophical, cultural, and scientific perspectives of the larger community. Emergent theory is tested and experimented with in the field. This relationship does not always produce results and is valuable in the testing process regardless of success or "failure." There are no short-cuts, no magic techniques; conditions are continually changing, necessitating changes or hybrids in established approaches. And so it is with working with people.

There are forms of public involvement practices that continue to work and are the basis for most interactions between designers and citizens. The designer has the responsibility to continually tinker and experiment with new hybrids.

Connections of theory to practice

I discovered two key sources of applied creative systems theory useful in design and public involvement processes. The first is in psychiatry, dealing with human relationships (Johnston, 1984/1986 and 1991). The second is found in school design programming processes (Verger, 1994). Johnston explores and experiments with ways to engage the interactions in human relationships, dealing in part with the recognition of (creative) differences among people (couples, groups, neighborhoods, staffs, etc.) and how those differences affect various levels of relationship. His Institute for Creative Development experiments with ways to identify the polarities separating those differences; develops means to define the temporary limits or containers of those polarities in order to begin potential dialogue; and defines the means to "bridge" those differences without compromise, expanding in turn the dialogue container. This work has a direct transference from small-group human relations to community interactions in relation to design and planning.

Verger explores the means to systemically manage and expand dialogue on complex design and budget issues, seeking resolution in group deliberations using a scale-descendant visual matrix process and progressing toward a thirdspace reality. I have also experimented with his techniques as a means to shift initial participant foci or agendas to another level of discussion, without asking for compromise. This also brings in principles discussed in *Thirdspace* (Soja, 1996) where the dialogue can seek a level different from the beginning, retaining key principles of participants and arriving at new and innovative outcomes. These principles are key components in understanding culture's role in the design of space. They can be based on cliché and rigid or packaged public involvement methods, or they can be open and creative and most definitely *uncertain in outcome.*

Key principles for public involvement processes:

1 *Working with people is an interactive process; there is no such thing as an interactive product without an interactive process ("sustainability" does not exist outside of an ecological process).*
   Many public involvement processes use techniques labeled "interactive" when in fact they consist of filler. *Interact* means to act on and between or among one another. The design and facilitation of public involvement activities has an interactive core that structures the presentation and discussion of information and ideas. The urban designer is a co-participant and guide working with citizens and stakeholders. Nobody says this is an easy or perfect process. Various ways and means of interactive formats are discussed in the case studies.

2 *Each participant brings an idea deserving of a place in the dialogue no matter how "outrageous."*
   At the outset of every meeting, workshop, intensive or gathering of people, ideas are brought to the table for discussion that can be contradictory, infuriating, off-base, out of context, and so on. They are considered options for inclusion in the dialogue. There are ways for the process itself to render many initial ideas as dead-ends, with no future value—let the process accomplish this task.

3 *The interactive process is guided by a principle of uncertainty: a journey without goals.*
   Here is a key principle: the result of every gathering is from the dynamics of the process, not from prescribed or predetermined outcomes that are to be "discussed" or "voted upon." This requires more, not less, preparation by the designers. This principle will have detractors regarding the "journey without goals," particularly from the planners. However, a goal is defined as an end one strives to attain. There are places for goals, as in games and structured interactions with strong rules of conduct. I argue that goals as ends to attain do not have a valid place in the phase of design where public authorship is desired. As scale levels become mature and more specific, as in the space programming phase, goals emerge as important benchmarks regarding function, budget, timing, etc., and have a value for the process—and yet, I argue, they require challenges and cannot dictate outcomes in each level. I use the words aspirations, notions, emergent patterns in place of goals to remove as much of the stigma of "predetermined outcome" as possible.

There are writers who engage the writing process, crafting sentence to sentence to paragraph to paragraph, allowing the story to emerge (with aspirations and notions). And there are writers who work from a set structure, filling in characters and plot sequences essentially knowing the outcome in advance. When I paint a watercolor I have a choice: try to wrestle the painting into an exact preconceived image that I began with or let it go and work with the fluidity, wetness, flow, drying, and serendipity as the painting emerges. You be the judge.

4   *As there is no goal, the aspiration is to maintain the creative energy and integrity of the process in order for the process to generate results.*

Being uncertain as to outcome places more responsibility on the energy and integrity of the process. This requires preparation. Having a structure of interactive activities for a workshop also means that change and alteration are critical if the workshop progress changes. Designing exercises that elicit ideas and interactive dialogue among people are a lot different than keeping people busy with feel-good, time-consuming games that are not interactive, simply entertaining.

5   *An interactive process is culturally specific.*

Community is not abstract. The patterns of human behavior as expressed in cultural patterns, traditions, and actions are space- and time-based as well. Every public involvement format and process addresses cultures and their differences as a basic requirement. A number of years ago, working with an architectural firm in Seattle on HUD VI (Housing and Urban Development Agency) housing projects, at any given meeting there may have been a dozen different ethnic groups requiring multiple translators and approaches. Asking simple questions such as "How do you and your family use the front yard?" became in-depth indicators of cultural differences with myriad responses, requiring the design team to reassess the question. *Culture, space, and time/history* are inherently intertwined.

6   *The process is scale-descendant.*

So much information and so many ideas are possible for dialogue that the structure of the dialogue requires a series of "containers" that are scale-relevant in order to work through the complexities of a given issue. In 1993, I was asked to design and facilitate a vision process, a prelude to a comprehensive plan, for the City of Bellingham, WA. The process was formatted as a sequence of five conferences approximately three weeks apart with a committed participant group of 250 citizens, providing consistency. The key point: the process was scale-descendant in space and topic. The first format began with historians, geologists, and others who provided the local audience of the "big picture" from the formation of Bellingham's land form from small fishing and logging towns to the geology and environment of Bellingham Bay and the four major salmon/trout-spawning streams emanating through the urban area from eastern foothills (this information was not known by a majority of participants). The big picture then led to a second session that described and discussed what *design* is, using specific examples. Session three then led to district-level scales regarding issues and potentials that then led to idea and strategy sessions. Session five led to a consensus vision.

7   *The process is spatially oriented, occurring in the context of specific places with representational media that describe layers of spatiality.*

All human activity occurs within a spatial context. No exceptions. As James Pettinari and I pursued in *Visual Thinking for Architects and Designers* (1995), understanding any dialogue in the context within which it occurs is crucial to the design process. How that context is understood, presented, placed into the dialogue is critical to enabling a quality discussion of issues and ideas. This principle is also scale-descendant, as Pettinari's Scale Ladder diagrams indicate, descending from a planetary view down to a room. Spatial information appears and is clarified at certain scales and disappears and has less relevance at other scales.

Rudolph Arnheim's (1969) description of the comprehension of reality revolves around the reality of sensory experience and the media of its representation. This is critical to all community dialogue processes. Visual media are more perceptual and verbal media are more intellectual. Both are critical to the process; the visual media form the foundation for increasing public awareness by placing ideas and concepts in spatial context. As discussed in Chapter 9, the use of non-objective art, graphic ornament, detailed argumentation or primarily narrative accounts, and precise technical imagery risks losing the relevance of what people see and understand. Spatially referenced plans, diagrams, axonometric drawings, and site sections are among the most effective visual formats for public involvement processes.

8   *The process is time-dependent.*

Sounds obvious! And yet the time periods for public involvement are critical to success or failure of the process for the following reasons:

- Too fast a time-frame can make people suspicious of the process—where fast methods lack depth and can lead to long-term problems.
- Too fast a time-frame may not provide the time required to work through the public process—a truly interactive process takes time and cannot be short-circuited.
- Too slow a time-frame can lead to a loss of participant attention and consistency—people often attend workshops and intensives after work or on a busy day with families, and are tired and less focused. Stretching out the process can lead to a loss of attention and a disruption in the learning curve most lay people encounter when dealing with design issues and strategies; if a consistency of participants is lost, the information learning curve is broken, requiring a constant iteration of basic information that can stall or delay the process unnecessarily.

History is relevant and cannot drive the process; the present is highly focused and often charged with emotion and reaction to current events; the future is uncertain. The designer's challenge includes identifying those historic aspects that are still connected to the present and/or have transferable lessons. In some cases, remnants from the past (see Appendix III) can be used as a bridging device between historic patterns and current issues to forge new design strategies; or at least an increased understanding of past actions to present form.

In the New Westminster case study, I discuss the challenge of a request by the New Westminster Downtown Development Association for a one-day charrette (design intensive). One day it was—with months of preparation. In "Visions for Bellingham," a five-conference (all day Saturday) time-frame proved successful with three-week preparation breaks. In AIA RUDAT design charrettes, a five day on-site intensive is needed to do an in-depth design process, preceded by a preparation team and followed by a team review one year later. Time is critical to the process.

9   *The process requires both quantitative and qualitative input and preparation.*

Working with people is an art, and requires specific and accurate background information and evaluation. "Winging it" may have short-term emergency success based on the designer's charm level but will certainly fail, as will drowning the public with data, charts, and "knowledge." Working with people is definitely a "both/and" model which is neither charm-based nor data-driven.

10   *Conflicts and differences are inherent to the process.*

Given the complexity of society, there is no assumed consensus at any gathering that focuses on future probabilities. Significant differences occur between seemingly strong allies. Serious conflicts often emerge as the scale of issues and the participants increase regarding a specific issue. In "Visions for Bellingham," of the 250 people in attendance at all five conferences, developers and property owners often clashed in "visions" with environmentalists and slow-growthers. "We have plenty of land so let's spread development out" was countered with "stop filling the wetlands and cutting the forested slopes for low-density residential subdivisions." Being prepared for conflict is critical and can be assisted by:

- smaller discussion groups followed by information sharing to the larger group
- scale-descendant structuring of issue discussion
- thirdspace techniques (see the "Community of Learners" case study, later in this appendix) to move the discussion away from negatives toward new discussion
- treating all initial ideas as viable options
- structuring the discussion with compromise referees to intercept and deflect compromise patterns in the dialogue (see Johnston (1991) for discussion on compromise resolution)
- letting the process absorb much of the conflict: this does not always work and with sufficient time can lessen or make mute key conflicts without confrontation; confrontation can only increase conflict and move toward compromise as a means of lessening anger.

I offer an example from City of Langley WA Comprehensive Planning Process (see Langley, 2009). During the comprehensive plan revision process in Langley, among many issues, two were critical to groups of residents (similar in profile politically and environmentally): one supported a green belt proposal around the urban area in the growth management area (GMA) and both agreed on the need for new residential subdivision regulations. A conflict emerged as the green belt group pushed for a zoning or regulatory classification and implementation strategy applicable to private lands in the GMA. This position created a negative base for the green belt topic to the point that the local forum and email communications began to insist on confidentiality and secrecy in green belt discussions. This conflict, among similar allied groups, is resolved by a community dialogue that moves the green belt issue to a different position, a broader position that can include a green belt component as part of a new subdivision strategy (and desire for conservation of more contiguous open space) and maintain the objectives of the GMA.

This led to a discussion of conservation design principles that retain GMA density objectives (six units per acre in many cases) and new design principles that maintain or conserve anywhere from 50 percent to 80 percent of land resources. The discussion on green belt per se created conflicts. By broadening the discussion to the larger issue of land resource conservation while meeting GMA objectives assisted in mitigating those (unnecessary) conflicts. And the conflicts are normal and understandable when good intentions manifest themselves in more narrowly focused strategies. As of this writing, conflicts remain over the details of subdivision regulation and the green belt issue has been absorbed into a larger dialogue.

There are conflicts in communities that are deeply engrained and may take years for resolution.

11   *Each scale level has a cluster of polarities that defines the limits of that level's initial dialogue.*

As in the previous discussions, conflicts and polarities do not have to be earth-shaking or between dire enemies. There are limits and differences in every discussion, no matter how civil or friendly.

They in fact define the initial container for discussion. I like to use the color wheel as an example of the "polarity cluster" idea: a color wheel is composed of 12 colors where the primaries red, yellow, and blue break down further into two variations of their secondary mixtures. For example, red and yellow make orange and the two variations exist as red-orange (closer to the red primary) and yellow-orange (closer to the yellow primary). Within the color wheel are color opposites, often called complementary colors because they can complement one another in their polarities. The opposite of any primary is the sum of the two remaining primaries and conversely the opposite of a secondary color is the remaining primary: red and green (yellow and blue); yellow and purple (blue and red); orange (yellow and red) and blue, etc.

When looking at the color wheel, there is much complexity in color represented by the circle and the potential mixtures that are possible. There are multiple "opposites" or polarities evident, including lesser opposites for the red-orange to the greenish-blue.

In design and planning, these "color opposites" are readily apparent in most meetings where conflicts over budgets, priorities, facilities, approaches, etc. differ significantly and in subtle ways among cohesive groups. There are methods and techniques for uncovering and identifying the many levels of opposites or polarities around a meeting table or in a workshop. An interview process or survey can be utilized to identify the positions and agendas of various individuals in a group—not typing them but seeking differing patterns, seeking the levels of polarity. Now there exists an understanding, as in Langley, that apparently similar participants can have very different positions on the same issue. This is a better place to start a meeting than one that is consumed in negativity: a negativity that can be resolved by merging to a new position.

The process can reach a place where both polarities are encompassed in a new and distinctly different and workable dialogue: thirdspace.

12 *Each scale level strives to generate an emergent reality or pattern that is carried to and helps define the next scale level.*

Attempting a quality dialogue with a room full of people is not advisable and does not lead to significant progress. As in "Visions for Bellingham," the scale can begin with a historic cultural/geological overview perspective working downward to neighborhood pedestrian design issues in smaller discussion groups; or, in larger group meetings, the scales are interspersed with a background session for the large group followed by small round-table sessions followed by large-group summaries, etc. Too many issues discussed at a large scale can dilute the critical issues and too many opinions in one concentration can dilute the quality of dialogue.

The scale-level concept is integral to the uncertainty principle. In small groups, working with compromise referees, a discussion can lead to new ideas and approaches that were not anticipated at the outset. These ideas are emergent realities or patterns that emanate from the process, not the facilitator or individual participants. They form the bridge between one scale and the next, providing the "next step" for expansion of the dialogue container and the topics of discussion.

13 *The larger the moral dimension the smaller the compromise permitted; and conversely the smaller the moral dimension the more compromise is acceptable.*

Significant material exists on the value of compromise. I use Johnston's compromise fallacy descriptions in preparing a referee for a workshop. The compromise fallacy consists of the following:

- unity fallacy (searching for one answer through dialogue)
- separatist fallacy (dividing and separating the issues into separate dialogues and formats)
- 50/50 fallacy (asking each polarity to give up 50 percent in order to "blend").

14   *The process seeks thirdspace as a separate and distinct outcome that embraces the creative differences of participants without compromising those differences.*

In the "Community of Learners" case study, as well as others utilizing the emergent reality matrix, the process is designed to accomplish the following:

- elicit dialogue from all participants without negative feedback
- document key components
- stimulate discussions using a referee to maintain the positive energy of dialogue away from compromise and negativity
- create a larger and more complex dialogue that emerges from small-group discussions; and is constructed outside of the small-group discussions with a visual matrix with new patterns emerging and separating themselves from individual positions and agendas
- shift focus of participants from personal attention and compromise to an emerging new pattern on the wall for all to observe.

15   *Consensus without compromise, seeking transaction.*

Transaction is the simultaneous and mutually interdependent interaction between multiple components (Capra, 1982, p. 267). This is an aspiration of an interactive public involvement process. Here is an area where new techniques and methods can be developed to achieve interaction. The *emergent reality matrix* is one such technique that uses the following objectives:

- Utilize scale-descendant issue containers to identify and expand information and ideas.
- Share those ideas using pattern-making graphic-visualization techniques by merging them in a larger visualization.
- Create a Gestalt structure wherein participants over time begin responding to the whole situation rather than individual parts.
- Identify and articulate new sets of relationships rather than components emerging from the Gestalt structure.
- Identify emergent consensus.
- Accept all input related to a defined scale and set of relationships.
- Employ a facilitator-referee to flag compromise fallacies.
- Synthesize key positions from dialogue.
- Separate positions from participants through construction of larger emergent reality matrix.
- Ascend or descend scale levels and repeat discussions and new synthesis.
- Expand matrix.
- Repeat as needed.
- Evaluate matrix and emerging patterns.

An interactive process uses a whole mind-body thought process, intellectual and incorporating cognitive perception processes.

Simply put, these interactive involvement processes require both an intellectual thought process and a cognitive perceptive approach using the senses. In most cases, graphic illustrations such as diagrams, three-dimensional perspectives, axonometric drawings, three-dimensional models, etc. are valuable in spatial orientation and referencing ideas and issues for participants. Great care must be used in this "representation of place," targeted for the participants and the context. Movement exercises, music, play-acting, and storytelling can all be effective in given situations as long as they do not drift into entertainment without interaction. Video games, computer games, etc. are less effective as they are less interactive.

16   *Every outcome is an emergent reality or pattern, immediately altered and changing as it is identified.* Each level of dialogue, including the event's conclusion, constitutes an emergent reality or pattern that is space- and scale-specific, in a real context (with multiple dimensions). Assume this outcome will begin to change again and is not static. The emergent pattern provides a new base for further actions and dialogues. Designers "make things" and are required to translate, interpret, design, and build based on these emergent outcomes. As Johnston points out in *Necessary Wisdom* (1991), one half of the creative process is observing what we design as it is placed in context, reflecting and learning as the process begins anew.

CASE STUDIES: NEW WESTMINSTER, BC; "A COMMUNITY OF LEARNERS", REDMOND, WA

Two case studies that include a design charrette or intensive process help conclude this section with descriptions of (not perfect) interactive processes that improve the final design recommendations: The New Westminster, BC experience and "A Community of Learners": the Redmond, WA experience.

New Westminster, BC Downtown Design Guidelines Charrette and New Westminster, BC Neighborhood Design Guidelines Charrettes, four neighborhoods

Client aspirations

Nettie Tam, Director of the New Westminster Business Improvement Association (BIA) (1996), requested a one-day design charrette process for the downtown to develop design guideline strategies. New Westminster is a dense urban area east of Vancouver, BC along the Frasier River.

I was contacted by John Talbot & Associates of Burnaby, BC to join the design/planning team for the charrette. My first reaction to John was "sorry . . . there is no such thing as a one-day charrette." Based on the client's insistence that we focus on a one-day event, the team prepared and facilitated the process described below. The process proved successful in numerous ways, including:

*   key interactive participation by 40 stakeholders
*   a set of consensus design guidelines produced at the charrette that were adopted and implemented by the city
*   a transference of the same process to each of four urban neighborhoods in the city, all with the same successful production (one day) and adoption of design guidelines.

Of course this process took more than one day; here's how.

Stakeholders

Nettie Tam obtained participation from 40 key stakeholders representing downtown property owners, merchants, residents, elected officials, city staff, and others. To ensure effective interaction between the city and the BIA, co-chairs were nominated from each organization to provide leadership for the process and the Downtown Action Team stakeholders.

Principle: consistency in participant attendance throughout the process.

Principle: diversity in stakeholder composition.

Principle: commitment by and coordination of key agencies and organizations.

Issue sessions

City planning staff organized and conducted six stakeholder issue sessions or visioning committees to obtain and document ideas, concerns, potentials, and constraints, from stakeholders and the general public at evening meetings organized by John Talbot. These sessions occurred between February and March 1995 to lay the foundation for the focus area or areas of concern from all affected groups, public and private. Each committee consisted of two chairs with between 10 and 20 business, community, and municipal members. A public meeting was held in June 1995 to review the first draft of the "Downtown Action Plan" issues and a revised draft was distributed in September 1995. The design charrette then occurred in November 1995.

Areas of focus included: downtown vision, social vision, transportation, downtown and waterfront development, arts/culture/heritage, and economic development.

Time-frames

A short time-frame, three months, aided in maintaining interest, freshness, and participant consistency in developing the issues or vision documents. Including public review and comment periods, the final issues documents took ten months from beginning to the design charrette event.

A one-year action plan resulted from the process, encouraging a strategy for near-term success in order to promote a longer-term implementation strategy.

Design charrette planning

Planning for the one-day charrette included a number of key tasks:

Assess background materials: background visual information was collected from numerous sources including three-dimensional models of the downtown, photographs, field surveys and visits, drawings, maps, and other graphic materials supplied by the BIA and city.

Prepare charrette base drawings: I enlisted four graduate students from the University of Washington to assist in the preparation of materials for use during the charrette event. The students prepared aerial oblique and eye-level perspective sketches, plan diagrams, and base maps of existing conditions for areas of concern or interest identified in the vision sessions. This step proved extremely valuable in that design team members were immediately able to access these base drawings and begin their design translation work.

Assemble design team: the BIA and city identified a number of local area architects all of whom designed projects for the New Westminster area. They were recruited to donate their skills and experience for the design event.[1]

Design team training session: I accepted a challenge from John Talbot and BIA/city to design and facilitate a training session for these area architects, knowing that, as one architect appearing to lecture to others, there may be resistance to the idea of "training" for such a talented and experienced group. Following some good-natured jabs and shared humor at one another, the training session began and was well accepted. "Sensitizing" is a better term than training and included:

- *Role and task of the designers:* translation and interpretation of what the stakeholders offer as well as the issues and visions put forth by the six vision committees.
- *Awareness of the role of the listener:* as architects, we all love to design and draw expressively, sometimes with so much energy and enthusiasm that we allow our own ideas to dominate the conversation; after all, we are designers. A quality discussion occurred with the design team as to the real authors of the process: the stakeholders and the communities they represented in New Westminster. The designers brought the following to the process:
  - experience in local context
  - experience in building typologies suitable for the local context
  - abilities to interpret and express ideas and notions from the stakeholders into concrete design solutions
  - a reasonable response with creative energy to the ideas and notions expressed
  - graphic visualization experience and skills.

Charrette event process

The charrette began at 9 a.m. and ended around 5 p.m. Yes! The process concluded with a presentation and discussion between the design team, charrette leaders, and stakeholders with consensus reached. City staff produced the final report for distribution and adoption.

The charrette occurred in an event–conference-type space with small-group tables and a separate area for the design team separated but still visible and accessible to the larger group. Graphics and photographs were displayed around the room for orientation and reference.

Sequence of events:

- Introductions and description of day's activities.
- Review of vision committee work.
- Small-group discussions with designers present at every small-group discussion *as listeners.*
- Group sharing of morning sessions.
- Stakeholders embarked on a field trip and treasure hunt.
- Stakeholders toured the project area by tour bus with facilitators from BIA/city/charrette team on board.
- Stakeholders were given cameras and asked to find areas and features that they liked and disliked, as well as selected features from the charrette team in order to further enhance their observations and understanding of contextual issues.
- The design team gathered in the "design studio" portion of the main room and began interpreting and exploring ideas from the vision committees and the morning's input from group discussions. The discussions allowed stakeholders to revisit the published results of the vision committees and add to that resource with new ideas. The design team worked for about three hours before rejoining the stakeholders returning from their field visit and treasure hunt.
- Designers presented ideas, translations, and interpretations to the stakeholders and listened to a stakeholder critique. The visualizations presented thus far, with base drawings provided by the graduate students, greatly increased the quality of the stakeholder response.
- Designers returned to the studio area and incorporated the comments and suggestions from stakeholders into the next iteration of design translations.

- Stakeholders proceeded to discuss further refinements and were then encouraged to visit and observe (not interrupt) the design team at work.
- Around 4:30 p.m. the design team pinned up all work, over 35 drawings, on walls for large-group presentation, discussion, and last comments.

Needless to say, the energy level was high and a creative and interactive atmosphere prevailed with a consensus achieved by stakeholders. The process was uplifting for all participants including the designers. Many commented to me that the ability to be involved in a creative intensive with such close interaction with the community was a rewarding experience.

The success of the "New Westminster Downtown Action Plan" encouraged the city to conduct four one-day charrettes, one for each of the four urban neighborhoods in the center of the city. The same process was used with adjustments made for topic and stakeholder makeup. Each charrette process concluded in adopted design guidelines.

New Westminster follow-up:

- divergent groups
- city staff leadership
- staff (or other professional) and peer facilitation
- local design community participation and sensitivity training
- selection of stakeholder group for diversity
- preliminary issues workshops
- technical database assembly
- technical context visualization preparation
- charrette process
- visual-based product outcomes.

"A Community of Learners": opportunities for the Redmond Elementary School site, Redmond, WA

(Prepared by the University of Washington Center for Architecture and Education, College of Built Environments, April 1996)

Background

In 1995, the Lake Washington School District with the City of Redmond, WA voted to lease the historic elementary school and site for future civic uses. The University of Washington Center for Architecture and Education proposed a public involvement process to envision the opportunity for the building, the site, and the surrounding area as a "community of learners". A multi-disciplinary team was assembled using faculty and graduate students from the College of Education and the College of Architecture and Urban Planning (now the College of Built Environments) to identify site opportunities and viable design options. The team was led by Ron Kasprisin AIA/APA, Department of Urban Design and Planning. The project process began in February 1996.

Public involvement process

The Redmond Elementary School process was designed in three parts:

1   a community workshop with educators, residents, parents, and city officials to be held on site in an all-day workshop format
2   a design charrette or intensive held at the University of Washington, Gould Hall, three weeks following the community workshop
3   a report preparation phase resulting in a brochure product for public distribution.

The design charrette phase of the Redmond project consisted of a one-day intensive. The architects and urban designers translated and interpreted the outcome from the community workshop into the final strategy for "A Community of Learners". Workshop participants participated as observers, input resources, and evaluators during the one-day event.

Of particular value in this case study is the design and facilitation of the community workshop; this is the focus of this section.

Workshop design

The workshop was designed in a scale-descendant manner:

• off-site activities
• site activities
• building activities.

Each scale level used the following user types as baseline evaluation criteria; each type was assigned three priority levels: (1) high, (2) medium, (3) low:

• children
• adults
• seniors
• community
• organization
• other.

These criteria were identified at the beginning of the community workshop.
The workshop outline is as follows:

• Team site walk.
• Introduction by facilitator to large group.
• Background presentations by city/school board staff.
• Subdivide into small-group discussions using multiple round-table sessions followed by a summary and idea-download by each small group, followed by a large-group sharing using emergent reality matrix and repeated again through all scale levels.

- Compromise fallacy guidance provided by facilitators at each table with separate recorder (staff person) taking notes.
- Each participant asked to "idea-download" after each session by printing in large letters on 5 x 7 note cards their three to five key points from each scale-level discussion.

Emergent reality matrix

Following each discussion, the note cards were given to two graduate students who assembled the cards on a large wall surface in matrix form. Three such matrices were constructed during the day, one for each scale level (off-site, site, and building).

As the discussions evolved during the course of the day, the matrices began to emerge on the wall with the following impacts:

- Topics and areas of focus were identified and prioritized (number of cards).
- Patterns of use began to emerge.
- New patterns were identified and highlighted within the wall matrix.
- More importantly, as the matrices became more complex and visually more pronounced regarding topics, patterns, and group preferences, the initial individual agendas and positions brought to the table became absorbed into the larger whole. Round-table discussions became more focused on the emergent reality matrix than on previously stated positions around the tables. In effect, the wall matrices shifted the attention from person-on-person and person-to-group to the emerging (wall) patterns. The visualization of the matrix became a new focus, lessening the person-to-person and participant-to-facilitator foci and dramatizing new group priorities, preferences, and directions.

The matrices were photographed in place, then disassembled for later cataloguing and quantification. This resulted in a list of prioritized activities by user type and priority for each type for each scale. Thus an emergent consensus resulted that did not require a final vote as the vote was inherent in the discussion process.

Off-site activities:

- transportation
- shuttle
- green belt walkways
- linkage, river trail
- visual connection
- center for community events
- traffic
- general business
- electronic information
- community sharing resources.

Site activities:

- outdoor events
- passive recreation

- active sports
- amphitheater
- interpretive trail
- parks/gardens
- flexibility future.

Building activities:

- performing arts/theater
- sports/informal recreation
- cultural, arts, and crafts
- emergency shelter
- library/media center
- meeting space
- adult/evening classes
- extended school activity/daycare
- administration space.

Conclusions and applications in practice

Why is this public process, *working with people*, important to the design profession?

- *It provides quality interactive connection with user–client as well as administrative–client.*
  Working with people is difficult due to personality characteristics, diversity, differences, agendas, etc. Designing and facilitating well structured yet meta-determinant (uncertain outcome) processes increases the education of the public and results in both quality engagement as well as quality outcomes.
- *It reduces unnecessary conflicts, misinformation, misunderstandings that enable more effort and energy on positive design issues and relationships as opposed to piecemeal arguments.*
  Many well-intentioned professionals in design and engineering are reticent regarding public participation. This can result in the use of methodologies that are entertaining, temporarily stimulating (as practiced by many public relations firms), hand-holding, and time-eaters. Not much gets accomplished. Meetings, workshops, and charrettes (to a lesser degree) can be disrupted by participants who lack key information or feel as if they are being talked down to or ignored. A poorly prepared graphic display, lacking in key orientation and reference, can disrupt a meeting and discussion just as poorly structured discussion sessions can drift in and out of compromise solutions and arguments, getting further away from the real issues. Interactive workshops with structure, flexibility, and visual aids can reduce unnecessary conflicts.
- *It identifies an in-depth space program that directly relates to time/historic and cultural factors of the community or urban meaning.*
  The results of a well-structured interactive session can reap rewards in the space program that describes the needs, desires, and potentials of the *urban meaning/functionality matrix*. The more quality information on "what and how much" for each level and cell of the matrix, the more rich is the design outcome. The more designers can respond to the complexity of the urban meaning matrix, while not perfect, the richer the composition of the built environment.

Key components of quality interactive public involvement for designers:

- designing for and with people (and their environments)
- utilizing cooperative learning process:
  - positive interdependence
  - face-to-face interactions
  - individual accountability
  - interpersonal and small-group skills
  - sufficient processing time
- sound preparation and visualization of data and information in laymen terms
- context-responsive
- visualizations of context: sensory perception of reality using visual languages
- identification of and respect for creative differences
- scale and spatial descendant levels and containers for dialogue
- meta-determinant process—the uncertainty principle:
  - aspirations are necessary
  - predetermined outcomes are potential disasters leading to compromise
- awareness of compromise fallacies:
  - unity fallacy
  - separatist fallacy
  - 50–50 or blending fallacy
- design for urban meaning: culture, space, and time/history as well as urban functionality
- people are the co-authors of and in the built environment.

Conflict resolution

Conflict is a natural and recurring ingredient in interactive public intensives. Here are some guides that can assist in managing conflict as a positive force in dialogue.

Three aspirations:

1 to have aspirations not goals
2 to maintain the creative energy of the process
3 to invoke the meta-determinacy principle.

Know the type of conflict:

- zero sum (pure win or lose)
- mixed-motive or trading
- pure cooperative or unification.

Face conflict rather than avoid it:

- Avoid denial.
- Resist circling the wagons.

- Avoid suppression.
- Disallow postponement.
- Avoid premature resolution (compromise).
- Respect yourself, your interests, and the interests of others.
- Accept cultural and creative differences.
- Distinguish between interests and positions.
- Identify common and comparable interests.
- Identify any need for third parties, such as:
  - facilitators
  - mediators
  - councilors
  - referees
  - recorders.

Polarity analysis: define conflicting interests and the limits or boundaries they set for the dialogue.

- Listen.
- Be alert to natural tendencies for bias, judgments, and compromises.
- Move dialogue whenever possible (emergent reality matrix) away from compromise.
- Use different skills for different conflicts.
- Know yourself and your personal perspectives.
- Be critical of ideas not people.
- Focus on the best decision or direction, not competitive winning.
- Encourage everyone to participate using oral and written methods as options, as not everyone is outgoing and verbally expressive.
- Restate if not clear.
- Facts on both sides are requirements for quality dialogue and issue exploration.
- Use a referee process to diffuse or deflect emotion-dominated dialogue.

Note

1 New Westminster Downtown Design Charrette Team: Nettie Tam, Executive Director BIA, John Talbot (John Talbot & Associates), Ron Kasprisin AIA/APA (Kasprisin Pettinari Design), Ken Falk (Creekside Architects), Doug Massie (Doug Massie Architects), Graham McGarva (Gaker/McGarva/Hart Architects), Eric Pattison (Decosse Pattison Architects), City of New Westminster Planning Department: Mary Pynenburg, Lisa Spitale, Stephen Scheving, Leslie Gilbert, Brian Coates, Lilian Arishenkoff, Augustine Wong, and Michael Kimelberg, University of Washington Graduate Students.

Bibliography

American Institute of Architects, 1992: *R/UDAT: Regional & Urban Design Assistance Teams:* Washington, DC.

Arnheim, Rudolph, 1969: *Visual Thinking*: University of California Press, Berkeley, CA.

Bellingham, City of, 1993: "Visions for Bellingham": City of Bellingham Community Development Department, Patricia Decker, Planning Director, Bellingham, WA.

Capra, Fritjof, 1982: *The Turning Point*: Simon & Schuster, New York.

Johnston, Charles MD, 1984/1986: The *Creative Imperative*: Celestial Arts, Berkeley, CA.

Johnston, Charles MD, 1991: *Necessary Wisdom*: Celestial Arts, Berkeley, CA.

Kasprisin, Ron and Pettinari, James, 1995: *Visual Thinking for Architects and Designers*: John Wiley & Sons, Inc., New York.

Langley, City of, 2009: "Wharf Street Form-based Code": Langley, WA (design team: Ron Kasprisin AIA/APA; Dr Larry Cort, Planning Director; Fred Evander, Planner).

New Westminster, City of, 1996: "New Westminster Downtown Action Plan": City of New Westminster, BC.

Redmond, City of, 1996: "A Community of Learners": University of Washington, College of Built Environments, Seattle, WA.

Soja, Edward W., 1996: *Thirdspace*: Blackwell Publishers, Cambridge, MA.

Verger, Morris, 1994: *Connective Planning*: McGraw-Hill, New York.

Webster's New World Dictionary, Second Concise Edition, 1975: William Collins & World Publishing Co., Inc.

APPENDIX III
REMNANTS, BRIDGING, HYBRIDITY, AND EDGES

Remnant patterns

Aren't remnants merely leftover icons, derelicts, or monuments from previous development periods? Why are they relevant for contemporary urban designers?

Remnant analysis

Remnant analysis asks whether or not a leftover or remnant pattern from previous cultures (or previous periods in same culture) can be useful in design as:

- a hybrid design outcome with new uses compatible with the form characteristics of the remnant
- a bridging device or action between the past and the emergent future, where a new use provides a valid and viable function to the historic remnant pattern
- creating a dialogue of urban form analysis for new adjacent or surrounding forms based on the remnant pattern; and presenting an opportunity for interconnections between the remnant and surrounding emergent forms
- providing a coherence or frame of reference within changing cultures
- providing a basis for comparison between old and new that enables the new to be more clearly identified.

Remnants

A remnant is an existing physical pattern (spatial entity as physical element, spatial structure, or spatial relationship) that has exceeded the functions of its original purpose, and whose existence may have potential for new functionality and meaning.

An artifact is a physical entity whose form has no transferability into another viable entity. The artifact can be preserved as a symbol of the past and cannot be reinvented as a bridge to the future.

Parent pattern (as system: CST)
The parent pattern of a remnant is the original time-specific spatial configuration or composition with cultural signatures, style, use, culture, and infrastructure technology (crafting) imprinted in the form. The pattern is a system of connected parts performing a societal need and function. For example, historic Fort William H. Seward in Haines, AK portrays the original fort constructed by the US Army around

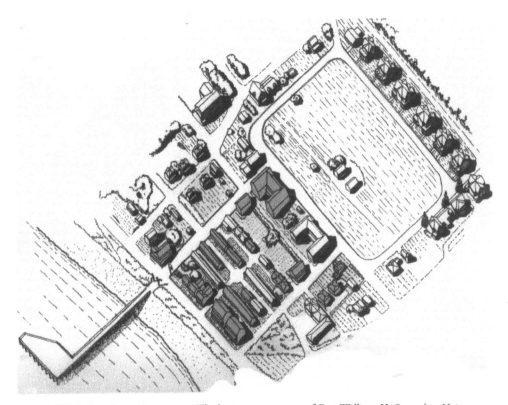

Figure AIII.1. Fort Seward remnant. *The basic parent pattern of Fort William H. Seward in Haines, Alaska exists to this day. The fort is occupied by artisans, a hotel, restaurants, residences, bed and breakfasts, vacant remnant buildings, and a few general commercial uses.*

1910 to monitor the Yukon gold-rush through Haines and Skagway (and possibly Teddy Roosevelt's "big stick" reminder to Canada and the British). Why the fort was constructed, and its varying uses until sale by the military after the Second World War, are critical to understanding the spatial configuration. This goes beyond historic or architecturally significant buildings and spaces. This is about the patterns that formed the framework for those significant elements in 1902 and it is about the evolution of the context to the present-day remnant (icon, monument, "thing"). Figure AIII.1 portrays the remnant fort as it currently exists, with an entirely different "story" or meaning in its current use: an intact parent pattern where the use and heart have changed, but enough of the original form remains as a historic remnant.

Classic remnant pattern

A classic remnant pattern is a historic pattern that has a use and form that transcends culture and time. I think that the Pantheon is one such classic pattern in that its original use, a religious structure, remains to this day. The style of religion has changed from a temple to numerous gods to a Christian church (at various times during the year). Pardon the tourists.

A more contemporary example is historic Creek Street in Ketchikan, Alaska—a boardwalk neighborhood overhanging Ketchikan Creek. In the 1800s and early 1900s, Creek Street served as an "entertainment" area for fishermen, loggers, and others working the waters and forests of the Inside Passage in southeast Alaska. Of course, the entertainment ranged from music to taverns to red-light

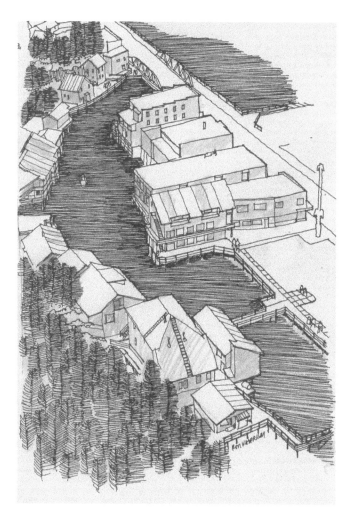

Figure AIII.2. Creek Street remnant.

facilities and their ladies of the night. There was a "married men's walk" on the rear hill for clandestine entry and exit. The key design form is the boardwalk itself, a remnant from the turn of the century that now structures the composition as an axial form moving along the bottom of a 60-feet-plus bluff. The axis holds together a collection of restored, reclaimed, and new structures that provide entertainment for present-day locals and thousands of cruise ship passengers. During the 1960s and early 1980s, the Creek Street complex was dormant, flanked by used appliances in the creek among the returning King Salmon— rescued by changing economies in the US/Canadian cultures.

Remnant container
This is the adequate historic boundary or contextual container with a new contemporary container overlain. The boundary is assigned based on the supporting systems associated with both the parent pattern and the contemporary context. The container has a locale or center area consisting of the physical location of the remnant and its immediate surrounds; it has a larger area of influence out toward its periphery.

Eroded remnant pattern

Over time, parent patterns lose original use and are affected by emerging changes within the surrounding contexts, eroding the parent and often obscuring the patterns. The parent is often uncovered through research and accident.

Transitionary remnant pattern

A transitionary remnant is where the original function still exists in some state and is being eroded or usurped by cultural changes; the parent pattern is dissolving, leaving remnants where original use is no longer dominant in the form; emergent meaning is uncertain.

Enfolded remnant pattern

Enfolded remnant patterns are two distinctly different period patterns folded into one, superimposed or entwined, retaining characteristics of each original pattern.

Emergent remnant pattern

Emergent remnants interact with emergent cultures and economies to produce hybrids which in turn create new patterns with viable uses respectful of the parent pattern:

*   satisfies a need and/or survival requirement
*   establishes a relationship with new supporting infrastructure
*   addresses cultural shifts
*   is profitable in its metamorphosis.

Remnants as bridges

Remnants can be a bridging device or action between past and emerging future. They may be obscured or made clear by time and context and are often overlooked as relics from the past rather than the remnants of past patterns (of culture in time reflected in space). In community design, remnants can be identified as remnant street patterns or railroad lines; as historic water recharges forests seen currently as woodlots; as portions of historic working waterfronts are surrounded and absorbed by cruise ship terminals and tourist facilities. They provide both elements as shapes and partial relationships in history for an emerging composition.

Remnants can be categorized for discussion as follows:

*   natural systems:
    –   watersheds
    –   recharge areas as forests and wetlands
    –   meadows and prairies
    –   floodways and plains
    –   sites
    –   settlements, current and historic
    –   districts and neighbors
    –   economic sites (canneries, mills, logging camps)
    –   migration routes

- infrastructure:
  - railroads
  - roads
  - boardwalks
  - piers and wharves
  - equipment (gold dredges, etc.)
- buildings
- symbols:
  - signage
  - cultural markings.

Hybridity

A hybrid is of mixed origin, unlike parts; a design made up of components from different styles of expression.

Hybridity can be an outcome of a thirdspace process, forming a design that moves beyond pre-existing conditions or issues, viewpoints, and development typologies to a new and different outcome that holds the integrity of the design process. Hybridity can be the pursuit of design coherence with context-specific and/or spatial program adaptations. It can be an adaptation of the original to a new environment, internal structural changes meeting external environmental influences. Innovations can emerge from an awareness of hybrid applications of conventional typologies. This is why typology is used as a starting point and not an end-point, beginning with design principles (as opposed to models) that have worked before in similar conditions and yet are altered by unusual or complex aspects of the specific reality context.

One of the more interesting examples of hybridity in urban design occurs in housing development, particularly infill housing in existing urban contexts. In Seattle, the Seattle Housing Authority's Scattered Site Housing program challenged local architects to design subsidized housing for existing neighborhoods with the stipulation that the new housing must fit and be integrated into the existing contexts. Housing types changed as a result of this contextual response, with triplex units designed as single-entry homes within urban blocks of single family houses; and with five-plex single-entry buildings designed for corner lots in the same single family context. Context provided the pressure to alter standard typology to meet both a stated program need and integrate that need as spatial entity into an established urban context.

Edges

Edges are multidimensional spatial entities that are both remnants and emergent patterns or realities. The beach is a transitionary pattern changing due to the wave and the upland point of departure (from the beach)—grass, cliff, wall, etc. The edge is the resultant effect of the "meeting," grounded in physics, and often formed by a dialectic of nature and industry.

An edge is a boundary of at least three spatial entities: black, white, and the line created by the meeting of the two.

Edges are transitional membranes. There is an external to internal transference of energy, a translation from one spatial language to another. Resources are taken from one and transferred and transformed to interlock with another; often as waste, product, or an entropic result (the shell on the beach becomes sand, the boulder was dislodged from the cliff, the wharf is reduced to isolated pilings). These transitional membranes are sources of creative capacitance: the floodplain absorbs the flood waters, the marshes absorb and filter runoff and incoming tides with nutrient production, and the public access facility connects human to water edge.

Edges are also barriers, as the dam and causeway, or the eight-lane highway traversing the water edge, cutting the community core from access to a historic waterfront. Transportation systems provide access and movement for people and goods, and are often planned in insulation from the larger urban reality, creating edge barriers that present serious future challenges for urban design.

Edges are always in motion, always emergent, and have both offensive and defensive responses to context. The motion factor is often overlooked in planning and design: over time, an urban edge sheds structure as uses (economy and culture) change, and can be proactive with additive uses and new structures. The historic riverfronts of mill towns in the Pacific Northwest, blocked from community access for decades, shed the industrial structures and wharves to be replaced by pedestrian trails, transient boat moorage, view platforms, kayak facilities, and ancillary uses such as restaurants and other water-attractive uses. Studying historic patterning in the built form reveals these changes and emergent patterns in edge conditions, providing clues and catalysts for design solutions.

The dynamics of edge energy are a major force in urban design, from the transition of urban waterfronts from industrial to human-friendly community resources; from the abrupt change of rural village to agricultural seams where pressure from residential subdivisions threatens the fragility of natural and cultivated landscapes. They offer opportunity for new development typologies and hybrids as the edge energy is integrated into the design process.

Components of edge

- natural
- manufactured
- length (more linear than vertical)
- depth (a graded or dissipative aspect with the release of energy from one entity to another)
- height
- structure
- organization
- portals
- multiplicity of layers
- solid
- porous
- transparent
- translucent
- framed/unframed
- emergent or entropic
- gravity relevant
- culturally influenced: social amity/enmity defense/privacy, economic, political, religious, etc.
- time period.

INDEX

Arnheim, Rudolph 12
Attoe, Wayne and Logan, Donn 93
axis 34; as structure 61

bridging: as structure 63; as tranformations 92–3;
    as historic connections 96–7; 166–8
Brosterman, Norman 3, 12

cantilever: as structure 63
Capra, Fritjof viii
Castells, Manuel viii
circle: as structure 58
clustering: as structure 66
cognitive perception 12
coherence 195
color 36–7, 105
complexity 2
composition 2, 45–7
compositional structures; defined and described
    51–67
compromise 93
concepts 191
conflict 147, 193–4; resolution 229
context 46; 107–9, 186
corners 103
creative urbanism 149, 184
creativity 190: creative 5; capacity for creativity
    5, 189
cross: as structure 56
crossroads: as typology 132
culture 6, 14; emergence of design in 15–19,
    186

design 11; Cartesian approach 15, language of
    20–27; parameters 27–8
diagonal: as structure 57
diagrams: design process diagram 7; plan 23;
    axonometric 25, 201

drawing: axonometric 25–6, 200; contour 26–7,
    202–3; orthographic 21; perspective 26;
    plan 21, 202; section 21–4, 203–5

edges 98–105, 236–7
eidetic: form 8; vision 12; as emergent reality 46
Eisenstein, Sergei 147
elements: dot 30–1; line 31; shape 31–3;
    derivative shapes 33; characteristics 37–8
emergent reality 14, 46

failing 5, 9
fear 3–5
Freidman, Jonathan Block 8
Froebel, Friedrich 12
functionality 46
ghost structures: see transparent
grid: as three-dimensional framework 70

Goldstein, Nathan 11
grounded theory 5

Hall, Edward 13
Human experience: need and measurement 15–16
hybridity 236

interlocking: as structure 67

Johnston, Charles viii, 5, 11

Kaku, Michio 13, 188

"L": as structure 54
Lazano, Eduardo 10–11
Lefebvre, Henri viii

meaning 46
matrix: CST 6–9; n-dimensional 6–9, 185–9

merging: as transformations 89–92
metric tensor 13
Modernist corporatism 18

Neruda, Pablo vii
New Technologies 17
New Urbanism 17
New Westminster, BC 222–5
nursery: as typology 132–3

order 9; as orders 79
organization 46

parts 46; analysis 195
perception 191
periodicities 14, 46
Pettinari, James viii, 26
place 6
planes 34
play 2–5
play-work 5
polarity: defined 47, 189; analysis 195
post-modern 17
postmetropolis 17
principles: defined 38–40
process 46
program: CST 6–9; architectural 6; 110
proportions 79

realities: see emerging realities; nested 188–9
Redmond, WA 225–8
regionalism: critical 17–18
relationships: defined 46; organizational 6–9,
47–8; remnants 14–15; structural 7, 48
remnants: as bridging connections 95; 232–6
Robbins, Tom 5
Rubin, Barbara 14
rurban *131*

Salmagundi 14
scale 79
Soja, Edward 1, 13–15, 186–7
space 6, 13–14, 186–7
Spreiregen, Paul 15–16
square: as structure 53
Strauss, Anselm and Corbin, Juliet 5–6,
184
structure 46; *see also* compositional structures
superimposition: as structure 65
surfaces 103

talent 4
templates 171–2
tension 97
theory 184, grounded 185
thirdspace 6, 187, 193
time 6, 14, 188–9
transparent: as structure 70
transformations: additive 83; bridging 92;
dimensional 81–2; merging 87;
subtractive 83
trialectic: culture, space, and time 6–9
typologies: defined 110–12

uncertainty 185
urban: defined 11
urban design: defined 10–12
urban form 13
urban functionality 6, 12
urban meaning 6, 12–15
uncertainty 5

value: in color 37
volumes 35–6

Webb, Frank 5
Wright, Mrs. Anna Lloyd 3